Banksy

My Autobiography

GORDON BANKS

MICHAEL JOSEPH
an imprint of
PENGUIN BOOKS

MICHAEL JOSEPH

Published by the Penguin Group

Penguin Books Ltd, 80 Strand, London WC2R ORL, England

Penguin Putnam Inc., 375 Hudson Street, New York, New York 10014, USA

Penguin Books Australia Ltd, 250 Camberwell Road, Camberwell, Victoria 3124, Australia

Penguin Books Canada Ltd, 10 Alcorn Avenue, Toronto, Ontario, Canada M4V 3B2

Penguin Books India (P) Ltd, 11 Community Centre,

Panchsheel Park, New Delhi – 110 017, India

Penguin Books (NZ) Ltd, Cnr Rosedale and Airborne Roads,

Albany, Auckland, New Zealand

Penguin Books (South Africa) (Pty) Ltd, 24 Sturdee Avenue,

Rosebank 2196, South Africa

Penguin Books Ltd, Registered Offices: 80 Strand, London WC2R ORL, England

www.penguin.com

First published 2002

I

Set in 12/14.75 pt Monotype Bembo
Typeset by Rowland Phototypesetting Ltd,
Bury St Edmunds, Suffolk
Printed in England by Clays Ltd, St Ives plc

A CIP catalogue record for this book is available from the British Library

ISBN 0–718–14582–8

My autobiography is dedicated to my family – Ursula my wife and the love of my life; our children Robert, Julia and Wendy; and our grandchildren, Matthew, Edward, Daniel, Eleanor and Elizabeth.

Contents

Illustrations

PICTURE CREDITS

Empics, 12; 15; 22; 23; 27; 28; 35; 40; 41; Colorsport, 14; 17; 24; 26; 34; 36; 37; Getty Images, 16; 25; 43; 44; Popperfoto, 20; 21; 31; 33; J. C. Thompson & Co. Ltd., 29; Chris Morphet, 30; Sporting Pictures, 32; Sentinel Newspapers, 38; H. W. Kokowski, 42; Mirrorpix.com, 45; NI Syndication, 46; Steve Merzer 48.

Every effort has been made to trace copyright holders and we apologize in advance for any unintentional omission. We would be pleased to insert the appropriate acknowledgement in any subsequent edition.

Acknowledgements

I would like to express my sincere thanks to the following people, all of whom have helped significantly in the production of my autobiography:

Julian Alexander and all at my literary agents Lucas Alexander Whitley; Barclays Bank plc, in particular Janice Hallam at Stafford; George and Alex Best; Ken and Jean Bolam; Chesterfield FC; Terry Conroy; Jimmy Greaves; Trevor Horwood; Roger Hunt; Sir Geoff Hurst; the staff of the *Leicester Mercury*; Leicester City FC, in particular club historians Dave Smith and Paul Taylor, authors of *Of Fossils and Foxes*; Simon Lowe; Manchester United plc, in particular Mike Maxfield; Jackie Marsh; Arthur Montford; Don Mackay; the staff of the Sheffield *Star*; Huston Spratt; Stoke City FC; Martin Taylor; Steve and Deborah Waterall; Rowland White and all at Michael Joseph.

For Sal, Lauren and Ruby.

A Note to Les Scott

My sincere thanks go to Les Scott for his invaluable assistance in writing this book. Les contributes regularly to the Stoke *Sentinel* and the *Bristol Evening Post*, has written extensively for TV and wrote the screenplay for the film *The Rose Of Tralee*.

He collaborated with George Best, Gareth Chilcott and Sir Stanley Matthews on their respective autobiographies, and when I made the decision to write my own I had no hesitation in asking Les to lend a guiding hand.

Thanks, Les. It has been a privilege to work with you and great fun.

1. Family Matters

The mark of a good goalkeeper is how few saves he has to make during a game. A spectacular save is the last resort when all else – positioning, anticipation, defence – have failed. But saves are always what we are remembered for. There is one in my career that people constantly ask me about; it is often spoken of as my greatest ever – though not by me.

It was 1970 and England prepared to play Brazil in the group stage of the World Cup, 1,500 metres above sea level under the relentless sun of Guadalajara. But the sweltering heat and lack of oxygen at such high altitude were the least of our concerns at the time. One man, bruised from Brazil's defeat four years earlier when they failed even to reach the quarter-finals, and intimating that this would be his last World Cup, was determined to make it a swansong to remember. This was a man who could single-handedly affect the outcome of a game at the highest level. He was, of course, Pelé.

In Brazil's opening group match against a talented Czechoslovakian side, Pelé orchestrated the game from start to finish. Brazil won 4–1 and Pelé had been the hub around which every Brazilian move had turned. In that game he displayed complete mastery of the ball, fantastic powers of acceleration, the cunning to veil his real intentions and the patience to bide his time before making his strike at the optimal moment. He kept the ball flowing, and his unselfishness continually brought his team mates into the picture.

The England squad attended Brazil's opening game. I watched Pelé with concealed awe: the finely tuned balance, his incredible skill on and off the ball and his uncanny ability to ghost into the right position at the right time. Once he played the ball it was as if he disappeared into the ether. The Czechs were taken up with trying to close down Jairzinho or Tostao, then, as if springing from a trapdoor, Pelé would suddenly appear in their penalty area to display his predatory skills to the full. The Czechs tried to put two, sometimes three, men on him, but such was the skill and technique of the man that he always found space to make the telling pass. Knowing Brazil were our next opponents I had watched Pelé closely. By the end of the game I didn't think he was just a great player. I knew he was *the* great player.

The opening ten minutes of England's match against Brazil, during which both sides sounded each other out, are best described as footballing chess. Brazil adopted a softly, softly approach. Consummate passers of the ball, they played it around among themselves at walking pace. Such precision passing meant that there was little we could do but watch. In that heat and at that altitude, to play a chasing game and try to close them down would have been suicidal. So we bided our time.

Then, just when I thought the game was settling down to a rolling, strolling classic, it suddenly exploded into life. Carlos Alberto played the ball out to Jairzinho on the Brazilian right. Jairzinho was a powerful, direct winger who could go through the gears like Michael Schumacher and cross the ball with Swiss-watch precision. I hit my toes as soon as I saw Jairzinho tearing down our left flank. We were caught on the hop. Bobby Moore had left Tostao free at the near post, Brian Labone was just outside our six-yard box and Alan Mullery, who had been pushing up, was sprinting back, anxiety creasing his face at the sight of Pelé heading towards our penalty box, unmarked.

When I saw Jairzinho arc around the ball, I knew the cross was coming. I moved two feet off my line, expecting him to cross to the penalty spot and believing that, since Pelé had now just entered our penalty area, I'd be first to the ball. Only Jairzinho didn't aim for the penalty spot. He whipped the ball across to a point just outside my six-yard box, a yard or so in from my right-hand post.

As I turned my head I saw Pelé again. He'd made ground fast and, such was the athleticism of the man, he'd already launched himself into the air. Sidestepping on my toes, I covered the ground to my right and was only two or three paces off the centre of goal when Pelé met that ball with the meat of his head. As an attacking header, it was textbook stuff. He rose above the ball and headed it hard and low towards the right-hand corner. The moment the ball left his head I heard Pelé shout, '*Golo!*'

Faced with a situation like that, you don't have time to think. All my experience and technique took over. The skills I had acquired through countless hours of practice and study had become what psychologists call 'overlearned' and what the rest of us call second nature. I suddenly found myself at a forty-degree angle with my right hand stretching out towards the post, my eyes trained on the quickly descending ball. One thing did flash through my mind: If I do make contact, I'll not hold this. Instinct, overlearning, call it what you will – I knew that if I made contact with the ball, I had to get it up in the air. That way Pelé, following up, would not be presented with a tap-in at my expense. The ball hit the ground two yards in front of me. My immediate concern was how high it would bounce. It left the turf and headed towards goal, but I managed to make contact with the finger of my gloved right hand. It was the first time I'd worn these particular gloves. I'd noticed that the Mexican and South-American goalkeepers wore gloves that were larger than their British counterparts, with palms covered in dimpled rubber. I'd been so impressed with this innovation that I'd invested in two pairs. Those little rubber dimples did their stuff: the bouncing ball didn't immediately glance off my hand and I was able to scoop it high into the air. But another thought flashed through my mind. In directing the ball upwards, I might only succeed in flicking it into the roof of the net. So I rolled my hand slightly, using the third and fourth fingers as leverage.

I landed crumpled against the inner side netting of the goal, and my first reaction was to look at Pelé. I hadn't a clue where the ball was. He'd ground to a halt, head clasped between his hands, and I knew then all that I needed to know. With the luck of the gods, the angle at which I'd managed to lift that ball was perfect and it had ballooned into the air and over the bar, out of harm's way for a corner.

As I stood up Pelé, ever the great sportsman, came up to me and patted me on the back.

'I thought that was a goal,' he said, smiling.

'You and me both,' I replied.

The TV footage of the game shows me laughing as I turn to take up my position for the corner. I was laughing at what Bobby Moore had just said to me.

'You're getting old, Banksy,' he told me. 'You used to hold on to them.'

Like hell I did.

When the wind blew from the south towards our terraced house in Ferrars Road, it was the only time you never saw washing hanging on the line. At the end of our street ran the main Sheffield to Rotherham road, on the opposite side of which stood Steel, Peach and Towser's steelworks. The works stretched for nigh on a mile and a half and what I remember most about it was the smell: an acrid mix of fired coal, sulphur-tainted steam and human sweat. Even when there was no wind the smell was ever present. When it did blow our way, the cosy rows of houses, and their occupants' washing, were immediately coated in a grimy film of raven-black soot.

On such days I can recall drawing comic faces in the muck that coated our windowsills. Washing windows and paintwork was a constant job in the Tinsley area of Sheffield where I grew up. Mam seemed to spend half her life with a bucket of water and wash leather in her hands, but it was a thankless and never-ending task, like painting the Forth Bridge.

That soot found its way inside every house and settled like a blanket on everything. It was part and parcel of Sheffield life in the 1940s. No one could remember it being any different. No one spoke about air pollution. The smell and the soot were just the by-products of what everyone aspired to – work. My dad worked in a steel foundry. My mother divided her time between cooking and washing. I was the youngest of their four sons, the others being David, Michael and John. John, the eldest, was always referred to as 'Our Jack', a term of endearment that was a source of bewilderment to me as a small boy, as I could never fathom its logic. 'Our Jack has eaten all his cabbage,' Mam would say, as if we might otherwise have confused him with another Jack.

Dad didn't earn much and with six mouths to feed money was always tight for us, as it was for all the other families in our neighbourhood. Tinsley folk may have been poor, but they were proud. I remember, one Sunday lunchtime, a neighbour appearing at his door to sharpen a carving knife on the front step to make us think they could afford a Sunday roast. He might have succeeded had it not been for the incongruous Sunday-lunchtime smell of frying fish wafting from their house as we played in the street. Fish was plentiful and cheap then, and that's all that the poorest could afford.

In the forties Tinsley families moved house rarely, if ever. Co-habitation was unheard of. A couple would never set up home together until they were married. That done, the vast majority stayed put until the time came for their children to call the funeral director. There were no nursing homes, no managed flats for the elderly. A house was bought or rented and turned into a home. At various times it was also a nursery, a hospital, a function room and, in the end, a chapel of rest.

Over time, people and their properties seemed to become one, each home taking on the character of its occupants. From either end of Ferrars Road the terraced houses all looked the same, but I soon learned the subtle individualities of each one. It was the small touches that gave them their characters: the highly polished brass letter-box on the front door of the Coopers; the pristine gold-leaf house number on the fanlight over the front door of the Dobsons; the net curtains in the front window of the Barbers, gathered rather than hanging straight as in every other home; the tiny red glass vase that balanced precariously on the narrow ledge of the Archers' window.

The Archers' red glass vase never contained flowers – few could afford such luxuries. Today that might be called minimalism. We were minimalists, too, in the sense that nobody had much of anything. Furniture and the wireless apart, what possessions people did have took the form of trinkets. Ornaments adorned every conceivable surface, including the walls, where lines of brightly coloured plaster ducks made desperate bids for freedom from nearly every front room.

For a Tinsley lad one of the few escape routes from a lifetime of work in the steel foundry or pit was sport. I had three childhood passions, the most important of which was football. In the forties it was quite common to watch both the Sheffield teams, Wednesday and United, on alternate Saturdays – if you could afford it. I rarely got the chance to see either, but at each of the twenty or so games I did get to see between the ages of seven and fifteen, I dreamed that one day I would be on the pitch rather than watching from the stands.

Tinsley County School was only a stone's throw from Tinsley railway shed, where steam trains were housed and serviced. On any given day there were up to fifty steam engines on shed, each belching smoke and steam in competition with that from Peach and Towser's. The phrase 'Go outside and get yourself some fresh air' was never heard from the teachers in my school.

The close proximity of the shed was a bonus to me, for my second passion was train spotting. The hobby is much ridiculed today, but in the forties, with no television, no computers and few toys, train spotting was a hobby taken up by most of the boys in our neighbourhood. Best of all it was free. All you needed was a copy of Ian Allan's *ABC Spotters Book*, a notebook and a pencil. I rarely ventured outside Tinsley and the sight of engines from other towns and cities always filled me with a sense of wonder. They may have come from faraway Newcastle or London, or just Wakefield or Bradford. It didn't matter. Simply to see them evoked in me a feeling of travel. Here was something from a town or city whose name I had only seen on a map. It was almost as if those places were visiting me. Though I never moved from my vantage point on that sooty brick wall by my school, I felt my horizons broaden.

At Tinsley shed my two greatest passions combined, for there was a class of locomotive named after famous football teams. I remember it always gave me a great thrill to see *Bradford City*, *Sunderland*, *Sheffield United* or *Everton* emblazoned above the centre wheel of the engine, with nameplate bearing not only the club's colours but a half caseball made of shining copper. Many of these plates now adorn the reception areas of their respective clubs.

Whenever I see them I am reminded of my schooldays at Tinsley County.

For quite another reason, the railway shed was a boon to many Tinsley families, mine included. In the shed yard was a coaling stage, under which steam engines stopped to have their tenders replenished. To one side of the stage was a large stockpile of coal, a magnet to families on the breadline. Many was the time my mam would send me and one of my brothers down to Tinsley shed with my old pram under cover of darkness. There was a well-known spot in the fence where the wooden panels had been loosened by countless others keen to put heat in their hearths. Once through, it was a simple matter of walking up and down the sidings on the lookout for windfall coal. (We never took it from the stockpile; Mam would have considered that to be stealing. Picking up stray lumps of coal that had fallen from a tender or spilled during refuelling she considered to be no more than helping to keep the engine shed yard tidy. Her view was not shared by the shed foreman.)

The pram was large and navy blue. We always had the hood down, because once the body of the pram had been filled with good-sized pieces of coal the hood was always a useful depository for the smaller stuff. Fully laden, we'd set off anxiously over the rough ground back to the fence. The weight of the pram and the cratered terrain made a speedy exit impossible, even if the foreman was bearing down on us, although the beam of his torch, visible from a hundred yards, always gave us sufficient warning to escape. Once through the fence my anxiety would dissipate and I'd chirp away merrily to my brother as we pushed our ill-gotten bounty back to Ferrars Road like hunters bringing home the kill. Mam would reward us with a supper of toast made on a fork in front of a blazing fire, courtesy of our night's work.

We had no bathroom, so the kitchen sink was where matters hygienic were attended to in the form of a twice-daily wash. On Friday nights a tin bath would be placed on newspaper in front of the living-room fire and laboriously filled by Dad with kettles of hot water. First to go was Dad, then Our Jack, then David, Michael and, finally, the youngest – me. Being the fifth user of the same bathwater, it's a wonder I didn't get out dirtier than I went in. The ritual of Friday-night bathing was not restricted to the Banks household. Everyone I knew had just one bath a week. It was also the only time I changed my vest and underpants. I wince at the thought now, but that's how it was, for me and for every young lad I knew. Our clothes were laundered once a week, every Monday, in the kitchen, Mam using a poss tub and dolly and a hand-operated wringer before hanging them on the line (or, if it rained, draping them over wooden clothes horses dotted around our living room). Come Tuesday they would be dry. On Wednesday they were ironed and then put away ready for us to wear again on Friday after our bath. For Mam, life must have been as monotonous as mutton, as regular as a roll on an army drum. That my childhood was always happy, secure and filled with a warm heart is all the more to her credit.

In the forties and fifties it was rare for parents to show outward signs of affection. Mam and Dad were caring and, in their own way, loving, but never tactile or overtly affectionate. It was a commonly held belief that to shower children with love and affection would make them 'soft' and incapable of coping with the daily grind of working life. Besides, there wasn't time. We shared Mam with the housework and Dad with the evening paper, though he would occasionally surface from the *Sheffield Star* to ask us, 'What have you been up to?' or to opine that 'They want locking up' when something in the paper appalled him.

Mam's opinions came from a kinder heart. 'I see the brother of the Earl of Harrogate has died,' she would say, as if the bereavement were personal. 'There's always trouble for somebody in this world.' To Mam life was indeed troublesome.

That I always felt settled in childhood was, I am sure, in no small way due to the small routines of home life. On a Saturday lunchtime, for example, we always had fishcake and chips, which it was my job to fetch. I did this on a bicycle that had more than a touch of Heath Robinson about it, cobbled together from spare parts found on a bomb-site. Riding that old bike was a precarious business at the best of times; with a string bag fully laden with six fishcake 'lots' (i.e. 'with chips') swinging from the handlebars it was downright dangerous. On one occasion the bag became tangled in what few spokes were in the front wheel and I was pitched head-first on to the cobblestones while dinner was scattered all over the street. Terrified to go home and ask for more money I simply scooped everything up and rewrapped it as best I could. I spent that dinnertime suppressing nervous laughter as I watched Dad bemusedly picking little bits of grit off his chips.

On Saturday mornings I'd fetch the groceries from Tinsley Co-op: flour, sugar, a pound of butter off the block, bread, eggs, a drum of Cerebos salt, Nice biscuits, Shippams paste, Oxo cubes, Bisto, Echo margarine, Carnation milk, Heinz beans, Ye Olde Oak ham and the only sort of salmon I knew existed – tinned. There was a lot more, but that was the core of the order every Saturday morning, the lack of variation testimony to the limited range available in a country still in the aftermath of rationing.

Mam worked part-time at the Big House, owned by one of the smaller steel magnates. I'm not sure what she did, exactly. 'A bit of cleaning and a bit of cooking', she said. The family must have treated her well, at least – she certainly wouldn't have stayed otherwise. Looking back, her life must have been awful. Dad rarely took her out, even to the local pub. That she made our draughty house a loving home is my abiding memory of her.

On Sunday lunchtimes, while Dad was in the pub, I'd help Mam cook the Sunday dinner to the accompaniment of *Two Way Family Favourites* on the wireless. I still smell roast beef whenever I hear 'With a Song in My Heart', its signature tune. The programme relied heavily on sugary sentiment from the likes of Dickie Valentine, Eddie Fisher, Vera Lynn and Alma Cogan, requested by mothers for their squaddie sons at BFPO 271 Cologne, BFPO 32 Cyprus or BFPO 453 Gibraltar – code words for faraway places that were a mystery to me.

This weekly reminder to the nation that Britain still had a military presence abroad served to maintain the misplaced notion that we were still a major power in world affairs when, in truth, the days of Empire were long gone. The plummy voices of Cliff Michelmore, Muriel Young and Ian Fenner were in sharp contrast to those of their listeners, the Sheffield folk whose expectations never extended beyond the steelworks or the pit.

Family Favourites was followed by an hour of comedy. First was *The Billy Cotton Band Show*, Billy's opening lines always being interrupted by a voice from the heavens shouting, 'Hey, you down there with the glasses . . . get orn wiv it.' Billy's response would be his catchphrase, 'Wakey! Wake-ho!', at which his band would strike up his frantic signature tune, 'Somebody Stole My Girl'.

Billy's show was followed by another half hour of comedy. Series came and went over the years – *Educating Archie, Round the Horn, The Navy Lark* – but one of my favourites was *The Clitheroe Kid*, with Jimmy Clitheroe. Jimmy's antics in a working-class family in the north-west of England were much more real to me than the Just William books I borrowed from the library.

When Dad got back from the pub, we would all sit down to our first course: a large piece of Yorkshire pudding over which had been poured a generous helping of Mam's wonderful gravy. Mam would then serve the Sunday roast followed by rice pudding sprinkled with nutmeg. Dad would sometimes round things off with more Yorkshire pudding spread with strawberry jam.

We ate well, but money was tight. It was an anachronism even in 1940s Sheffield, but I wore clogs to school to which my father, in an attempt to extend their life, had fixed steel bars across the soles. This made me very popular, since I could be dragged across the playground to make sparks fly from my footwear. I've often wondered if my exceptional reach is a result of being constantly pulled about that playground.

Football and train spotting apart, the other great love of my childhood was the cinema. Our local fleapit, situated next to Tinsley Working Men's Club, rejoiced in the name of the Bug Hut. There I would sit spellbound on a Saturday afternoon watching Gene Autry or Roy Rogers, Arthur Askey, George Formby or Old Mother Riley among row upon row of grimy kids. All pals together.

Our Jack suffered chronic kidney problems and also had a bone-marrow defect that affected his legs. Jack never grew above five feet tall and for much of his childhood was confined to a wheelchair. I used to push him to and from the Bug Hut. When we arrived I would wheel Jack down to the front and then take one of the sevenpenny seats at the back. On one occasion I became so engrossed in the film that I went home without him. He wasn't best pleased, and neither was Mam.

When I was about eleven Dad bought two decrepit lorries and set up his own haulage business. He worked impossibly long hours, but the business soon folded because the lorries were forever breaking down. Undaunted, he decided to launch a new business, one he knew plenty about – gambling. For a number of years Dad had supplemented his meagre income by running an illegal book on horse racing. Licensed betting shops were still to come and the only legal place to bet in the late forties was at the racetracks themselves. Dad, knowing the steel workers liked a flutter, reckoned he was on to a winner opening up his own betting shop, and he wasn't wrong.

We moved from our Tinsley home to Catcliffe, a mining village on the Sheffield–Rotherham border. Our new house adjoined a series of arches, like those under railway viaducts. Dad decided one of these would be ideal for his 'flapper' betting shop, so we cleared it out and cleaned it up.

The business did well, our increased standard of living more than compensating for the odd court appearance and £40 fine. Fortunately, the local Bobby was one of Dad's drinking pals, so we received plenty of warning when a raid was imminent. The Bobby, in return, received a Christmas turkey and a bottle of whisky which Dad mysteriously found in the shop each year and which, of course, had to be taken in as lost property.

The shop that did so well, however, also brought tragedy upon us. One day in the early fifties Jack was heading home with the day's takings when he was set upon by two robbers. In spite of his disability, they beat him up badly as well as making off with the takings. Jack spent weeks in hospital, his health deteriorated and, tragically, he died. He was a great guy, a loving brother, and we were all devastated at his passing. Nothing was ever again the same. For the first time in my life I experienced the loss of a loved one. I grieved for months, mourned for years and miss him to this day. That his attackers eventually received lengthy jail sentences was no compensation for losing a dear brother and a great friend.

My childhood footballing heroes were always goalkeepers. On my infrequent visits to Hillsborough or Bramall Lane it was always they who captured my imagination. Keepers such as Wednesday's Dave McIntosh, a Girvan-born Scot whose centre parting was old fashioned even in the early fifties, and United's Ted Burgin, a Sheffield lad like me and my inspiration that one day I too would be good enough to play professionally. McIntosh and Burgin apart, there was Manchester City's Bert Trautmann, unique in that he had been a German prisoner of war who had stayed on in Britain to make a career for himself in football. A worthy successor to the great Frank Swift, Bert had been signed from non-league St Helens Town and developed into one of the very best goalkeepers of his day. I used to marvel at his anticipation, courage and agility, attributes also present in another boyhood hero of mine, Bert Williams of Wolves and England, who proved to me that you didn't necessarily have to be tall in order to be a good goalkeeper. Another favourite was Blackpool's George Farm. In the fifties, Blackpool, boasting the great Stanley Matthews, Stan Mortensen and Jackie Mudie, were the equivalent of today's Manchester United. Their appearance always ensured a full house. Most, understandably, turned up to see Matthews weave his magic, but the attraction for me was George Farm. Farm had an unorthodox style, catching the ball with one hand over and the other underneath it. But what interested me was the way he'd shout instructions to the defenders in front of him. Farm took it upon himself to organize his defence, which was very unusual for a goalkeeper at that time.

At the age of fourteen, my appearances in goal for my school side earned me a call-up for Sheffield Schoolboys. I was thrilled and honoured to have been chosen to represent my city, but my memories of playing for Sheffield Boys are tainted by the fact that I was suddenly dropped with no explanation after seven or so games. It wasn't in me to complain, so I simply accepted my lot and concentrated on playing for my school.

I wasn't a great scholar. On leaving school in December 1952 I got a job as a bagger with a local coal merchant. It was dirty, hard, physical graft conducted in all weathers. Though I didn't appreciate it at the time, the work served to make my upper body and arms muscular, which is a great advantage for a goalkeeper.

I was fifteen, still developing physically, and the eight-hour day bagging coal left me tired out by the weekend. I was still in love with football, but by Saturday I felt too exhausted to do more than spectate at one of the many amateur games played in our area. One Saturday afternoon I went to watch a team called Millspaugh. Their trainer approached me before the start of the match:

'You used to play in goal for Sheffield Schoolboys, didn't you?' he asked.

The Millspaugh goalkeeper hadn't turned up. Would I fancy a game?

My tiredness rapidly disappeared and I immediately raced home to collect my football boots. I should have fetched some shorts as well, since the trainer had only a goalkeeper's jersey to offer me on my return. Too late now, so I played in my working trousers. I still recall the bemused looks on the faces of my new team mates when a cloud of coal dust shot up from those trousers as I blocked a shot with my legs.

The game ended in a 2–2 draw. I felt pleased with my first taste of open-age football. I was only fifteen and the majority of those playing were in their mid to late twenties. I must have impressed the Millspaugh manager because after the game he asked if I would like to be their regular goalkeeper. I had no hesitation in saying yes.

I had been playing for less than a season with Millspaugh when Rawmarsh Welfare asked if I would sign for them. Rawmarsh played in the Yorkshire League, which was a much higher grade of football and one well thought of in local footballing circles. I made my debut for Rawmarsh in an away game against Stocksbridge Works. Any thought I may have had of making my name in what was then the highest non-league level of football in the county was quickly dispelled when we lost 12–2. Following a second game, a 3–1 home defeat, the Rawmarsh manager let me down gently, saying, 'Don't bother coming again.'

The following Saturday found me back on the touchline watching Millspaugh at the local rec. Before the game the Millspaugh trainer approached me.

'Goalkeeper hasn't turned up,' he said. 'Fancy a game?'

Oddly enough, I did.

I gave up coal-bagging to be an apprentice bricklayer with a local building firm. Much of my time as a rookie was spent hod-carrying for the experienced brickies, which was even harder graft than the coal-bagging. No sooner would I have delivered one load of bricks than my brickie, who was on piece work, would be screaming from up top for more. I was still only fifteen and knew better than to complain. In the run-up to Christmas the brickies, intent on earning more for their families, worked even more quickly. Health and safety considerations were non-existent. I never wore a hard hat, for example. One day a falling brick gave me a mighty whack on the side of my head. I stopped midway down the ladder, blood streaming down my face. The brickie was very sympathetic. 'Get an effing move on! Yon brick was only on yer 'ead for a second.'

They were hard men and hard task masters, those brickies, but they had hearts of gold. Come pay day, many was the time my brickie would slip me a few bob out of his own pay packet as a tip for helping him achieve his piece-work bonus.

Like coal-bagging before it, hod-carrying served to make my upper body strong and muscular, while constantly running up and down ladders strengthened my legs. I may have been only in my mid-teens, but I was no gangly youth.

I didn't recognize the man in the overcoat watching Millspaugh from the touchline. After the game he introduced himself as a scout from Chesterfield. He said I might have some potential as a goalkeeper, and that he'd be prepared to give me a run in Chesterfield's youth team. The season had six games to go. If I played well enough in those six games, I might be offered terms.

This was it: the chance I had dreamed of. Come next season I could be a professional footballer.

2. Aspiring Spireite

Chesterfield were a small club, but even so they enjoyed an average attendance of around 9,000, twice that of today. The first team played in Division Three North, the reserves played in the Central League and the youth team in the Northern Intermediate League. Both these minor leagues were very strong and invariably Chesterfield finished the season near the foot of both.

The Central League included the second XIs of clubs such as Manchester United, Liverpool, Everton, Blackpool and Newcastle, and it was not uncommon to line up against First Division and even capped players.

In truth, Chesterfield were way out of their depth in such company, so it's probably just as well that one of the Chesterfield directors was a key member of the Central League Management Committee. The Northern Intermediate League included junior teams from Newcastle United, Sunderland, Middlesbrough, both Sheffields, Leeds and Wolverhampton Wanderers.

I had my sights set on no more than a place in the youth team when I first arrived at the club's Saltergate ground one rainswept evening at the end of March 1953. I'd been told to report to the ground at 6.30 p.m. for training. Chesterfield's gym turned out to be a small space underneath their sloping grandstand, no more than twenty-five feet by twelve. Its ceiling was a network of steel girders supporting the seating above. From one girder hung a plank of wood on a rope. This was for sit-ups. There were two old mats on which players did press-ups, a short bench and a set of weights. A medicine ball and a punchbag were suspended from two more girders. It wasn't exactly what Arsenal were used to.

The trainer set me to work pummelling the punchbag and in time I had not only strengthened my wrists, hands and arm muscles, but also improved my sense of timing and co-ordination. In later life, when jumping to punch a ball clear, I rarely missed and usually got good distance. I am sure those early workouts in the Chesterfield gym were the reason.

As promised, I was picked for the six remaining Northern Intermediate games left in the season. I must have done something right because I was asked to report back for pre-season training in July 1953. When I did, Ted Davison, the manager, offered me a contract as a part-time professional player. I was to train at the club on Tuesday and Thursday evenings and play for whichever team I was selected for on the Saturday. My wages would be £3 a week. On signing the contract I was ecstatic. I couldn't have been happier if I'd been offered full-time terms with Manchester United.

My performances for the Chesterfield youth team earned me a promotion to the A team, then the reserves. I'd allowed myself to dream but the reality of Central League football woke me up with a bump. In 1954–55 we finished bottom with just three wins to our name. I conceded 122 goals: an average of three per game.

In spite of the constant hammering, my enthusiasm never waned. I loved playing in goal, especially in the Central League where just about every week I'd come face to face with a hero of mine. Against Leeds United I faced the great John Charles, who was having a run-out with the reserves on his way back from injury. Known as the Gentle Giant, John was blessed with a magnificent physique and was equally at home at centre half or centre forward. In the air he was peerless and his passing was magnificent, his vision enabling him to see openings invisible to others. He had a shot like an Exocet and could score from any angle, even when off balance. Above all, he was a great sportsman.

Knowing I was a young lad with only a handful of reserve team games to my name, John Charles came up to me as the players took to the field.

'Now, don't you worry, son,' he said. 'You do your best out here today. I won't hurt you and I won't go up with you for a ball with my arms flailing. Enjoy yourself and do your best for your club.'

We lost that game 5–0 and I think I'm right in saying that John scored three. He was true to his word, however, and never gave me any rough treatment. As a 16-year-old I would have been a pushover for him, but he played it fair and he played it straight. That was Big John, a player whose great talent for the game was in keeping with his tremendous sense of sportsmanship.

On another occasion, following a seven-goal defeat at Wolves, I was soaking my aches and bruises in the Molineux plunge bath when one of the Chesterfield directors emerged through the pall of steam alongside one of the Wolves board.

'I just had to come and offer my congratulations,' said the Wolves man. 'You let in seven today, but if it weren't for you, it could have been double figures. That was as good a performance in goal as I've seen in many a year. Take heart from that.'

I did.

By the time their careers are over, today's Premiership stars have usually amassed enough money to retire from playing altogether. In the days of the maximum wage it was a different story, and First Division players often dropped down a division or two in order to extend their working lives. I came across countless seasoned pros who had played top-flight football during my time in the Chesterfield reserves. We even had a couple of our own – most notably, Eddie Shimwell.

Eddie had played in three FA Cup finals for Blackpool, including what many consider the greatest ever, that of 1953 when they came from 3–1 down to beat Bolton Wanderers 4–3. That final was dubbed the Matthews Final because of Stanley Matthews's scintillating play on the wing. It was also the game in which Blackpool's centre forward Stan Mortensen scored a hat trick, and when Matthews came to write his autobiography in 1999 he insisted that the chapter relating to the 1953 final be called 'The Mortensen Final'.

Eddie Shimwell had been a very good right back whose assets were his strength, stamina and timing in the tackle. He signed for Blackpool for £7,000 from Sheffield United in 1946 and became the first full back to score in an FA Cup final when he netted against Manchester United in 1948. In recognition of his services, Blackpool gave him a free transfer in 1957 and he joined Oldham Athletic before arriving at Chesterfield for his swansong.

As any old pro will tell you, you never lose skill – it's the legs that go. Eddie had never been the quickest player and when he arrived at Saltergate it was evident that he was slowing up. So much so that he found it difficult to stake a claim in the first team. Eddie was also plagued by a troublesome shoulder injury, but still he kept on playing.

I remember one reserve team game when, having received the ball deep in our own half, Eddie took off down the right wing. He hadn't run more than a few yards when his upper body suddenly and violently quivered. At first I couldn't see what the problem was, but on taking a closer look I noticed Eddie's left shoulder jutting through his shirt at an acute angle. Unbelievably, his shoulder had popped out of its socket. I glanced across to the Chesterfield bench and saw our trainer take to his feet, then back to Eddie, who amazingly was still running with the ball. It was then that I saw something even more astounding. Eddie simply carried on running and with his right hand reached across and yanked his left shoulder back into place! I'd heard many a story of old pros playing on through injury, but this was the first time I'd witnessed it. I could only marvel at his fortitude and resolve. At the same time, though, I also felt sadness. Eddie obviously loved football, but there was no way a seasoned and respected pro like him should have had to play with such a debilitating injury just for the money. When I see a player writhing around in simulated agony today I always wonder what Eddie would have made of such amateur dramatics.

Two very good friends at Chesterfield were Barry Hutchinson and Paul Brown, an ex-Sheffield United player. The three of us travelled together from Sheffield for both training and matches. As we waited one day for the team bus I was amazed to see my boyhood hero, the former Sheffield United goalkeeper Ted Burgin, walking by on the opposite side of the road. Browny called his old team mate over. To my surprise, he was just an ordinary bloke on his way to the chip shop. He even spoke with the same accent as

me. Burgin was no less my hero in terms of his expertise as a
goalkeeper, but from that moment I saw him in a different light. It
would be an exaggeration to say that my age of innocence was
suddenly over, but I did sense that something from my childhood
had died.

My career with Chesterfield was interrupted when I received my
call-up papers for National Service. I joined the Royal Signals and
after weeks of square-bashing at camps in Catterick and Ripon
found myself posted to Germany. Fate had another wonderful
stroke of luck in store for me, for it was during my time there that
I met a beautiful young German girl called Ursula. I fell in love
with her then and I'm even more in love with her now. Ursula and
I have been married for over forty years, and have three children
and five grandchildren.

   While in Germany I managed to play quite a lot of football, first
for my squad, then for my regimental team. We managed to win
the Rhine Cup, a very prestigious trophy at that time.

   Chesterfield must have kept tabs on me because on being
demobbed I received a letter inviting me back. Ted Davison had a
surprise waiting for me: a contract as a full-time professional. It
took me all of five seconds to sign. My dream had come true.

Many of the reserve team were still young enough to play in the
FA Youth Cup and we found to our delight that the experience of
playing against seasoned pros and the occasional international in
the Central League made us more than a match for players of our
own age.

   In 1955–56 I was the keeper for both the regular reserve team
and the FA Youth Cup team. I'd suffered a fractured elbow early
in the season, but surgical expertise and a young body's healing
capacity meant that within seven weeks I was back between the
posts and keen to show what I could do.

   The FA Youth Cup was a relatively new competition. The
inaugural winners in 1952–53 were Wolverhampton Wanderers
and the current holders were Manchester United, who had also

won it in 1953–54. In theory, a team doing well in the Youth Cup should have a rosy future as those players progress to first-team football. This didn't and doesn't always work in practice, of course, but managers and directors nevertheless showed keen interest in their youth teams' progress.

We set out on the trail of the FA Youth Cup in 1956 as minnows and surprised not only the Chesterfield supporters but also ourselves by reaching the final. Our opponents were the holders, Manchester United, who included in their team Wilf McGuinness, Alex Dawson and a blond-haired lad on the left wing who possessed a humdinger of a shot, Bobby Charlton.

The final was over two legs, the first at Old Trafford. As our coach drew into the Old Trafford car park I was taken aback by the sheer number of supporters milling about. I was left in no doubt that this was a big occasion.

Manchester United produced a special programme complete with potted biographies of each player. I well remember sitting in the dressing room and reading them. The pen portraits detailed how the United players had been spotted playing for England Schoolboys, or the North of England Schoolboy Representative XI, or even England Youth. Mine said I had been spotted playing for a works team on Tinsley Rec.

As I ran on to the pitch I was dumbfounded to see around 34,000 people in the ground, all but a handful of whom were supporting United. From the kick-off those United supporters got right behind their team. United forced us on to the back foot and within minutes I knew how those Texans must have felt at the Alamo. The United pressure was relentless, shot after shot rained in at my goal. I caught them, parried them, tipped them over the bar and blocked them with any part of my body I could. But for all my efforts and those of my team mates, such constant pressure had to pay off and just before half time United scored twice.

After the interval United picked up the same script and soon we found ourselves three goals adrift. There was little we could do to stem the pressure. Inside right Harry Peck and centre forward Bob Mellows, whose goals had been instrumental in our reaching the final, were playing so deep I thought they'd end up with the bends. With twenty minutes to go United took their foot off the gas and I enjoyed a welcome break from Bobby Charlton's machine-gun shooting as our forwards went deep into largely uncharted territory. To my delight we managed to pull a goal back. Then, with five minutes remaining, we broke away and nicked a second: 3–2. I couldn't believe it and I doubt if the United players could either. It had been smash-and-grab stuff and I left Old Trafford in great spirits, feeling we had gained a moral victory.

A crowd of over 14,000 turned up at Saltergate for the return leg, some 5,000 more than the average attendance for a first team game. The second leg was another humdinger. This time we had more of the play but, in spite of our pressure, couldn't claw back the deficit. The game ended 1–1, which gave United a third successive FA Youth Cup. We may have lost, but I gained a great deal of satisfaction from our performances as a team, and was happy with my own efforts. I was looking forward to further progress at Chesterfield.

The following season my youth team days were largely behind me, and along with team mates Harry Peck, Keith Havenhand and Bob Mellows I was selected for a Northern Intermediate League Representative squad to play the 1955–56 NIL champions, Sunderland, at Roker Park. As it turned out, I didn't play, and the goalkeeper's jersey went to Alf Ashmore of Sheffield United. However, just being in the squad had boosted my confidence.

In July 1958 Ursula gave birth to our first child, Robert. Needless to say, we were blissfully happy. It wasn't the done thing for fathers to attend births, so in time-honoured tradition I hung about outside while Ursula did all the hard work. I had been told that the birth of a child changes your life. The arrival of Robert certainly changed ours. I don't think I've ever been as tired as I was in those first six weeks and, of course, compared to Ursula's my role was easy. Becoming a father was the most wonderful feeling imaginable, and I was consumed by a general feeling of well being. We were now a complete family and I felt that both my marriage and my life had been redefined for the better.

I tried to do my bit. I changed nappies. I rocked Robert to sleep when Ursula was exhausted. I did more around the house. Ursula was a marvellous mother, full of confidence and vigour, which was no mean feat considering what she had been through. I have always had the utmost respect for womankind, but seeing how naturally Ursula took to motherhood enhanced that respect tenfold.

Robert was the first of three. Ursula later gave birth to two beautiful girls: Wendy, who arrived in 1963 just before I was about to play in an FA Cup final, and Julia, who was born in 1969 a few days before I was to play a match for England. My family mean the world to me. Of all the gifts that life has bestowed upon me, they are undoubtedly the greatest.

In the 1958–59 season my performances in goal for Chesterfield reserves saw me pushing the long-serving Ron Powell for a place in the first team. Ted Davison had been replaced as manager by Duggie Livingstone and it was he who finally gave me my big chance in November 1958, when I made my debut in a home game against Colchester United in the newly formed Third Division of the Football League.

I thought Duggie Livingstone would take me to one side the following day and tell me what was expected of me, but I should have known better. Like most managers in those days, tactics and man-management were low on his list of priorities.

In fact, Duggie was more like a headmaster than a boss. I remember one occasion when three of us missed a match after being directed on to the wrong train by a railway attendant. Not only did Duggie give us a rollicking and dock our wages, he also made us drive to Sheffield Midland station to point out the errant attendant in order to back up our story. Luckily he was on duty, and admitted misdirecting us. We never did receive an apology, but I exacted revenge of a sort when, some time later, Duggie asked for a lift in my clapped-out van. A combination of racetrack driving and pre-MOT mechanics scared the living daylights out of him.

'Gordon. Don't ever let me ask you for a lift again!' he said, and meant it.

The night before my league debut I couldn't sleep. My mind was racing and I played the forthcoming game over and over in my mind. On the first occasion we won 1–0 and I saved a penalty. Then we won 3–0. I was worn out before I got up.

The programme from the game against Colchester made much of the fact that Ron Powell was set to make his 300th consecutive appearance for the club. My selection, of course, was going to deny him that milestone. Ron himself was fine about it, but I wondered what reaction I would receive from the Chesterfield faithful when they saw me run out in the goalkeeper's jersey. The very fact that Ron had been dropped in the first place taught me a lesson about football: there is no room for sentiment in the game.

Near the back of the programme was a small paragraph headed 'Special Note'. It read, 'The opening paragraphs of Saltergate Chatter were printed before team selection. We now welcome and congratulate Gordon Banks as goalkeeper for today's match. Ron Powell will receive congratulations on his 300th appearance soon, on the appropriate occasion.' I took that to mean that they weren't expecting my elevation to the first team to be a lengthy one!

Also making his debut that day was inside right Arthur Bottom, bought from Newcastle United with money raised by supporters' clubs through a series of whist drives, bingo, pie and pea supper nights etc. at which I and other players were invariably in attendance. As you can see, everything operated on a much smaller scale in those days.

Colchester United had been in the Third Division South, so were rare visitors to Saltergate. We players knew next to nothing about them, and neither did Duggie Livingstone. His pre-match team talk comprised a few clichés about 'taking the game to them' and 'playing to our strengths', the latter meaning nothing to me as nobody had told me what our strengths as a team were. The sum total of managerial guidance I received that day was, 'Good luck, son.'

Thus versed in my expected role I sprinted down the tunnel and out in front of the 7,140 fans present to witness my league debut.

The result was a 2–2 draw, our goals coming from Bryan Frear and Maurice Galley. Despite conceding two goals I came off the field quite satisfied with my own performance, feeling that neither goal I had let in could be described as resulting from a goalkeeping error. In the dressing room my team mates were full of praise, which raised my spirits even more. Even Duggie Livingstone said 'Well done.'

'Played it just like you told me, boss,' I replied.

I was selected for the following league game, a 1–1 home draw against Norwich City, and during the remainder of the season missed only three games, through injury.

There were some sizeable attendances in the Third Division in those days. I played in front of over 11,000 at Wrexham, 13,000 at Carlisle United, 15,000 at Notts County, in excess of 17,000 at Plymouth Argyle and 20,505 at Norwich City. Even our home attendances picked up. Most noticeably against Hull City and Mansfield Town, against whom we drew crowds of over 10,000.

That season we finished a respectable sixteenth – way off the promotion places but well clear of the relegation trapdoor. I was enjoying my football immensely and loved the camaraderie of my team mates, a number of whom are good friends to this day.

Back in the fifties, unless you were a player destined for a club in a much higher division, there was little to be gained from moving clubs. Players in the Third Division were all paid more or less the same. Marginally more in the Second Division, less in Division Four. Unless a First Division club came in for you, there was little financial incentive to change clubs. The rule at that time was that a player only received a cut of his transfer fee if he had not asked for a move. If he requested a transfer, he got nothing. As a result, the fruit rarely fell far from the tree.

In January 1959 *Charles Buchan's Football Monthly*, the most popular football magazine of its day, surveyed the origin of players in the Third and Fourth Divisions. The statistics showed that in the thirteen Third Division clubs in the North and Midlands there were only twelve players of southern origin. In the Fourth Division the situation was even more pronounced: seventeen clubs and seven players, respectively.

In those days both the teams and their supporters were largely home grown – a far cry from the situation today, when 'one-club men' can be counted on the fingers of one glove.

Unfortunately, such loyalty was not always a two-way street. The Blackpool board didn't even think fit to award Stanley Matthews a testimonial, for example. Today, we have millionaire Premiership players being awarded testimonial games after, in some cases, just six years of service at a club. The decision by Niall Quinn to give away the proceeds from his testimonial at Sunderland in 2002 to children's charities was a gesture as laudable as it was rare.

My Chesterfield team mates were a super bunch of lads who played no small part in helping me to establish myself in the first team. To a man, they always encouraged me and, when I did make a mistake, advised me not to worry and just get on with it. To a young goalkeeper experiencing league football for the first time, their encouragement and support were invaluable.

I was learning my trade not in training but out on the pitch. You might think that's a very dangerous way to do it, and you'd be right. But in those days there was no such thing as a goalkeeping coach. I was embarking upon a career which, certainly in those early years, was self-taught.

In total I played in twenty-six matches. With each game my self-assurance grew and come the final few games I was confident enough not only to shout instructions to team mates but to organize the defence in front of me. I told the full backs when to push on and when to drop back and even started to tell big Dave Blakey when to drop in and pick up. Goalkeeping apart, I felt I was making a positive contribution to the team and took heart from the fact that in the final five matches of the season I kept three clean sheets and conceded only three goals.

My horizons at this time didn't extend beyond playing for Chesterfield. I had, after all, only those twenty-three league games to my name, so it came as a shock during the summer of 1959 when Duggie Livingstone called me into his office and introduced me to a dapper man with wavy black hair who said he wanted to sign me.

The man in Duggie's office was Matt Gillies, the manager of

First Division Leicester City. Duggie informed me that Leicester had offered Chesterfield £7,000 for my services.

'We don't want to sell you,' said Duggie. 'You have outstanding potential and we see your future here at Chesterfield. Whether you sign for Leicester or not is entirely your own decision. Here's a pen.'

Chesterfield were, as ever, strapped for cash and the money was just too good to turn down.

My knowledge of football at the time was hardly comprehensive. You might not believe this, but I was unsure what division Leicester City played in, let alone exactly where Leicester was. What I did know, however, was that Leicester were a much bigger club than Chesterfield and that they played at a higher level. The very fact that they were willing to pay what was at that time a decent fee for an unknown goalkeeper was to me an indication of their confidence in my ability and potential. I reached for the pen Duggie Livingstone was jabbing in my direction and signed.

By now Ursula and I were living in Treeton, a small mining village just outside Chesterfield. As I arrived home I suddenly realized that I had committed our future without consulting my wife. But I needn't have worried, she was delighted for me.

'How much are they going to pay you?' asked Ursula.

I drew a deep breath. 'Fifteen pounds a week!' I said triumphantly.

Ursula clasped her hands together in joy and took to her feet, and we danced around the kitchen together in celebration of our good fortune.

3. Learning My Trade

The summer of 1959 was memorable. BMC launched the Mini, Fidel Castro became president of Cuba. I was clicking my fingers to Bobby Darin's 'Dream Lover' and curling my lip to Cliff Richard's 'Living Doll'. This was the new music of the time and I liked it. Rock 'n' roll was here and we young people took to it in a big way. Pop music was changing and so was my life.

My sale to Leicester had caused a great deal of discontent among Chesterfield's supporters, many of whom felt that my fee of £7,000 had been too low. I felt flattered.

That summer Maurice Galley and Ivor Seemley were also put on the transfer list. The money received from my move resulted in no notable signings. Following my exit Ronnie Powell had come back as first-choice goalkeeper and, in need of cover, Duggie Livingstone signed a lad called Ted Smethurst from non-league Denaby United. Chesterfield's other signing that summer was Brian Frost, a forward from another non-league team, Oswestry Town. I was pleased to see Brian get his chance in league football because I had been at school with him. We were two of five lads from Tinsley County School who went on to play professional football, an unusually high number from one year at a single school. (The others were David 'Bronco' Layne, who became a prolific goal-scorer with Sheffield Wednesday until his career was ended through his involvement in the infamous bribery scandal of 1963, Bob Pashley and Terry Leather.)

I arrived at Leicester in July 1959 full of high hopes and enthusiasm. It was the first day of pre-season training and I immediately knew I'd joined a top club when I saw the Leicester training ground. Situated on the outskirts of the city, the ground was purpose built and had a wooden pavilion containing changing rooms, a shower block and a weights room. There were also three full-size pitches. I was impressed; I'd never known such luxury.

I decided to improve my knowledge of football in general, which I was sure would assist me greatly in my quest to make my mark as a First Division goalkeeper. My £7,000 fee had given me the idea that I would soon be knocking on the door of the Leicester first team. That notion was immediately dispelled when the trainer, Les Dowdells, arrived to tell us there was going to be a press photo call and began to distribute shirts. Les began by handing out six green tops. I hadn't realized that Leicester played in green. Only when he started to dole out blue shirts as well did it dawn on me that I was just one of six goalkeepers at the club challenging for a single place in the first team.

I soon discovered that Johnny Anderson, who was from Arthurlie, and his fellow Scot Dave MacLaren, who had been signed from Dundee, were the two main contenders for the first team goalkeeper's jersey. Of the three other keepers I can recall only two: Tony Lines, a promising youngster whose potential had been spotted when playing for the Lockheed works team, and Rodney Slack, a lad from Peterborough who had been scouted at his local youth club team.

Chesterfield had given me the chance of playing league football, but Leicester City gave me the opportunity of carving a career at the highest level of the game. I'd worked as a coal-bagger and hod-carrier, often getting up at 5.30 in the morning, and there was no way I wanted to go back to that life. I was determined to give my all at Leicester and buckled down to pre-season training. The fact that I was just one of six concentrated my mind wonderfully. I knew the club couldn't justify six full-time professional goalkeepers indefinitely and I was determined that, come the day Matt Gillies decided who was to stay, I would be included.

I did all that was asked of me in training, and in the pre-season friendly games I felt I gave a good account of myself. On the Friday morning before the first day of the 1959–60 season I trained as usual with my team mates, after which we all headed to the club noticeboard to find out the teams for the opening day of the season.

That's how it was back then. There was no squad-rotation system. No horses for courses where a player might be picked because his style was considered suited to a specific game plan, or thought to be problematic to a particular team or opponent. The manager picked his best eleven for the first team, his second best eleven for the reserves and so on.

As I scanned the team sheets my spirits soared. I was in the reserve team. This was a tremendous boost to my confidence. Having arrived at the club with high hopes I'd been brought back down to earth when I realized I was sixth-choice goalkeeper. Now, after only six weeks and four friendly matches, I was number two. Dave MacLaren had been chosen to keep goal for the first team at West Ham United. The reserves were at home to Southend. Hardly a classic game in the making, but one I was looking forward to greatly.

In the previous season Leicester reserves had been champions of the Football Combination. For me to make it into that side at the first time of asking was a great boost to my spirits and made me feel I was making headway. However, even I was to be taken aback by how quickly my progress was to gather momentum.

I kept a clean sheet on my debut (we drew 0–0 with Southend) and also in my second game, a 4–0 victory at West Ham – my first ever game in London. There followed a 5–2 win against Bristol City and a 0–2 home defeat to Chelsea reserves. Although we lost against Chelsea I came off the pitch feeling I'd had my best game to date. I wasn't the only person to think that.

The Leicester first team were due to play Blackpool at Filbert Street the following Wednesday. The team for that game was pinned up after Tuesday morning training. I was still in the changing room drinking tea and chatting with some of the lads when one of my team mates from the reserves, Richie Norman, sauntered in.

'Dave MacLaren's injured. You should go see who Mr Gillies has picked in goal,' he said.

And on the noticeboard there was my name, in goal against mighty Blackpool the following day. I suddenly felt the whack of Richie Norman's hand on my shoulder.

'Well done, Gordon,' he said. 'Well deserved.'

A crowd of 28,089 witnessed my Leicester City league debut. It bore certain similarities to my first game for Chesterfield in that the manager said little apart from 'Good luck and do your best'. Matt had obviously waited until the last moment before making a decision about Dave MacLaren's fitness because it was the Scot's name that appeared in the match programme. I wasn't mentioned at all. Not that it bothered me; I had other things to occupy my mind, not least of which was a very lively Blackpool forward line that contained Jackie Mudie and Bill Perry, both of whom had played in the famous FA Cup final of 1953, and rising stars Ray Charnley, Arthur Kaye and Dave Durie.

I was a little disappointed to learn that the great Stanley Matthews wasn't included in the Blackpool team, as I would have loved to have played against the maestro. Stan was forty-four years of age but still eminently capable of playing First Division football. He had, in fact, been a member of the England team only two years previously. His mere presence in the Blackpool team used to lift the players and would have put up to 7,000 on the gate.

The Leicester crowd gave me their full support that night, as did my new team mates. As a young debutant I couldn't have asked for more from my defence. Len Chalmers, Joe Baillie, John Newman, Tony Knapp and Colin Appleton encouraged me for the duration of the game, saying 'well done' to just about everything I did. Whenever I had the ball in my hands, Len and Joe would run out wide and make themselves available while centre half Tony Knapp kept me calm.

Our inside left, Ken Leek, put us in front, but that wily little predator Jackie Mudie pulled a goal back for Blackpool. I think it was Blackpool's Arthur Kaye who played the ball into our penalty box from the right. Jackie Mudie latched on to the pass and I quickly came off my line to close down his vision of goal. Jackie, shrewd and calculating, spotted a small gap to my left and simply stroked the ball down that channel and into the corner of the net. There wasn't much power behind his effort; there didn't need to be. Mudie knew I wouldn't reach the ball and went for accuracy rather than venom. The game ended in a 1–1 draw and I was happy to have gotten through it without making a serious error.

I retained my place for the following game, a 2–0 defeat at Newcastle United, but with Dave MacLaren once again fit found myself back in the reserves when Leicester travelled to Blackpool for their return fixture.

While I was concentrating my efforts in the Football Combination, the Leicester first team began to leak goals. A 3–3 draw at Blackpool was followed by a 4–3 victory at Birmingham City. There then came a 1–1 draw with Spurs, a 4–1 defeat at Manchester United and a 3–2 home defeat at the hands of Blackburn Rovers. Fourteen goals had been conceded in five games. For the next game, away at Manchester City, I found myself recalled to the first team. I wish I could say I came back into the team and suddenly Leicester became watertight in defence, but I can't. We lost 3–2 at Maine Road, drew 2–2 at home to Arsenal, then suffered the ignominy of a 6–1 defeat at Everton. Six! It was like being back with Chesterfield reserves.

Although my presence in the team hadn't stemmed the tide of goals, I felt that with each game my performance was improving. Following our defeat at Everton I kept my place for the game against Sheffield Wednesday and was to be an ever-present in the team for the remainder of that season. We lost games, of course, but never again were we on the receiving end of a hammering. The emphasis was still very much on attacking football at this time, but in only two games in the new year did we concede more than two goals: a 3–1 defeat against Birmingham City and a 3–3 draw with Everton.

Leicester finished a creditable twelfth in the First Division, not bad considering we had had a poor start with only four victories from our first twenty matches. Our form in the new year gave rise to great optimism and I had taken heart from my own performances. After that very disappointing start to our campaign, we lost only six of our remaining twenty-two league games. Since my arrival at the club as sixth-choice goalkeeper it had taken me just over a quarter of a season to establish myself in the first team.

Progress had its price, of course. I was my own greatest critic and I placed great demands upon myself, both physical and mental. I wanted to continue improving as a goalkeeper and became single minded in this aim. After my normal training (which, in fact, was the same training every other player at the club did, irrespective of which position he played) I'd ask a couple of the youth team players to stay behind at the training ground to practise shooting at me. I was keen to develop, even evolve, the practical side of goalkeeping. Sometimes I'd ask these young lads to ping shots at my goal from a variety of angles. On one occasion all I asked them to do was either chip or lob the ball towards goal. I took up a position halfway between the penalty spot and the edge of the area. Constantly running backwards to get to the ball enabled me to work out the best position I could take up relative to the kicker in order to backpedal and still make the save.

Players at both Chesterfield and Leicester tended to work to their strengths rather than their weaknesses. To my mind, this was the opposite of what they should have been doing. I made a concerted effort to work on my weak points – taking crosses on my left, for example. I also worked on different ways to punch the ball clear when under pressure: I discovered there were seven. I had no idea how good a goalkeeper I could be, but I was determined to find out. I worked hard at every aspect of my game until, by the end of the 1959–60 season, I knew enough about goalkeeping to realize just how much I still had to learn!

I was aiming high and so too were Leicester City. Unfortunately the club's finances were rather more down to earth. During 1959–60 the club made unsuccessful offers for John White of Falkirk (who eventually opted for Spurs), Hibernian's Joe Baker (who was signed by Italian giants Torino) and a centre forward who had been scoring a lot of goals for Second Division Middlesbrough, Brian Clough. Clough signed for near neighbours Sunderland, going on to score 251 goals in 274 games before a bad knee injury curtailed his career at the age of twenty-seven.

I suppose I was one of Matt Gillies's successful signings that season, but I wasn't the only one. The club had also signed Albert

Cheesebrough from Burnley. Albert went straight into the first team and was virtually ever-present that season. Albert's £20,000 fee, a considerable one for Leicester, proved to be money well spent.

Another young player also made his mark during my first season at Leicester – Frank McLintock, a Glaswegian who had been signed from Shawfield Juniors. As a young player he combined the toughness of a Gorbals upbringing with a fine footballing brain to emerge as a stylish wing half whose great vision was the catalyst to many a Leicester attack. At twenty-two he had the guile and nous of a much more experienced player, and his skilful repertoire was an indication of a great player in the making. When Frank eventually left Leicester, for Arsenal in 1964, the £80,000 Leicester received was a club record. Frank's enthusiasm for football was to play no small part in my development as a goalkeeper, for which I will always be grateful.

Our good form in the new year gave rise to hopes of a good run in the FA Cup. In round three we won 2–1 at Wrexham, with goals from Albert Cheesebrough and Ken Leek. (The headline writers then were no better then than they are today: 'Cheese and Leek Give Wrexham Food for Thought'; 'Wrexham Leek Early Goal then Are Cheesed Off'.) In the fourth round we beat Fulham 2–1 at Filbert Street to set up a fifth-round home tie with West Bromwich Albion – the first ever all-ticket match at Leicester.

Someone had the bright idea that cup tickets would be sold on the turnstiles at the reserves' Football Combination fixture against Bournemouth. A bumper crowd of 22,890 turned up to see the reserves that day, while I played in front of fewer than 17,000 in the First Division.

A near-capacity crowd of 38,000 was at Filbert Street for the West Brom tie. Tragedy struck at half time when the match referee, Jack Husband, collapsed in the officials' changing room and died. Amazingly the game continued, a former referee in the crowd running the line and one of the linesmen taking over as referee. We won 2–1, though there were few celebrations. That the game was allowed to continue speaks volumes about the nation's attitude to death in the aftermath of the Second World War. Nowadays we would all be shocked by such an event, and rightly so, but to people with the carnage of war fresh in their minds it seemed hardly to warrant a second thought. The best defence people had erected against six years of destruction was simply to 'get on with it'. So we did.

A crowd of 39,000 saw us bow out of the Cup against Wolverhampton Wanderers. It turned out to be a classic quarter-final, full of cut and thrust. Peter Broadbent put Wolves ahead only for Tommy McDonald to equalize for us. Len Chalmers, two years older than me at twenty-four, had recently been appointed captain. Len played exceptionally well that day but towards the end of the game couldn't get out of the way of a low centre and deflected the ball past me and into the net. In the dressing room after the game Len was inconsolable. I told him, 'It's gone now, Len, so forget it. Your luck will change next season.' Nothing could have been further from the truth.

Wolves went on to win the FA Cup that season, beating Blackburn Rovers 3–0, though they were denied a third consecutive League Championship when Burnley pipped them on the last day of the season. The success of Burnley and Wolves was a triumph for attacking football, still very much in vogue in 1960 as evidenced by Wolves' goal tally of 100 plus for the third successive season. We played Burnley twice towards the end of the season when they really had their tails up and the Championship within their reach. We lost by the only goal at Turf Moor, but dented their progress by winning 2–1 at Filbert Street. Our good form in the second half of the season and the fact that we had given the eventual champions a good run for their money home and away made me believe that Leicester could go on to bigger and better things the following season. I wasn't wrong.

4. From Number Six to Number 1

The dawn of the sixties was a time of change, both for me and for the game. My weekly wage rose to what was then the maximum, £20, so at last we could afford a TV set. On it we watched Real Madrid beat Eintracht Frankfurt 7–3 in the European Cup final – their fifth consecutive success in the five-year-old competition.

Real's domination of European football led many British clubs to adopt similar coaching methods, and the FA's coaching school at Lilleshall received a whole new intake as a result. Jimmy Adamson, Tommy Docherty, Frank O'Farrell, Dave Sexton and Bob Paisley were all in the Class of '61, as was Bert Johnson, who, as Leicester first-team coach, was to play a significant part in my development.

What the players wore changed too, old-fashioned thick cotton strips being increasingly rejected in favour of lightweight nylon and boots becoming lighter and lower slung.

Ursula and I took our first holiday around that time – a week at Butlin's in Skegness – while on the other side of the country Bill Shankly became manager of struggling Second Division Liverpool.

We bought a new house, a semi in Kirkland Road, Braunstone, in which we rattled around like two peas in a drum. I was doing the only thing I wanted to do, play football, and was being paid for it. Life was great.

Apart from the considerable thrill of having established myself as Leicester's first-choice goalkeeper, the events surrounding my first season at Filbert Street had not been remarkable. All that was to change, however. In 1960–61 Leicester embarked upon one of the most notable seasons in their history and football was rarely out of the headlines as a result of events both on and off the pitch.

When I reported back for pre-season training, revolution was in the air. The vast majority of players were deeply unhappy about the maximum wage limit and so was the players' union, the PFA.

There was talk of strike action in order to free ourselves from contracts that bound us to a club for life and put a ceiling on what we could earn.

Nationwide, supporters were grumbling as well. During the close season the Football League had announced that admission prices for adults were to rise to a minimum of 2s. 6d. (12½p). Following the post-war boom when total annual crowds were in excess of 40 million, attendances had been in gradual decline and many supporters believed the increased admission price would only make matters worse. (They were right: 1960–61 saw attendances fall to 28.6 million from 32.5 million the previous season.)

There was discontent in the media, too, with a number of stinging articles comparing the quality of the English game unfavourably with that played abroad.

But in 1960–61 English football began the process of catching up. The benefits of the FA's coaching school began to filter through and the newly introduced apprenticeship system meant that, for the first time, many clubs had a properly structured youth policy. Changes such as these played no small part in our winning the World Cup just a few years later.

That summer also saw the birth of the League Cup, conceived by the then FA Secretary Sir Stanley Rous and delivered by his Football League counterpart Alan Hardaker. Although the competition was initially unpopular among clubs and supporters alike, I was all in favour of it. In time it was to repay my enthusiasm with a treasure chest of golden memories.

In the close season Matt Gillies had added two new players to the squad: George Meek, a winger from Leeds, and George Heyes, an understudy goalkeeper from Rochdale. Both Johnny Anderson and Dave MacLaren had been transferred, further boosting my confidence that the manager had every faith in me and easing my fears that one small mistake in a game could cost me my place.

Matt had also tried and failed to sign Arsenal centre forward David Herd and Pat Crerand from Celtic, both of whom were to opt for Manchester United, and Dundee's Alan Gilzean, who eventually moved to Spurs. Matt obviously felt we needed a replacement at centre forward for Derek Hines, a prolific goalscorer who had joined Leicester in 1947 and was now nearing the end of his career. In the end he found the player he was seeking in Leicester's reserve team: Ken Leek, a stylish, skilful centre forward whose speed off the mark was breathtaking and who did a terrific job for us up front.

Our opening game of the season bore certain similarities to my debut for the club. It took place at Filbert Street, the opposition were Blackpool and the score was 1–1. We followed that with a fine 3–1 win at Chelsea, courtesy of goals from left winger Gordon Wills (2) and Jimmy Walsh, who had taken over from Len Chalmers as captain. On the train back home the team were in optimistic mood.

But we lost our next four games and Matt Gillies began to ring the changes: Ken Leek for Derek Hines, Ian King for Len Chalmers at right back, Frank McLintock for Ian White at right half and Howard Riley for George Meek at outside right. The team picked to go to Old Trafford on 10 September had a very different look to it from the one that had started the season just a few weeks earlier.

With the likes of goalkeeper Harry Gregg, Maurice Setters, Bill Foulkes, Bobby Charlton, Johnny Giles, Albert Quixall and Dennis Viollet, Manchester United were a team of real quality. Johnny Giles put them ahead, but Jimmy Walsh equalized for us after forcing Jimmy Nicholson into a mistake in the second half. The game ended 1–1. We had put an end to a sequence of four successive defeats but, more significantly, Matt Gillies's wholesale team changes were beginning to bear fruit: we lost only four of our next thirteen league games.

Good as United were, the 1960–61 season was dominated by one club – Tottenham Hotspur. Spurs were magnificent in every respect. Their 11 consecutive wins at the start of the season was a record, as were their 31 victories in 42 league games, their 16 away wins (including 8 in a row) and, equalling Arsenal's 1930–31 total, their tally of 66 points.

We met Spurs at Filbert Street in mid-September, losing a close encounter by the odd goal in three. When we travelled to White Hart Lane for the return fixture in February, Spurs were top of Division One and well clear of their nearest challengers, Sheffield Wednesday and Burnley. We were sixth, but arrived in London on the back of a six-game unbeaten league and cup run that had seen us beat Everton 4–1 and Manchester United 6–0.

In Terry Dyson, Les Allen and Cliff Jones, Spurs possessed three of the speediest players around at that time. We were very much aware of this and set about denying those three possession, believing that if we cut out their source of the ball, in the main from Danny Blanchflower, John White and Dave Mackay, we stood a good chance of nullifying what the press had dubbed 'the unstoppable force'. That worked, up to a point. Spurs scored twice through Danny Blanchflower (penalty) and Les Allen, but our own forwards, prompted by Frank McLintock and Colin Appleton who teamed up magnificently with Jimmy Walsh in midfield, gave the Spurs defence a torrid time. Jimmy Walsh scored twice and a Ken Leek goal gave us a memorable 3–2 victory. It was only Spurs' third defeat of the season and their first at home. We were ecstatic. We had beaten the best team in Britain in their own back yard. Leicester City had come of age as a team.

We knew we'd never catch Spurs in the League, but we had high hopes of lifting England's other prestigious trophy, the FA Cup. We had already beaten non-league Oxford United 3–1, then Bristol City 5–1 in a replayed game that had been abandoned when a torrential downpour swamped the Filbert Street pitch, and were due to face Birmingham City in the fifth round. City proved difficult opponents. Before a crowd of 54,000 at St Andrews Howard Riley gave us the lead only for me to be beaten by a penalty from Birmingham's centre forward Jimmy Harris. In the replay we squeezed out a 2–1 win in front of a capacity 41,916.

The quarter-final draw paired us with Barnsley, then a mid-table Third Division side. The Barnsley manager, Johnny Steele, had told the press his side 'would not roll over and die'. They certainly didn't.

The game at Filbert Street ended goalless and the replay at

Oakwell was an equally close affair. Barnsley at this time did not have floodlights and the game took place on a Wednesday afternoon. A crowd of 39,250 packed Oakwell on what would normally have been a working afternoon to see the Third Division side belie their lowly status by taking the game into extra time. Howard Riley scored for us, Ken Oliver for Barnsley, but a typical piece of opportunism from Ken Leek saw us progress at the expense of the gutsy home side.

The semi-final draw had already taken place on the Monday prior to our replay against Barnsley. We were to meet Second Division Sheffield United at Elland Road, while Spurs had been drawn against Burnley.

Over 52,000 turned up at Elland Road to witness a tight and taut goalless draw. The replay, at the City Ground, Nottingham, was no better, neither side possessing the temerity or wherewithal to break the deadlock, and the 0–0 scoreline sent us to St Andrews for a second replay.

The first twenty minutes of our game at St Andrews provided more drama and excitement than both previous encounters combined. Within minutes of the start I was diving full length to tip away a stinging drive from the United centre forward Derek Pace and moments later was happy to see a swerving shot from Len Allchurch clear my crossbar by inches. Down at the other end the United goalkeeper, Alan Hodgkinson, saved well from both Ken Leek and Jimmy Walsh. Both teams had set out their stall and both were going for victory.

Our centre half, Ian King, missed a penalty early on, but we took the lead midway through the first half when Jimmy Walsh, a player who seemed to hang in the air when he rose to the ball, headed in. Just before half time I thought we had the game wrapped up when the prolific Ken Leek made it 2–0.

Our second-half plan to contain the Sheffield side was working a treat when we gifted them a penalty on 65 minutes. Their penalty taker, Graham Shaw, repaid Ian King's earlier generosity by shooting wide, though, let it be said, I went the right way! And that was that. When the final whistle blew I looked up to the darkened skies above Birmingham and thanked my lucky stars. Two and a half years ago I had broken into the Chesterfield first team. Now I was about to play in an FA Cup final at Wembley. Could this really be happening to me? It could and it was.

5. Into Europe

In the space of a year my life had changed dramatically. My performances for Leicester City had come to the attention of the England manager, Walter Winterbottom, and during Leicester's FA Cup run I was called up for the England Under-23 squad. (In those days the England manager was responsible for not only the full international team, but also for both the England Under-23 and youth sides as well as being the FA's head coach.)

I played twice for the England Under-23s, against Wales and Scotland. The team line-up illustrates just how important it is to have young players coming through, for nearly all of us went on to greater things. For the game against Wales, the England outfield players were John Angus (Burnley), Gerry Byrne (Liverpool); Bobby Moore (West Ham), Brian Labone (Everton), John Kirkham (Wolves); Peter Brabrook (Chelsea), John Barnwell (Arsenal), Johnny Byrne (Crystal Palace), Les Allen (Spurs) and Clive 'Chippy' Clark (West Bromwich Albion), with Alan Mullery (Fulham) in reserve. And English football was supposed to be devoid of quality players!

For the game against Scotland, George Cohen (Fulham) came in for John Angus at right back. Mick McNeill (Middlesbrough) was at left back for Gerry Byrne, Mick O'Grady (Huddersfield Town) for Peter Brabrook and Peter Dobing (Blackburn Rovers) for John Barnwell. Our opposition for those two games included such stars in the making as Mike England (Blackburn Rovers), Arfon Griffiths (Arsenal), Pat Crerand and Billy McNeill (both Celtic), Alan Gilzean and Ian Ure (both Dundee) and a young blond lad from Huddersfield Town, Denis Law.

Rubbing shoulders with some of the very best young players in British football made me even more determined to improve my technique as a goalkeeper. I knew I was still a long way off recognition at full England level, but those two appearances for the Under-23s gave me hope that, with hard work and diligence, I might one day be good enough.

For now, though, I was happy to concentrate on our forthcoming FA Cup final. While we were making hard work of defeating Sheffield United in one semi, Spurs were breezing past Burnley 3–0 in the other. Burnley were the reigning league champions who, along with Sheffield Wednesday and Wolves, had clung to Tottenham's coat tails in the race for the Championship, but the Spurs team of that season was in a different class altogether. Still, we had managed to beat them at White Hart Lane, and we really did fancy our chances against them at Wembley.

Spurs were managed by Bill Nicholson and captained by the great Danny Blanchflower, who also skippered Northern Ireland. Danny was an articulate and deep-thinking player who not only played a good game, but talked one too, and Spurs' success in 1960–61 resulted in no small part from Blanchflower's theories on football and the way it should be played.

Danny also had a ready wit. Before one Home International match, when asked what his plan against England was, the Northern Ireland captain revealed that 'We're going to equalize before England score.'

Both Nicholson and Blanchflower were masters of tactics and improvisation. Yet we had out-thought both of them at White Hart Lane. Could we do so again at Wembley?

Before we could find out, Matt Gillies was to make a decision that would grab the headlines for all the wrong reasons and throw our preparations into turmoil when, three days before the final, he dropped the player who was our best hope of winning it.

On the Wednesday before the final, Ken Leek had gone to a pub for a couple of pints with some friends. Matt interpreted this as a gross breach of club discipline, a wholly unprofessional act in the week before a Cup final. And perhaps it was, but Ken's punishment was severe in the extreme. Matt Gillies dropped him from the team for Wembley. His replacement was to be our reserve centre forward, 21-year-old Hugh McIlmoyle.

I felt a mixture of shock and disbelief, as did the rest of my team mates. Ken was the best centre forward we had at the club. Even at full strength, with everyone playing to the best of his ability, we knew Spurs would be very difficult opponents. Gillies had used a guillotine to cure dandruff. Yes, Ken should have known better than to go out in public for a beer three nights before the FA Cup final, but it was hardly a case of Gazza in the dentist's chair or Roy Keane at his most opinionated. He'd been home and in bed by eleven.

The manager had punished not only the player but also the team, for we all knew that, without Ken, the odds against us winning had just lengthened considerably.

To play in an FA Cup final is the pinnacle of many players' careers. It was certainly the greatest moment of mine at the time. I was twenty-three years of age, had only been at Leicester for two seasons and couldn't believe the good fortune that had befallen me. Three years previously I had been playing in the Chesterfield reserve team; now I was about to play at the most famous football stadium in the world in the final of the oldest cup competition in the world.

For such an important game, everything is planned to the last detail. Before setting off for Wembley each player received an itinerary from club secretary Charles Maley detailing what time the players had to meet at Filbert Street, the time the coach left the ground for Leicester station and its arrival at same to the minute. It even denoted what time we would be served sandwiches on the train and what the sandwich fillings would be. It's a pity that the game itself couldn't have been as rigorously enacted, for it took only fifteen minutes for our plans to go awry.

To anyone with a passion for 1960s football, the Spurs team of that day rolls off the tongue like a litany: Brown, Baker, Henry; Blanchflower, Norman, Mackay; Jones, White, Smith, Allen and Dyson. We lined up alongside them in readiness to be presented to the Duke of Edinburgh: Gordon Banks, Len Chalmers, Richie Norman; Frank McLintock, Ian King, Colin Appleton; Howard Riley, Jimmy Walsh, Hugh McIlmoyle, Ken Keyworth, Albert Cheesebrough.

Both teams caused a minor sensation by breaking with tradition and wearing tracksuits when taking to the pitch. Ours were pale blue with a fox's head stitched on to the left breast; Tottenham's were white.

I remember glancing around the stadium and being impressed by the sheer number of Leicester City fans present, especially in view of the fact that Spurs were the best-supported club in the country – the combined attendance figure of 2.5 million people at the club's league and cup games that season remains a record.

The Cup final had been given an extra edge by the fact that Spurs were chasing 'the impossible double'. No team had won both the League Championship and the FA Cup in the same season throughout the century. Newcastle United in 1905, Sunderland in 1913 and Manchester United in 1957 had each won the League Championship but lost in the FA Cup final. Most people believed that the heavy fixture programme and the intense competitiveness of the modern game were such that no team could win both the First Division title and the Cup in the same year. I just hoped they were right.

If Spurs felt under pressure, it certainly didn't show. The previous evening they had gone to see *The Guns Of Navarone* at the Odeon, Leicester Square, after which they all enjoyed a couple of beers back at their hotel. We had all been in bed by ten thirty.

When a reporter from the London *Evening News* queried the wisdom of this, it was Danny Blanchflower again who came up with the quotable quote: 'I can only tell you the story of the golfer, Walter Hagen. Hagen was up late before a crucial play-off match, and a reporter told him, "I suppose you know your opponent has been long in bed?" "Sure," said Hagen, "but do you honestly think he's getting any sleep?"'

Spurs were confident, but so too were we. Our game plan, such as it was, had Jimmy Walsh and Ken Keyworth closing down Danny Blanchflower and Dave Mackay, while young Hugh McIlmoyle was to play deep as a centre forward in the hope of dragging the Spurs centre half Maurice Norman out of position and creating space for Jimmy and Ken to exploit.

And that's how it went for those first fifteen minutes. We set about Spurs with some verve but, after a quarter of an hour, disaster struck. Our right back, Len Chalmers, sustained an injury to his knee ligaments. It wasn't the result of a bad tackle, just bad luck. The damage was so bad that he should have left the field immediately, but there were no substitutes in those days, and he carried on gamely.

Len couldn't run, so Matt switched him to the wing, with Howard Riley dropping back, but we were effectively playing with ten men.

Looking back, it appears that events had conspired against us winning the Cup in 1961. We were without the spearhead of our attack, Ken Leek, and within fifteen minutes were effectively a man down. With all due respect to Hugh McIlmoyle, had we had Ken to worry the hell out of Maurice Norman and been at our full complement of eleven fit players, I believe we could have done it, for even with our handicaps, Spurs found us as hard to break down as we did them.

At half time it was goalless, but as the second half progressed the fact that Len was a passenger began to take its toll. We tired a little on the sapping pitch and Bobby Smith put Spurs ahead after sixty-nine minutes. Latching on to a great through ball from Spurs winger Terry Dyson, Smith controlled the ball, for once beat Ian King and hit a hard drive that was too far to my left for me to get a hand to.

Eight minutes later the game was effectively over when Smith returned the compliment. Terry Dyson met his cross from the right at the far post to plant a firm header into my net. There was nothing I could have done about either goal, but at 2–0 I knew that Spurs had done the double.

After receiving our medals, in recognition of Spurs' remarkable achievement we stayed at the mouth of the players' tunnel until they had completed their lap of honour. As the ecstatic Tottenham players made their way back, we lined up on either side of the entrance and applauded them on their way to the dressing room. It seemed the sporting thing to do, and I think they appreciated the gesture.

To lose a cup final is awful. When Leicester lost a league match I couldn't wait for the next game and the opportunity to rid myself of the disappointment. You can't do that after a cup final. The depression and general feeling of disappointment last for weeks. And of course, it's the same for the supporters. More than once during the club's post-match banquet at the Dorchester Hotel on Park Lane, I spared a thought for the crestfallen City fans travelling home.

In the papers, Matt Gillies was insisting that Ken Leek had been dropped owing to lack of form. I didn't and don't believe that for a second. I'm sure that Charles Maley's board-meeting minutebook would back up my opinion, too, were it not for the fact that the relevant pages have rather surprisingly gone missing.

Following the Cup final Ken asked for a move. In June he was transferred to Newcastle United, but spent only five months on Tyneside before moving to Birmingham City. From there he went to Northampton Town, then Bradford City before moving into non-league football.

As for Hugh McIlmoyle, the unwilling and unwitting participant in this controversy, the burden of responsibility of leading our line rested too heavily on his young shoulders. Unable to hold down a regular first-team place, within a year Hugh moved on to Rother-ham United and was to become a footballing journeyman in every sense of the word. His subsequent career included three spells at Carlisle United interspersed with appearances for Wolves, Bristol City, Middlesbrough, Preston and Morton. Hugh developed into a fine player and a prolific goalscorer, all in all scoring 200 league and cup goals on his travels.

The 1960–61 season marked a watershed for professional foot-ballers. The Football League agreed to the demands of our union, the Professional Footballers' Association, that the maximum wage and the so-called 'slavery contract' be abolished. The PFA had been engaged in a long hard battle with the Football League and our victory, which simply gave us the rights enjoyed by all other workers, was due largely to the efforts of PFA Chairman Jimmy Hill and our union secretary Cliff Lloyd, a former solicitor.

The maximum wage had long been a bone of contention among footballers. According to the Football League, it allowed all clubs to hold on to their best players. That is why relatively small clubs often managed to keep a world-class player for the duration of his career: Preston and Tom Finney, Blackpool and Stanley Matthews, Bolton Wanderers and Nat Lofthouse, Middlesbrough and Wilf Mannion. The system may have benefited the clubs, but certainly not the players.

Freedom of contract came about as a result of a test case when Arsenal's George Eastham sued his former club, Newcastle United, for restraint of trade in refusing him a transfer. George and the PFA won their day in court. The rest is history.

Johnny Haynes of Fulham became Britain's first £100-a-week footballer, but not every player saw a huge increase in his wages, even when the time came for a new contract. One of the first Leicester players to renew his contract following the abolition of the maximum wage was Richie Norman. Everyone was eager to know what Richie had managed to negotiate with Matt Gillies.

'Say hello to Leicester's first three-figure-a-week footballer,' said Richie on entering the dressing room.

Everyone was slack jawed. Jimmy Walsh asked Richie what his new wage was to be.

'Thirty pounds, twelve shillings and sixpence,' replied Richie.

Matt Gillies was particularly difficult to negotiate with where wages were concerned and treated the club's money as if it were his own. Rather than suggest an amount, Matt always asked how much I wanted. Whatever I suggested, Matt would pull a face, sigh, then say, 'I'd love to pay you that, Gordon, believe me I would. But . . ' After ten minutes of Matt's excuses I'd feel so bad about asking for a rise that I was almost ready to play for free.

The most I ever earned at Leicester was £60 a week in 1966, when I was England's first-choice goalkeeper. I should imagine David Seaman is glad he wasn't born thirty years earlier.

6. Wembley Again

In the summer of 1961 ten football journalists were asked to predict who would be amongst the honours in 1961–62. The consensus of opinion was that Spurs would retain their league title, Aston Villa and Birmingham City would contest the FA Cup final, Everton would win the League Cup, Liverpool and Sunderland would be promoted from Division Two and Queens Park Rangers would win Division Three. Well, at least they got Liverpool's promotion right.

One of football's great attractions is that the game is so unpredictable. Following our improved league form and our Wembley appearance of the previous season, I was convinced that Leicester City would win some silverware in 1961–62. I was so wrong that I could have been writing for the national newspapers.

The close season had seen a flurry of activity on the transfer market and some notable moves. Jimmy Greaves eventually completed his £99,999 record move from AC Milan to Spurs, Brian Clough left Middlesbrough for Sunderland for a fee of £45,000, while at Leicester Ian King followed Ken Leek through the door when he signed for Southampton for £27,500. Another transfer of note was completed in October when Stanley Matthews left Blackpool and signed for his hometown club Stoke City for the second time in his career. On the managerial front, former Wolves and England captain Billy Wright took over from George Swindin as manager of Arsenal.

As Spurs couldn't play themselves in the Charity Shield they faced instead an FA Select XI in the season's curtain-raiser. Spurs were as formidable as ever, winning 3–2 against what was more or less the current England team before a White Hart Lane crowd of 36,595.

Spurs' double success also benefited Leicester City, the FA ruling that, as losing finalists, we would participate in the European Cup-Winners Cup. It would be my first venture into European football and I was looking forward to it with great enthusiasm.

In the close season Leicester toured South Africa and Rhodesia (now Zimbabwe) – my first trip abroad – where we won four matches and drew one.

Our domestic programme began at Manchester City, where we lost 3–1, swiftly followed by a 1–0 home defeat by Arsenal that put a major dent in our early-season optimism. Still, a football season is a long haul; in time we would surely hit a vein of consistent form and swiftly rise up the table.

It never happened. Only once did we string three victories together (against Manchester United, Cardiff and Chelsea in April – that little run ended with a considerable bump when we lost 8–3 at Aston Villa), and we ended the season in mid-table. Combined with a third-round FA Cup exit, the 1961–62 domestic season was a big disappointment to everyone.

The highlight of a dismal year was our involvement in the European Cup-Winners Cup. None of the Leicester players had any experience of European football, and our first-round tie against Glenavon from Northern Ireland did little to change matters. This unglamorous though gentle initiation (we won 7–2 on aggregate) was followed by the plum draw everyone had been hoping for: Atletico Madrid. Everyone connected with the club was licking their lips at the prospect, but on the day of the first leg at Filbert Street I found myself in a situation that today defies belief.

Two weeks previously I had been training with the rest of my Leicester team mates when I was called over by Matt Gillies.

'Good news, Gordon,' said Matt, 'Walter Winterbottom has included you in the England squad for the Portugal game.'

This came as a huge surprise. To be called up for England was a quantum leap in my career. It was an even bigger surprise when I discovered that England were due to play Portugal on the same day that Leicester were playing hosts to Atletico Madrid!

I couldn't let the club, my team mates and the Leicester sup-porters down, yet to decline Walter Winterbottom's invitation

1. A Coronation street party in Ferrars Road and not a car in sight. Our house was the first one in the third block on the left. You can just make out the steel-works at the end of our road.

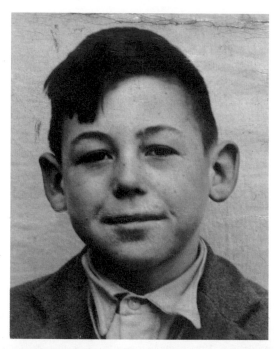

2. Me, aged about nine, during my days as a coal liberator. My idea of bliss was a slice of bread and dripping.

3. Mam and Dad out walking in Sheffield city centre. Needless to say, the car was not theirs!

4. Dad doing a bit of on-course turf accounting at Doncaster. For the steelworkers and coal miners of Sheffield, a trip to Doncaster was a major undertaking.

5. Me at fourteen. The jerkin I am wearing was at the time the height of Sheffield fashion.

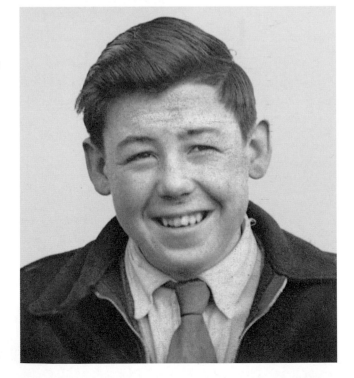

6. On holiday in Scarborough. I was aged about sixteen. Dad is obviously in the holiday mood – he's taken off his jacket and tie.

7. Mam and Our Jack at Scarborough.

8. In goal for Tinsley County Secondary School. Immediately to my left is Bob Pashley, who went on to play for Bolton Wanderers and both the Sheffield clubs. Far right on the back row (next to the teacher) is David 'Bronco' Layne, who became a free-scoring centre forward with Sheffield Wednesday. Centre front with the ball at his feet is Terry Wheighway, who was on the books of Sheffield United. The lad on my immediate left became the only person I've ever known to have a full-length photograph of himself in a passport.

9. Tinsley Rec, where my career as a goalkeeper began. When it rained, it was like a quagmire. When it was cold, the pitch became so icy that the teams had trouble turning round at half time.

10. A dispatch rider with the Royal Signals in Germany. I still have the helmet and wear it if ever I go to Hampden Park for a Scotland–England game.

11. *Below*: My debut for Leicester City reserves against Southend United in 1959. A City supporter ran into the goalmouth and took this photograph. Notice what appears to be a very healthy crowd for a match against Southend reserves!

12. The 1961 FA Cup final. Terry Dyson (out of picture) scored for Spurs. The other players are Bobby Smith (partly obscured by the far post), Colin Appleton, Cliff Jones and Ian King.

might mean that I would never get another chance at international level. There was only one thing to do: I would attend both games.

Some years earlier the Arsenal goalkeeper, Jack Kelsey, had played on a Wednesday afternoon in Cardiff for Wales against England, then hurried back to London to play for his club in a prestigious friendly against Juventus. I reasoned that if Jack Kelsey could get back from Cardiff to London, I could make it from London to Leicester.

England beat Portugal 2–0. Portugal's young number 8, Eusebio, was absolutely fantastic and gave every indication of being a great player in the making. Twice, from distance, he smacked powerful shots off the post with the first-choice England keeper, Ron Springett, floundering on the ground. Ron was a super goalkeeper, but on that day was lucky to keep a clean sheet.

Within twenty minutes of the final whistle I was on my way back to Leicester in my small Ford van (not the same one with which I had terrified Duggie Livingstone at Chesterfield). I arrived at Filbert Street just half an hour before the kick-off.

Atletico Madrid, like every other club in Spain – in the world, for that matter – lived in the shadow of Real Madrid. In the first round of the Cup-Winners Cup Atletico had beaten the French side Sedan by the same aggregate score as we had achieved against Glenavon. Though this was Atletico's first time in the Cup-Winners Cup, they had played in the 1958–59 European Cup, having finished runners-up to the holders Real in the Spanish First Division. A storming campaign eventually ended in a replayed semi-final against – that's right – Real Madrid. They had also defeated Real in the Spanish cup finals of 1960 and '61. We certainly had no illusions about their calibre as a team of quality and fighting spirit.

Despite my mad dash from Wembley I was raring to go, and so were my Leicester team mates. Matt Gillies had not been to see Atletico play, nor sent anyone to watch them. We knew nothing about their style of play, how they might approach the game or the best way to play against them. Atletico, however, had been to see us. One of their coaching staff had watched our previous game, a 2–0 home defeat by Blackpool.

In the absence of any better plan, we set about Atletico as we did any side visiting Filbert Street. We took the game to them from the start and laid siege to their goal. Atletico were quite happy to soak up the pressure and try to catch us on the break. A standard European pattern, as familiar today as the *Match of the Day* theme, but a new and puzzling tactic to us then. It looked as though they'd come for a goalless draw – which of course they had.

But they didn't get it. Ken Keyworth put us ahead and had a second disallowed when the referee pulled back play because Ken had been fouled en route to goal. That was European lesson number two for me. Foreign referees interpret the rules differently from British officials.

None the less, it seemed as if Ken's goal was going to be enough. With less than a minute remaining, however, we were taught European lesson number three. During the closing stages we should have played possession football and killed the game off. Instead, we staged one last assault on the Atletico goal in the hope of extending our lead to make life difficult for them in the return leg. Our attack broke down; Atletico's Ramiro brought the ball quickly out of defence and played it up to their number 8, Adelardo; he played a pass inside to Mendoza, who swept the ball into the net. Within seconds of the restart the referee blew for time; we'd fallen prey to a classic sucker punch.

The return leg was a belter. It wasn't in our nature to sit back and absorb pressure, so we adopted Matt Gillies's usual game plan: 'Get out there and give it a go'.

In front of over 50,000 vociferous Spaniards in the Vicente Calderón stadium we gave a good account of ourselves, but it was not to be our night. At home, Atletico were far more positive in their approach and I soon found myself busy. Eventually their pressure bore fruit when Atletico were awarded a penalty following a foul on Mendoza. Fortunately, I anticipated correctly and managed to save Collar's waist-high spot kick to my right. The respite proved temporary as Atletico were later awarded a second penalty. Again Collar shot to my right, and again I anticipated correctly. But this was a much better penalty, fired high towards the roof of the net. There was no way I could get even a finger to the ball and 50,000 Spaniards roared their approval.

Howard Riley and Ken Keyworth both went close to equalizing but when Atletico added to their tally in the second half they were content to see out the match playing keep-ball. Leicester's first European adventure was over, but there was no disgrace in losing to Atletico Madrid. They were a very good side, one much more experienced in the ways of European football than us, and eventually won the competition, beating Fiorentina of Italy in a replayed final that was finally decided in September of the following season.

With Jimmy Greaves in their ranks, everyone expected Tottenham Hotspur to retain their league title in 1961–62. They didn't. Ipswich Town had been promoted from Division Two the previous season and their manager, Alf Ramsey, worked a minor miracle in guiding his unfancied side – largely the same one that had won promotion – to the First Division title.

Alf Ramsey proved himself to be a great motivator of his players and a wily strategist, qualities that, in time, would greatly benefit both England and yours truly. Throughout the season Ipswich vied with Spurs, Burnley and Everton for the top spot in Division One. Both Spurs and Burnley were involved in Europe and both enjoyed runs in the FA Cup that eventually saw them meet in the final. Ipswich had no such diversions; they concentrated on the League and when Spurs and Burnley both faltered at the wire, Burnley winning only one of their last seven games, Ipswich's fresh and fluent football reaped handsome dividends. They finished three points ahead of Burnley and four ahead of Spurs to be arguably the most unlikely Football League champions in the history of the game.

The next year, 1963, was a remarkable one, both personally and historically. This was the year of the Cuban missile crisis, Concorde, Dr Beeching's axe, the Profumo affair, the Great Train Robbery, the Beatles and James Bond. (Who could forget the sight of Ursula Andress emerging glistening from the sea in the first Bond film,

Doctor No?) Before it was over I was to be in the running for the League and Cup double, make my debut for England in the most important game in our international calendar, and follow that up by facing the best international side in the world.

The summer of 1962 had been a frustrating one for me. My hopes of being in Walter Winterbottom's squad for the World Cup in Chile were dashed when he picked both Sheffield goalkeepers instead – Wednesday's Ron Springett and Alan Hodgkinson of United. I was on stand-by. At Leicester, Charles Maley retired as secretary, being replaced by Eddie Plumley. Matt Gillies had made no close-season signings, although towards the end of the previous season he had bought Mike Stringfellow, a lithe and speedy winger from Mansfield Town, and a mercurial midfielder, Davie Gibson, who joined us from Hibernian.

But there was no reason to suppose that the coming season would be very different from the last. And there was certainly nothing to suggest that we'd end it as contenders for the League and Cup double.

I had a nightmare of a game at Craven Cottage on the opening day of the season, not helped by the fact that I broke my nose when diving at the feet of Fulham's Graham Leggat. As if to rub salt in the wound, he went on to score both of Fulham's goals in our 2–1 defeat.

Unlike the previous season, however, we quickly put that opening-day setback behind us. We drew 3–3 with much fancied Sheffield Wednesday, then defeated Nottingham Forest 2–1, Mike Stringfellow proving himself to be a fine player with keen predatory skills. We then beat Wednesday 3–0 at Hillsborough, Mike taking his goal tally to six in four games.

It was an encouraging start, and our form was to get even better. We lost only one of our next nine games, Leicester's best start to a First Division campaign since 1925–26. Things were looking up.

Leicester's chief scout, Bert Johnson, having completed his FA coaching course at Lilleshall, was appointed first-team coach. Bert's input had an immediate effect. As a team we became better organized and the players' individual talents were at last moulded into a cohesive pattern of play. Jimmy Walsh and Davie Gibson were encouraged to track their opposite numbers back to our penalty area to provide extra cover when we were under attack. The midfield rotated to greater effect.

European lesson number one was implemented, and instead of taking the game to our opponents we became more patient in our build-up. Confident of our defensive qualities, we were content to soak up pressure and then use the speed of Mike Stringfellow and Howard Riley to counter swiftly. We worked on dead-ball situations, the offside trap, game plans – you name it and we had a strategy for it.

'Tactical awareness' was the new big thing on training pitches throughout the land, not least at West Ham where Geoff Hurst's innovative ploy of running in from deep to meet free kicks resulted in many goals for his club and, on one especially important occasion in 1966, a first-half equalizer against West Germany. (With all due respect to Alf, that one was pure Ron Greenwood.) The origins of organized football date back to the Victorians, but the origins of the game we know today can be traced back to the work of those Lilleshall graduates in the early sixties.

The winter of 1962–63 was dubbed by the press the 'Big Freeze'. Fixture lists were decimated, no complete programme of football being possible between 8 December and 16 March. Only three of the thirty-two third-round FA Cup ties were played on the day they were scheduled. Fourteen cup ties were postponed ten times or more, the match between Lincoln City and Coventry City being postponed a record fifteen times while that between Middlesbrough and Blackburn Rovers, originally scheduled for January, wasn't played until mid-March. Bolton Wanderers played no football at all between 8 December and 16 February. Over 400 matches fell victim to the weather.

Clubs became desperate for money. Queens Park Rangers moved to the aptly named White City in the hope that the pitch there would prove more playable. Halifax Town, with their pitch at The Shay covered in a three-inch layer of ice, at one point opened it as a skating rink. Blackpool used army flame-throwers on the pitch at Bloomfield Road while Chelsea employed a highways tar burner. Birmingham City rented a snow-mover from Denmark and Wrexham covered the Racecourse Ground pitch with 80 tons of sand.

At Leicester we managed to avoid too much disruption owing to a combination of good luck and determination. The previous summer the Filbert Street pitch had been re-laid using top soil containing a chemical fertilizer-cum-weedkiller. Fortunately, the chemicals generated a little heat which helped keep the frost at bay. Our dogged groundsman built on this by depositing oil drums filled with burning coke around the pitch the night before a game.

Even so, the pitch would be half-frozen come three o'clock, and completely so by the end of the match. I and several others used to file down our studs to the nails attaching them to our boots (the exposed nail-heads gave better grip on the frozen surface). I don't think we'd get away with *that* today.

The fact that we were playing regularly when other teams were not must have given us an edge as far as match fitness was concerned. Whatever, we embarked upon an unbeaten run of sixteen league and cup games, of which fourteen were won. On 8 April a 1–1 draw at Blackpool saw Leicester City at the top of Division One for the first time since 1927, and with an FA Cup semi-final against Liverpool to come, we had high hopes of achieving the double.

Our excellent run of form ended at Easter, at West Ham, when Bobby Moore's side beat us 2–0 courtesy of two goals from Alan Sealey. But we immediately bounced back to earn a 2–2 draw against Manchester United on Easter Monday, and the following night beat United 4–3 in front of a packed Filbert Street in the return fixture, a result that saw us regain top position in Division One. Following our next game, a 1–1 draw at Wolves, we set off for Hillsborough, the venue for our FA Cup semi against Liverpool.

Hillsborough was packed to the rafters, a capacity crowd of 65,000 roaring their approval as the teams took to the pitch. I remember looking up to the alp-like terracing and being amazed at the sight of that heaving, swaying mass of humanity. The noise was deafening. An alarming, volatile collective roar that made the hairs on the back of my neck stand on end. As I took up my position in the goalmouth for the pre-match kickabout, I did so to a backdrop of bedlam. The Leicester fans repeatedly chanted 'Cit-eee – Cit-eee' while the Liverpool supporters replied with the recent Beatles hit 'From Me To You'.

When the game got under way the mosaic of red and blue banked on the terraces once again erupted. It was pandemonium and such a highly charged atmosphere communicated itself to the players. The early exchanges were fast and furious. Liverpool seemed hell bent on taking an early lead and within minutes I found myself pressed into action time and again. We defended valiantly; we had to, the Liverpool pressure was relentless.

I dived low to my right to collect a shot from Ian Callaghan. Moments later I was at full stretch to save from Ian St John. Then Peter Thompson tried his luck, St John again, then Roger Hunt and Ron Yeats. I felt as if I was performing at the back of a fairground shooting range.

After about twenty minutes of this we eventually broke out of defence. Howard Riley and Graham Cross interchanged a series of passes on our right and, when the ball was eventually played into the Liverpool penalty area, Mike Stringfellow rose majestically to head the ball into the net.

I couldn't believe we had taken the lead with our first attack. Even more unbelievably, that first attack was also, more or less, our last.

Our goal served only to annoy Liverpool, who then laid siege to my goal in their efforts to equalize. Liverpool's army of supporters roared them on, while the City supporters were no less vociferous in their encouragement of our rearguard action. Liverpool poured forward and my team mates in the Leicester defence went into overdrive to keep the red tide at bay, which we somehow did until half time.

In the second half Liverpool redoubled the pressure. I don't know exactly how many times during the course of the game I was called upon to make a save. All I can say is, never in my entire career did I make so many saves in a match as we stuck to our task of defending the slender lead Mike Stringfellow had given us.

As ninety minutes approached, Liverpool hit us with everything they had. For the umpteenth time I went down at the feet of the marauding St John. John Sjoberg put himself in the way of a stinging drive from Ian Callaghan. Frank McLintock denied Roger Hunt with a timely sliding tackle. The ball broke to Callaghan; somehow I managed to get my fingertips to his rasping drive, but still we couldn't clear our lines. The ball ricocheted around my penalty area like a pinball. Shots were deflected by outstretched Leicester legs. I blocked efforts with any part of my body I could. Still Liverpool came at us as we desperately clung on to the slenderest of slender threads.

In the dying seconds Liverpool won a free kick just outside my penalty area. Ian St John ran up to the ball, stepped over it and kept on running while Gordon Milne played the ball into his path. St John angled a shot at goal that I managed to deflect up and away. The ball bounced midway between my six-yard box and the penalty spot; red and blue shirts converged. Suddenly I saw the ball rocket skywards in the general direction of heaven. As far as I know it's still going, because for the first time in ninety minutes, I took my eyes off it. The long drawn-out shrill of the referee's whistle cut the air and I immediately fell to my knees in a combination of joy, relief and sheer exhaustion. We'd done it!

According to that Sunday's *News of the World*, Liverpool had had thirty-four attempts on goal. We'd had one. That semi-final performance against Liverpool was, in my opinion, my best ever in a club game, as well as my busiest.

One distasteful footnote came as I, laughing with relief, and Ian St John crying in despair, left the pitch. Though each experiencing our emotions separately, we were close enough to appear in the same press photograph which was cruelly slanted to depict me laughing at the distraught Scot. Needless to say, the next time I played at Anfield I was pelted with boiled sweets, orange peel and worse. The vitriol directed at me by the Liverpool fans was remarkable. Of course, Ian knew I had been set up. On seeing the photograph he kindly contacted me and told me not to worry about it. It's just a shame he didn't tell the Kop!

Almost unbelievably, following our semi-final success against Liverpool, Leicester didn't win another league game that season. Our failure was due to a number of factors, not least of which was a crippling injury list. After the Liverpool game we were full of confidence but very much aware that we would have to apply ourselves totally in every one of our remaining five matches if we were to achieve our dream of the double. Immediately following our success in the semi-final we played West Bromwich Albion at the Hawthorns. Jimmy Walsh came in for the injured Ken Keyworth only for me to break a finger diving at the feet of Albion's Ken Foggo. Our trainer taped up my fingers but we lost 2–1, Albion's winner coming from a Don Howe penalty.

That injury put me out of our three remaining league games, but I wasn't the only player missing in action: Mike Stringfellow, Ian King and Davie Gibson were also crocked. Their replacements were decent players, but the cohesion and fluidity of the team were affected, and the fact that we had to play three crucial league games in the space of a week didn't help. We were attempting to fire on all cylinders when we couldn't field the same team consecutively in any of our remaining matches, and we contrived to lose each one to finish fourth in Division One – an excellent position in normal circumstances, but to us it felt like relegation.

The champions were Everton, who clinched the title in front of nearly 70,000 fans at Goodison Park when they beat Fulham 4–1. The newspapers dubbed Everton the 'Cheque Book Champions' because they had spent £180,000 on five players, most notably Tony Kay, who cost £80,000 from Sheffield Wednesday, and Alex Scott, a £40,000 purchase from Glasgow Rangers. Kay and Scott proved more than useful additions to a side managed by Harry Catterick, but for me the key players in that successful Everton team were their young centre half, Brian Labone, and Roy Vernon and Alex Young, who between them scored fifty goals that season.

The bookies had made us odds-on favourites to win the FA Cup final. We had enjoyed a good, though ultimately disappointing, season in the First Division while our opponents, Manchester

United, had had a torrid time. On paper, United looked a good side; Bobby Charlton, Denis Law, Johnny Giles, Albert Quixall, David Herd, Pat Crerand and Bill Foulkes were all extremely gifted players, as was their captain, Noel Cantwell. Yet United had barely escaped relegation to Division Two, finishing just three points ahead of their doomed neighbours Manchester City. In their semifinal, United had made hard work of beating Second Division Southampton by a goal to nil. Almost to a man, every sports writer said it was going to be Leicester's year for the Cup.

On the day, however, just about every Leicester player, myself included, underperformed. In contrast to our lacklustre showing, United displayed exemplary teamwork, while also giving full vent to their considerable individual skills.

I was at fault for United's opening goal. Twelve minutes into the game the United goalkeeper, Dave Gaskell, threw the ball out to Johnny Giles, who swiftly moved it crossfield for Bobby Charlton to shoot. I could only parry Bobby's shot and there was the United centre forward, David Herd, to accept the gift.

The result was never in doubt after United's second. I saved from Bobby Charlton but my intended throw out to the right wing was intercepted by Paddy Crerand, who beat Richie Norman before slipping the ball to Denis Law twelve yards out. Colin Appleton went to tackle him, but Law was far too elusive. He skipped away, then swivelled through 180 degrees to fire a low right-foot shot that I had no chance of reaching. It was the twenty-ninth minute, Law's twenty-ninth goal of the season and his twenty-ninth in all cup competitions.

With ten minutes left a wonderful diving header from Ken Keyworth put us back in the game. Minutes later, however, Denis Law rose like a Green's cake before planting a firm header to my left. I was beaten, and couldn't believe my luck when the ball hit the post and rebounded straight into my arms. Four minutes from time, though, I was less fortunate when I jumped to collect a Johnny Giles cross. On landing I jarred the heel of my boot and the ball spilled from my hands for David Herd to poach another goal. At 3–1 there was no way back. For the second time in three seasons I tasted the disappointment of losing a Wembley cup final.

The club's post-match banquet was again at the Dorchester on Park Lane and, as before, was a low-key affair. Our disappointment was, if anything, greater than two years previously. Then we had been the valiant losers of an unequal struggle, but this time everyone had expected a Leicester victory. That we had all played so badly on our big day was a mystery to everyone. As our skipper Colin Appleton said at that dinner, 'We learned an important lesson today, lads, but for the life of me, I don't know what it is.'

7. England Calls

Since joining Leicester I'd made a concerted effort to study goal-keeping and its role. Like every other club, Leicester had no goalkeeping coach or specialist training routines. I trained with the rest of the lads and, while I was happy enough to do all the long-distance running to build my stamina and sprinting to enhance my speed off the mark, this type of training was hardly suited to my role in the team. I needed routines that were tailored to my requirements.

I was quite willing to put in the extra hours, but I could hardly practise saving my own shots. I needed some help, and fortunately two of my good friends and team mates were there to provide it.

In the early sixties both Frank McLintock and Davie Gibson lived in digs. Davie had joined Leicester from Hibernian and was still doing his National Service with the King's Own Scottish Borderers when he arrived at Filbert Street. He was a fine ball player, quite the artist, and his creativity coupled with granite-like hardness made him formidable on the pitch. Davie had an uncanny feel for the ball, and his inch-perfect forty-yard passes to Ken Keyworth or Mike Stringfellow were a joy to watch.

I liked Davie a lot, as both a player and a friend. When he left the game he stayed in the Leicester area and became a postman before he and his wife opened a residential home for the elderly, which they still run today.

Frank and Davie were very keen to develop their game and, being single lads, had the time to do it. The three of us used to put in some extra training at Filbert Street on Sunday mornings, the pair of them pinging shots at me from all angles.

We practised week in, week out, and my positional game improved by leaps and bounds as a result. Whenever an opposing forward was about to shoot, I knew at what angle and height the ball would come and could adjust my stance accordingly. I began to anticipate shots on target, moving to restrict my opponent's view of goal before he let fly. Goalkeeping for me was no longer an art. It had become a science.

Of course, it was not an exact science. I still conceded goals, but progressively fewer each season. In the five seasons from 1958–59 to 1962–63 Leicester conceded 98, 75, 70, 71 and 53 goals, respectively. It would be unfair of me to take all the credit – we had a very good team and I had quality defenders in front of me – but I'd like to think I played my part in reducing our goals-against tally.

Having worked on position, I next had to improve my reactions. For example, I'd ask Frank and Davie to half-volley the ball at me from five yards, never telling me which side of the goal it was going. I spend countless hours improving my ability to stop shots from within the penalty area and discovered that I had to position myself differently and make different types of saves according to exactly where in the area the ball had been struck. It was all very complicated, but in time it became second nature.

I made a concerted effort to try to read situations, to anticipate an opponent's intended cross or pass by adjusting my position quickly, so making him think again.

When Matt Gillies appointed Bert Johnson as first-team coach, I asked Bert if I could have some extra practice sessions after normal training. Bert was all for it and soon had half a dozen of the first team lads helping me out. We worked on defending corners to the near post, devising a system whereby two defenders took responsibility for that area, which left me free to concentrate on the remaining two-thirds of my goal. I decided I didn't need any other defenders in the six-yard box – that was my domain and no one else's. Bert immediately saw the advantage of this. Leaving opponents unmarked in or around our six-yard box at the time of a corner left the likes of Richie Norman, Ian King and Colin Appleton free to pick up anyone making runs from deep, and Ken Keyworth or Mike Stringfellow available to receive a quick throw out from me. In short, we found we had a numerical advantage when defending corners, hence Leicester City's reputation as masters of the counter-attack.

I also discussed defending free kicks with Bert in some detail and we came up with a number of ways of minimizing the danger. One idea I had was very simple, but proved highly effective for a time. Whenever Leicester conceded a free kick some forty or fifty yards from goal, our defenders would position themselves on the edge of my penalty box as normal alongside their opposite numbers. I would watch the man taking the free kick like a hawk, and just as he was about to strike the ball I would scream, 'Now!' Immediately they heard this, the Leicester back line would take to their toes and sprint upfield, leaving the opposing attackers in an offside position.

My constant practice, development of goalkeeping technique and specialized self-training helped me enormously. With every day that passed, I learned a little more. I trained a lot, but I was always careful not to overdo it; the last thing I wanted was to suffer mental or physical fatigue during the course of a game.

At no time did I consider myself to be particularly special as a goalkeeper, but I did believe the role of a goalkeeper in a team to be special. That's why I continually worked at my personal game. In the main, it was a journey of self-discovery. There were no books about goalkeeping technique, no specialist coaches and not everything I tried worked. It was, in the main, uncharted territory and there was an element of hit and miss about what I did. If an idea didn't work, I simply ditched it and tried to think of something else.

I studied the styles of as many other goalkeepers as I could and tried to learn from them. I devised my own training schedules that were geared not only to improving my technique, but also to enhancing my agility, strength, reactions and focus. My improvement was constant, but I was never satisfied and kept working at my personal game. It paid dividends. In 1963, Alf Ramsey selected me for the full England team.

It is widely believed that when Walter Winterbottom resigned as England manager in 1963, the FA immediately turned to the Ipswich manager Alf Ramsey, and that the rest is history of the most glorious kind. That wasn't exactly how it went. The FA at first offered the England job to Jimmy Adamson, who had been Walter's assistant during the 1962 World Cup in Chile. Jimmy turned down the job, seeing his future not as a manager but as a coach. (Jimmy did eventually turn his hand to management, with his beloved Burnley, Sunderland and Leeds United, but coaching was his real strength.)

So the FA looked to their second-choice candidate, Alf Ramsey. In his time as a right back for England, Alf had seen at first hand the effects of team selection by committee. He was adamant that no official would wield such influence again and became the first England manager to have sole responsibility for team affairs.

For sixteen years Walter Winterbottom had had to put up with a Selection Committee who had sometimes never even seen their selections play. Quite often a player was awarded a cap in recognition of his services to the game, or, as Walter once said, 'Because the Committee thought him a decent and deserving chap'.

In 1959 he persuaded the England Selection Committee to pick a batch of young hopefuls for a game against Sweden at Wembley. Middlesbrough's Brian Clough and Eddie Holliday, Tony Allen of Stoke City, Trevor Smith of Birmingham City and John Connelly of Burnley were added to a team that also included the youthful Jimmy Greaves and Bobby Charlton. Sweden won 3–2. Before that game England had lost only once on home soil, that watershed defeat at the hands of the Hungarians in 1953. Walter found himself back at square one as the Selection Committee reverted to the old regime of panel picking.

When Alf Ramsey succeeded him, all was to change. The Ipswich Town directors had never interfered in the selection of the Ipswich team. Alf had had sole control of team affairs at Portman Road and he knew that, if he was to make a success of his new role as manager of the national team, the dinosaur that was the Selection Committee would have to go. The FA bowed to the inevitable and Alf took the job.

I was reserve goalkeeper in the squad Alf selected for his first game in charge, a European Nations Cup match against France. The Nations Cup was the forerunner of the European Championship and in 1962–63 took the form of two-legged knock-out ties rather than group games. Under Winterbottom England had drawn 1–1 against France at Hillsborough and when the return leg was played in Paris, in February 1963, we still had high hopes of progressing past the first round of the tournament.

Alf introduced only one new cap for the game in Paris. Ron Henry of Spurs came in at left back and I once again found myself understudy to Ron Springett. The game turned out to be a nightmare for England, for Alf and for Ron Springett. France won by five goals to two to send England tumbling out of the tournament and give Alf Ramsey much food for thought. At least he now had some idea of the magnitude of the task ahead of him.

Alf gave debuts to three players in England's next game, at Wembley against the 'auld enemy', Scotland. To my considerable delight I was one of them along with the Liverpool pair Gerry Byrne and Jimmy Melia.

The England–Scotland game was a fixture in the now defunct annual Home International Championship, which also involved Northern Ireland and Wales. Football was rarely seen on TV in those days, and the Home Internationals afforded people in Cardiff, Belfast and Glasgow a rare opportunity to see the top players in action.

The match was the first to be played at Wembley since it had been redeveloped, over £500,000 having been spent on a new roof that swept around the stadium. Whether the new roof had anything to do with it I don't know, but as the teams emerged from the tunnel I was taken aback by a deafening noise so intimidating it almost brought on palpitations. Wembley was filled to capacity, and most of the 100,000 crowd seemed to be roaring for Scotland.

As we walked out, Jimmy Greaves turned to me. 'I knew they'd rebuilt this place,' he said, 'but I didn't know they'd shifted it up to bloody Glasgow!'

I could have wished for better fortune on my England debut. All seemed to be going well for me until our right back, Jimmy Armfield, uncharacteristically decided to pass the ball across our back line. Scotland's left half, Rangers' Jim Baxter, thought it was

Christmas. Latching on to the gift we had presented him with, he bore down on goal.

I raced off my line to cut down Baxter's view of my goal, but he swayed like a bird on a twig. I put all my weight on my left foot and Jim rolled the ball to my right and into the net. Debutant I may have been, but I let the more experienced Jimmy Armfield know exactly what I thought of his crossfield pass. To his credit, Jimmy held his hand up and took full responsibility for his mistake.

Jim Baxter started to run the game, while our defence was all over the place. In a moment of desperation, Ron Flowers of Wolves took the legs from under Rangers winger Willie Henderson and the referee, Leon Horn from Holland, had no hesitation in pointing to the penalty spot.

Jim Baxter approached the ball as if he were on a leisurely stroll in the park and casually placed it into the left-hand corner of my goal as I dived the wrong way. Once again a tidal wave of noise swept down from the terraces as the Tartan Army jigged as one in celebration.

We played better in the second half and enjoyed the lion's share of the play, but could only manage one goal in reply, from Blackburn's Bryan Douglas. During this second period Jim Baxter gave full vent to his swaggering skills. At one point, he received the ball out on our right and, to the amazement of everyone, progressed down the wing juggling the ball up and down on his left foot. The Scottish supporters were in raptures. In the heat of furious combat there was 'Slim Jim' playing keepy-uppy as if frolicking in his own back garden. Baxter, however, reserved his party piece for last. Having juggled the ball down our right wing, he then nudged it forward, swung his left foot over the ball and turned round so that he was facing his own goal. Baxter than brought his right leg behind his left and chipped the ball across into my penalty area. Ian St John met Baxter's cheeky centre with his head but I managed to collect the ball underneath my crossbar. The Tartan Army went wild and even we England players shook our heads in wonder at Baxter's artful arrogance.

Following the final whistle, as both teams headed towards the tunnel Jim stuck the ball up his shirt and swaggered off the pitch. For all true lovers of football, Baxter's artistry that day was a joy to behold. It was just my luck that he had chosen my England debut as the occasion on which to produce the greatest performance of his career!

One month later, in May 1963, Alf picked me for England's game against Brazil, despite the finger injury I'd picked up at West Bromwich just four days earlier. Having already lost a cup final at Wembley and been on the losing side on my international debut, I was praying for better fortune against the World Cup holders who were, without doubt, the best international side in the world.

Despite being without the world's best player, Pelé, who was injured, Brazil still had enough class and quality in their ranks to offer the severest of tests for England in what was Alf's third game in charge. The England team was Gordon Banks (Leicester City); Jimmy Armfield (Blackpool), Ray Wilson (Huddersfield Town), Gordon Milne (Liverpool), Maurice Norman (Spurs), Bobby Moore (West Ham); Bryan Douglas (Blackburn Rovers), Jimmy Greaves, Bobby Smith (both Spurs), George Eastham (Arsenal), Bobby Charlton (Manchester United). The Brazilians fielded Gilmar; Lima, Edoiardo; Zeuinha, Dias, Rildo; Dorval, Mengalvia, Coutinho, Amarildo, Pepe.

Brazil were unbeaten on their tour of Europe. Alf had watched them in action and had really done his homework. He had noticed that Brazil liked to play the ball into the feet of their centre forward, Coutinho, so he told Gordon Milne to take up a position in front of Coutinho when Brazil were in possession to stop this happening.

Alf warned me to be on my toes if ever Brazil were awarded a free kick outside our penalty area. 'They are fantastic strikers of the ball, Gordon,' he told me, 'and can bend and swerve it either way.'

Mindful of Alf's words, I paid particular attention to lining up the wall of defenders in front of me when Brazil were awarded a first-half free kick twenty-five yards out. I took up a position just to the right of centre and positioned the wall so that it overlapped my left-hand post. It was all to no avail. The Brazilian inside left, Pepe, sprinted up to the ball and with tremendous power sliced his left foot across it. I'd never seen a ball cut through the air at such a trajectory. It flew over the wall heading for the left side of the goal. Naturally, I moved to my left, only for the ball to then veer to my right and into the net. I simply couldn't believe that anyone could make a ball move so much in the air. It was a terrific goal and I consoled myself with the thought that there wasn't a goalkeeper in the world who would have got anywhere near it.

At half time, however, Alf was not best pleased. 'I warned you about their free kicks,' he said, 'be on your toes!' I made my excuses, but I could tell from his stern expression that he thought I should have at least got a hand to it.

I made up for it in the opening stages of the second half, though. First I managed to claw away a fierce downward header from Coutinho, then hold on to a long-range effort from Amarildo that was heading for my goal like a snake. Minutes later I saved from both Dorval and Mengalvia. Not conceding another goal during that spell of Brazilian pressure turned the game. As the second half progressed we began to assert ourselves and only some desperate defending by the South Americans kept the score at 1−0. England were not to be denied, however. With minutes remaining our concerted pressure paid off. Blackburn's Bryan Douglas latched on to a great through ball from Bobby Charlton and calmly beat Gilmar.

I felt the draw was no more than we deserved. After a shaky start to both halves, we had grown in confidence and, at times, more than matched the World Champions. On my third appearance at Wembley I finally left the pitch without the taste of defeat in my mouth and Alf Ramsey, in his third game as England manager, had gained a highly creditable draw against the best in the world. I guess both of us were looking to the future with some optimism. I know I certainly was.

My performances for Leicester and my inclusion in the England team led to a number of clubs enquiring about my availability. Newcastle United, Wolves and Aston Villa made official approaches to Leicester regarding a possible transfer but Matt Gillies and the

City board were adamant. I wasn't for sale. That suited me fine as I was very happy at the club and with life in Leicester. Another club seemingly impressed by my performances was Arsenal. Their manager, the former Wolves and England captain, Billy Wright, appeared before the Football League accused of making an illegal approach to me. In Billy's defence, I can honestly say that I have no recollection of this. He certainly didn't telephone me at home because Ursula and I didn't have a telephone! All I can think of is that a bit of gentle nudging on the part of Arsenal's George Eastham, who'd often told me that I'd enjoy life at Highbury, had been blown out of all proportion.

In the summer of 1963 I joined the England squad on their continental tour. The tour was highly successful and offered concrete proof that, after a disappointing start to his career as England manager, Alf Ramsey was getting it right. We began with a terrific 4–2 win in Bratislava over Czechoslovakia, who had given Brazil a good game in the World Cup final just twelve months previously. We then beat East Germany 2–1 in Leipzig and rounded off the tour in some style with an 8–1 win over Switzerland in Basle, Bobby Charlton scoring a hat trick. Alf picked me for all but one of those games, which was a great fillip to my confidence. I felt that Alf now saw me as England's number one goalkeeper, and I was determined to work hard and continue my development in order to prove him right.

8. Down South America Way

Leicester City kicked off the 1963–64 season at West Bromwich Albion with the same team that had played against Manchester United in the previous season's Cup final, only the second time in the history of the club that a team which had concluded one season had begun the text.

A hard-earned 1–1 draw at the Hawthorns was followed by a 3–0 home win against Birmingham City, and when Arsenal were beaten 7–2 three days later, we once again had high hopes of enjoying a very successful season. But, as so often, our form was to ebb and flow.

Apart from a sparkling spell between 21 December and 18 January during which we registered five successive wins in the League, including a fine double over reigning champions Everton, we never realized our true potential. Our wayward form resulted in us losing more games at home (8) than we did on our travels (7), which is no way to win the League. However, it was the League Cup that was to occupy our minds during the months ahead.

In the three years since its introduction in 1960 the League Cup had come on a bit. It would never possess the ivy-covered venerability of its big brother, the FA Cup, but after three finals it was beginning to grow in importance in the minds of club officials, players and supporters alike.

Having received a bye in round one, we began our League Cup campaign modestly enough with a 2–0 win over Fourth Division Aldershot. The club's youth policy was beginning to bear fruit and Matt Gillies took the opportunity to blood one of our aspiring youngsters, Bob Newton, who scored our opening goal. Newton's appearance against Aldershot showed that Matt was not afraid to bring youngsters into the first team. Moreover, some of these youngsters were to play important roles in our League Cup success.

In round three, Tranmere Rovers were beaten 2–1, one of our goals coming from Bobby Roberts, for whom Matt had paid a club record fee of £41,000 to Motherwell. Bobby was a terrific competitor with a cannon-like shot, but his accuracy rarely matched his power and his wayward shooting was often a source of frustration to Bert Johnson: 'One of these days, Bobby son, you'll knock the hands off the town hall clock.'

Wayward finishing apart, Bobby was a super player and, once established in our midfield, proved himself to be one of real class. Today he is widely regarded by Leicester supporters as one of the club's all-time greats and deservedly so. He is still involved in football, as chief scout for Derby County.

Following our defeat of Tranmere, Gillingham were our next victims, which set up a quarter-final meeting against Norwich City, winners of the League Cup in its second season. A Howard Riley goal cancelled out one from Ron Davies for Norwich and, with a semi-final against West Ham beckoning both teams, we met again in the replay at Filbert Street.

It was Norwich's first visit to Filbert Street for twenty-seven years. The last meeting between the two clubs had taken place in the FA Cup at Norwich in 1954. They proved to be tough opponents and included in their ranks Tommy Bryceland, a hugely gifted inside forward, Bill Punton, a speedy and tricky left winger, and the Welsh centre forward, Ron Davies, one of the best headers of a ball in football at the time. The game turned out to be a typical cup tie, full of blood and thunder and played at breakneck speed. With the score at 1–1 and the game into extra time, Howard Riley settled it to send us through to meet West Ham in a two-legged semi-final.

West Ham's style was in marked contrast to the 'up and at 'em' approach of Norwich City. Prompted by Bobby Moore, their build-up from the back was like distant thunder at a picnic. Just when we thought we were having a good time of it, the ominous presence of Moore would gather in midfield and the off-the-ball running of Johnny Byrne, Geoff Hurst, Ronnie Boyce and John Sissons would soon swamp us. We'd score, only for West Ham to come straight back at us. Their attacks were sophisticated. When coming out of defence they always did so by passing the ball along the deck with slide-rule precision. Rarely, if ever, did the ball go in the air. When West Ham moved the ball into our half of the field, the darting runs of Hurst, Boyce and Sissons rocked us on our heels. A combination of skill and silky passing was their only arbiter, and the quality of football displayed by both sides gave the game the flavour almost of an idyll. Rarely had the expectation of a football treat been more thoroughly roused than it was on this night, and rarely has it been so completely satisfied. A tremendous game of football ended 4–3 in our favour, but we still had much work to do.

As a footballing spectacle, the second leg at Upton Park was, if anything, even better. Frank McLintock gave us the lead. Then Bobby Roberts for once managed to keep his head over the ball when shooting to give us the considerable comfort of a two-goal lead on the night and 6–3 on aggregate. To their credit, West Ham refused to panic or resort to shabby tactics and continued to play the purist football they were so well known for. Their valiant efforts, however, were to no avail and we marched on to a two-legged final against Stoke City, conquerors of Manchester City in the other semi-final.

The first leg was at the Victoria Ground. Matt Gillies was continuing with his policy of giving promising young City players a chance. Richie Norman was injured and, with Colin Appleton assuming Richie's role at left back, the youngster Max Dougan played on the left of midfield. Another young player, Terry Heath, replaced the injured Frank McLintock, though with Graham Cross dropping back, Terry enjoyed a more forward role in midfield.

We never really got into our stride against a very wily and experienced Stoke side which included Peter Dobing, Dennis Violett, John Ritchie and Jimmy McIlroy. There had been a lot of rain and the pitch was very greasy. (We were later told that the muddy conditions so suited Stoke that their manager, Tony Waddington, had persuaded the local fire brigade to water the pitch further on the morning of the game!) Such greasy conditions are always troublesome for a goalkeeper. The ball tends to skid off the wet surface at an alarming speed, which makes judgement difficult. I found myself in just such a predicament when going down low to save from the Stoke full back Bill Asprey. I thought I had the ball covered, but it shot up and it was all I could do to claw it away from goal. The Stoke left winger, Keith Bebbington, needed no second invitation and promptly buried the loose ball in the back of the net.

Though we never reproduced the stylish fluent football of our two semi-finals against West Ham, we were never out of the game and when Terry Heath blocked an attempted clearance by a Stoke defender, there was Davie Gibson to pounce on the loose ball and equalize.

For the return leg, Matt brought in another youngster of promise, Tom Sweeney, in place of Terry Heath. With Richie Norman fit again, Colin Appleton resumed his normal role at the expense of Max Dougan. A crowd of over 25,000 turned up at Filbert Street with great expectations of seeing us win the club's first major trophy.

We didn't disappoint them. Mike Stringfellow scored a cracking goal to give us a half-time lead. Two minutes into the second period, however, Dennis Viollet, one of the original Busby Babes, put Stoke level, only for Davie Gibson to restore our lead with a glancing near-post header. When Howard Riley added to our tally, I knew there was only one destination for the League Cup. With just seconds remaining, Stoke City's George Kinnell, a cousin of Jim Baxter, pulled a goal back, but by then it was academic. The 3−2 scoreline gave Leicester City their first major trophy since their foundation as Leicester Fosse back in 1884.

It's an odd-looking trophy, the League Cup. For a start it has three handles, though I have never discovered why. Unlike the FA Cup, it has neither a lid nor a plinth. The three handles take the form of serpents, though again, I have no idea why. For winning the League Cup, each player received an inscribed tankard rather than a medal, which I found a little disappointing. The tankard resembles any other you might see hanging up at the back of a public bar. That the League Cup had yet fully to capture the imagination of football in general did not detract from our joy at having won it. As individuals we were delighted, but even more so for the club and its supporters.

My international career really took off during this season. I became England's regular goalkeeper and received the ultimate honour when I was picked to play for my country against the Rest of the World in a game celebrating the centenary of the Football Association. I'm such a patriot that I would have played for my country for nothing; for the opportunity of playing against the Rest of the World I would have willingly paid the FA.

Such was the interest in this game that Wembley had sold out six weeks before the match was due to take place. When I walked into the dressing room, picked up one of the complimentary match programmes and looked at the team line-ups, my eyes nearly came out on stalks. Playing against us were some of the greatest names ever to have graced the game. Eusebio of Portugal, Alfredo di Stefano and Paco Gento of Spain, Denis Law, Jim Baxter, Raymond Kopa of France, West Germany's Uwe Seeler, the magical Magyar, Ferenc Puskas, and one of my all-time heroes, the Russian goal-keeper Lev Yashin.

Yashin was known throughout the world as the Black Octopus. (He invariably wore all black when playing and the assimilation with an octopus came from his superb handling of the ball.) No matter how hard a shot, irrespective of the angle, he always seemed to get a hand to the ball. And what hands they were. Lev Yashin had hands like shovels and fingers like bananas; in my entire career in football I don't think I ever saw a goalkeeper with bigger hands. When he jumped to punch the ball clear, he achieved incredible distance. Little wonder: physically he was very strong and when he balled one of his massive hands into a fist, it was like a ham-shank.

He played seventy-eight times for Russia and his performances and great sportsmanship resulted in him being awarded the two highest honours the Soviet government could bestow on a civilian, the Order of Lenin and Honoured Master of Soviet Sport.

He appeared in three World Cups, the last in 1966, when his goalkeeping helped Russia reach the semi-finals. When he eventually retired from football in 1970 his club, Moscow Dynamo, played a Rest of the World XI in his testimonial and a crowd of 120,000 turned up at the Lenin stadium to see it.

I met him on a number of occasions. Though obviously aware of his world-wide fame, he was a very modest man, quietly spoken and extremely polite. For someone who was supposedly a Russian policeman and played for a club with strong links to the KGB, he had a great sense of humour and would often make light of the harsh realities of Russian life.

He died in 1998, but his legend lives on, not only in Russia but throughout the football world, where his name will for ever be synonymous with great goalkeeping.

Though they were playing together for the first time in what was billed as a friendly, I had no doubt whatsoever that the Rest of the World team would provide stern opposition and a severe test of Alf Ramsey's progress at the helm. Their starting line-up was Yashin (USSR); Santos (Brazil), Schnellinger (West Germany); Pluskal, Popluhar and Masopust (all Czechoslovakia); Kopa (France), Law (Scotland), di Stefano (Spain), Eusebio (Portugal), Gento (Spain).

It had been decided that substitutes would be allowed for this game and the Rest of the World bench was formidable in its content: Puskas (Hungary/Spain), Baxter (Scotland), Seeler (West Germany), Soskic (Yugoslavia) and Eyzaguirre (Chile).

The England team comprised Banks (Leicester City); Armfield (Blackpool), Wilson (Huddersfield Town); Milne (Liverpool), Norman (Spurs), Moore (West Ham); Paine (Southampton), Greaves and Smith (both Spurs), Eastham (Arsenal) and Charlton (Manchester United).

The game was in keeping with the occasion. It produced a feast of football and was a personal triumph for Jimmy Greaves, who in such illustrious company showed that he, too, was a world-class player. All the goals came in the last twenty minutes. Terry Paine gave us the lead only for Denis Law to combine with Puskas and di Stefano before sliding the ball under my legs as I came out to cut down the angle. Jimmy Greaves wrapped the game up for England with seven minutes remaining. Milutin Soskic, who had replaced Yashin for the second half, could only parry a thunderbolt from Bobby Charlton and in nipped Jimmy to score a typical poacher's goal. Jimmy had an even better goal disallowed by the referee, who, rather than letting it stand, gave us a free kick following a foul on Jimmy.

It may only have been a friendly to celebrate the centenary of the FA, but our victory was a benchmark for England in general and for Alf Ramsey in particular. The press saw it as ample evidence that Alf was making good progress in his quest to put England back at the top of world football. It had been ten years since Hungary had arrived at Wembley and put Billy Wright's team to the sword. Following our victory over the Rest of the World XI, there was a feeling that English football was on the point of being great again.

One swallow doesn't make a summer, and one victory over a World XI didn't make England the best in the world, but I had the feeling that we were on our way back.

It was around this time that I had my second experience of how underhand certain members of the press can be at times. To be fair, 99 per cent of all the column inches written about me have been honest and objective, sometimes even giving me more credit than I deserve, so I found it both shocking and extremely hurtful to be the victim of some misleading sensationalist reportage.

A journalist from a Sunday redtop approached me regarding a story ostensibly about footballers' diets. After a half-hearted interview during which he hardly made a note, he got up to leave.

'Oh, by the way, I hear you're in dispute with Leicester over money,' he said.

I told him that 'dispute' was too strong a word for what was simply the ongoing renegotiation of my contract. At this time I was on £35 a week. I felt I was giving good service to both club and country and was worth a bit more. After all, it was below half what Tottenham Hotspur's players earned, and a good deal less than what just about every other First Division club was paying at the time. I told the reporter I was confident that the matter would quickly be resolved to everyone's satisfaction. He asked Ursula if she thought I deserved a bit more money and, of course, she told him 'yes'.

'If Gordon gets a rise, I suppose the extra money will enable you to put a bit more food on the table,' said the reporter.

'I suppose it will,' said Ursula as the two of us saw him to the door.

When I saw his article, my heart sank: ' "I Can't Live on £35 a Week" Says Gordon Banks' Wife'.

I was furious, not so much because I had been duped but because I knew the trouble and grief his scurrilous piece would bring to my wife. Sure enough, the next time Ursula went to do the weekly shop she ran a gauntlet of angry women who told her, in no uncertain terms, how fortunate we were to have such a high income and how they had to manage on much less. All I could do was tell her to maintain her dignity and ride it out. With time, the matter would be forgotten, if never forgiven.

The 1963–64 season saw a landmark in the history of Wembley: the first match to be played there under floodlights. No longer would midweek internationals be played at the grand old stadium on Wednesday afternoons when most supporters had difficulty in attending because of their work commitments. I played for England in that game: an 8–3 victory over Northern Ireland. Jimmy Greaves scored four and Southampton's Terry Paine also helped himself to a hat trick.

Another first was achieved when Jim Fryatt of Bradford Park Avenue scored the fastest goal on record. His goal against Tranmere Rovers was timed by the referee at just four seconds.

But football was dragged through the gutter that year with revelations in the *Sunday People* of a bribery scandal. The paper revealed that a number of players had been paid by a gambling syndicate to fix matches. It was a major news story which involved several players, most notably Peter Swan and David 'Bronco' Layne of Sheffield Wednesday and their former team mate, Tony Kay, who had by then joined Everton. The *People* alleged that the trio had taken part in arranging the outcome of a Sheffield Wednesday game at Ipswich Town in December 1962, which Wednesday had lost 2–0. Other players of lesser note were also said to have been involved in match fixing, and all were subsequently arrested and tried in a much-publicized court case.

The key defendant was Jimmy Gauld, a former Everton, Charlton and Swindon Town player who was revealed as the ringleader. The players were charged with conspiracy to defraud. Ten were subsequently jailed, and banned from football for life by the FA. Jimmy Gauld received the heaviest sentence, being jailed for four years and ordered to pay £5,000 costs. The other nine players were jailed for between four and fifteen months.

I was deeply shocked and saddened by this scandal, not only because it besmirched my profession and the game I loved, but also because it involved my old school mate David Layne. His involvement abruptly terminated what I, and many others, believed would have been a very successful career in football.

During the summer of 1964 I was a member of the England party that toured North and South America, and it was during this tour that I first lost my place in the England team, albeit only briefly.

The tour began well when we beat the USA 10–0 on a dustbowl of a pitch in New York, a result that went some way to avenging England's humiliating defeat at the hands of the Americans in the 1950 World Cup. The margin of our victory was especially pleasing to Alf Ramsey, who had been a member of that defeated England side.

I hardly touched the ball and spent the vast majority of the game spectating. Liverpool's Roger Hunt scored four and, on his debut for England, Blackburn's Fred Pickering scored a hat trick. Fred was a very tall and powerful centre forward, not the sharpest or most mobile of strikers but awesome in the air and very difficult to knock off the ball. Fred knew where the goal was and in only three games for England scored five times. It is indicative of just how many quality forwards were then playing in English football that five goals in three matches wasn't enough to earn Fred a fourth cap following his move to Everton that summer.

Following our convincing victory over the USA we flew down to Brazil to take part in a four-team tournament with the hosts, Portugal and Argentina. This tournament had been billed as the 'Little World Cup' and was seen as a true test of our ability to compete against the very best in world football.

Our opening game was against Brazil, but my dream of finally playing against the great Pelé was dashed when Alf Ramsey took me to one side after our first training session. Alf told me he thought my form had suffered of late and that he was going to play Tony Waiters of Blackpool in goal. I was very disappointed, but as a player you must accept and respect a manager's wishes. Alf asked me if I was happy with his decision to play Tony. I told him I was far from happy. 'Good,' said Alf, 'because that's the right attitude to have. If you had told me it was OK, I would know you were either lying or that you didn't have the mental attitude that I'm looking for in my players.'

I watched the game from the sidelines as Brazil gave full vent to their mercurial footballing powers. For much of the game England were the equals of Brazil, but with twenty minutes remaining the Brazilians stepped up a gear. We conceded three free kicks outside our penalty area and Brazil produced the sort of wizardry that had deceived me at Wembley in the previous season. The final score was 5–1. Back in the dressing room, Alf was not a happy man and I harboured high hopes of a quick recall to the fold.

Two days later Brazil took on Argentina and Alf insisted we all went along to watch and learn from two of the top four FIFA-rated sides in the world (the others being Portugal and West Germany). We sat on benches by one of the touchlines in the cavernous bowl of the Maracanà stadium. Behind us a formidable fence separated us from the massed ranks of volatile Brazilian supporters. We soon discovered that English footballers were not the most popular people in the eyes of the Brazilian fans. Even as we walked down the touchline towards the benches we were assailed by non-stop verbal abuse; once we had taken our seats, those fans proceeded to throw the contents of a greengrocer's shop in our general direction. We didn't learn much about either team because our attention was constantly being diverted as we ducked and dived to avoid the oranges, apples, tomatoes, bananas and nuts that rained down from the packed terraces.

Argentina were on fire and raced into a three-goal lead. When the third Argentinian goal went in, Ray Wilson was hit on the shoulder by a tomato. Ray immediately took to his feet, turned to face the Brazilian fans and held up three fingers on one hand and none on the other to remind the Brazilian supporters of the scoreline.

'That's right, Ray,' said Jimmy Greaves, 'you try and appease them.'

That did it. Hundreds of livid Brazilians began pulling at the fencing as if trying to bring it down. Those who couldn't get near to the fence angrily gesticulated at us with fingers or fists, and you didn't have to possess a working knowledge of Portuguese to know what they were insinuating. The atmosphere was turning very, very ugly and Alf Ramsey, a model of self-control, got to his feet.

'Gentlemen, there is no cause for alarm, simply sit and –'

Alf never finished what he had to say. An apple rocketed through the air and hit him square on the back of the head. It was too much, even for Alf. Still exuding calm authority, Alf bent down, picked up the offending missile and carefully placed it on a bench.

'Gentlemen, be so kind as to follow me,' he said.

Follow him we did, and at more than a casual pace as he led us down the touchline to relative safety behind the Brazilian goal, where the distance between us and the supporters was too great for us to be troubled by anything thrown from the terraces.

From our new vantage point I was able to concentrate fully on the game. Pelé was coming in for some really shabby treatment from his Argentinian marker, who stuck to him like a leech. Pelé was hacked and kicked, at times even when he didn't have the ball. In the end it all proved too much for him. With play deep in the Brazilian half of the field, Pelé was coasting about in the middle of the park when an Argentinian defender thought fit to run his studs down the back of one of Pelé's calves. The great man snapped. He turned quickly and landed a 'Glasgow kiss' right on the nose of his tormentor. As head butts go it was a good 'un. The Argentinian defender went to ground like a parachute with a hole in it, his nose broken.

Probably wisely, the referee chose to ignore the assault and, as opposed to the guy with the broken nose, Pelé remained on the pitch. To have dismissed him would in all probability have sparked off a full-scale riot. Perhaps fresh in the referee's mind was the knowledge that, less than a fortnight earlier, 301 people had been killed during a riot at the national stadium in Lima, when Peru's opponents had again been Argentina.

Alf Ramsey recalled me for our next game in the series, a 1–1 draw against Portugal. In our final match we were up against Argentina, who needed a draw to win the competition. This was a very closely contested game between two evenly matched sides, but on the hour Alfredo Rojas sent a stinging low drive into the right-hand corner of my net. In contrast to the rough-house tactics deployed against Brazil, Argentina had concentrated on playing football against us. In so doing, they showed what a very good side they could be.

Of the three teams we came up against in Brazil, Argentina impressed us most. Technically they were our superiors and their level of skill and organization had been very impressive. We were all of the mind that Argentina would be a major force in the 1966 World Cup. We'd been particularly impressed with the skill and general performance of the Argentine captain, who had proved himself to be a world-class player. Alf Ramsey even went as far as to tell our trainer, Harold Shepherdson, to take a special note of him in the dossier they were compiling on possible qualifiers.

'What's his name, again?' asked Harold.

'Antonio Rattin,' replied Alf.

9. Chelsea Blues

We kicked off the 1964–65 season against a newly promoted team who were managerless and had a 15-year-old in goal. After six seasons in the Second Division Sunderland had just returned to the top flight, but before a ball had been kicked the club was in turmoil. On 31 July manager Alan Brown had left for Sheffield Wednesday. Then their first-choice goalkeeper Jimmy Montgomery, an England Under-23 international, sustained a hand injury which ruled him out for two months and reserve keeper Derek Kirby was injured in a pre-season friendly. As the loan system had yet to be introduced, Sunderland had no alternative but to play Derek Foster, their untried youth-team keeper. At fifteen years of age he became the youngest goalkeeper to appear in the Football League and, by a matter of days, the second youngest player ever in the First Division.

An exciting end-to-end game finished in a 3–3 draw in which Derek acquitted himself remarkably well for one so young. Sadly, he never fulfilled his early potential, making only eighteen first team appearances in nine years at Roker Park.

Back at Filbert Street the club's wage structure was still a major bone of contention. Frank McLintock was so unsettled that he put in a transfer request, while Bobby Roberts and Davie Gibson refused to accept the terms they were offered. Leicester were offering me £40 a week. To put this in perspective, Southampton of the Second Division were paying their first team players a basic wage of £45, and even those at Fourth Division Bradford Park Avenue could earn £40 a week with bonuses. Frank and I were current internationals; to be paid the lowest basic wage in the First Division simply wasn't on.

The matter was finally resolved in December, when the club offered me £60 a week and I immediately accepted. Why they couldn't have done this in the first place is beyond me.

The contract I negotiated included a bonus of £5 for every home gate in excess of 30,000. I thought I'd be quids in as the capacity at Leicester was 40,000. As it turned out, until my departure from the club in 1967 Leicester were only to attract more than 30,000 to Filbert Street on seven occasions. My total crowd bonus over three seasons was £35!

Frank McLintock's unhappiness led to him joining Arsenal in October 1964 but Leicester's miserly reputation made it difficult for Matt Gillies to spend the £80,000 we received for him on quality players to bolster our squad. In 1964–65 Matt was frustrated in his attempts to sign Colin Bell from Bury, Southampton's Martin Chivers and Francis Lee from Bolton. What success might we have enjoyed had those players joined Leicester?

After an encouraging start to the season in which we remained unbeaten until our seventh game, our form once again ebbed and flowed. We enjoyed a double over Liverpool (if ever Liverpool had a bogey team it was us), Fulham were beaten 5–1, Spurs 4–2 and there was a thrilling and hard fought 2–2 draw against Leeds United, a team that had quickly gained a reputation as hard men following their promotion from Division Two. But our final position of eighteenth in Division One was a disappointment to everyone, though we did enjoy good runs in both cups.

Our penultimate game of the season was at White Hart Lane. It was a meaningless end-of-season fixture and both sets of players were relaxed enough to display one or two party pieces for the 33,000 spectators.

With ten minutes of the game remaining, we were trailing 5–2 when Spurs were awarded a penalty. I stepped back into the goal to rub my hands on the long grass to clean them (I never wore gloves until 1970). As I was bending down with my back to the play Jimmy Greaves, ever game for a laugh, dinked the ball off the penalty spot and sent it bobbling into the goal. I turned and started laughing, as did the rest of the players. The Spurs supporters on the terraces gave an ironic cheer. Jimmy walked up to retrieve the ball so that he could take the penalty properly when, to the amazement of everyone, the referee blew his whistle and raised an arm to signal a goal.

I was furious and raced up the pitch after the referee while the Spurs players fell about laughing.

'Played advantage,' he informed me.

'From a penalty?'

'Advantage. Best law in football,' he said. 'It allows you to ignore all the others for the good of the game.'

Even referees like their end-of-term practical jokes, it seems, and this one was well and truly on me!

That incident brings to mind another that occurred during my early days as an international. At a training session, the press were anxious to obtain a shot of England's new goalkeeper in action and Jimmy said he'd hit one chest-high to my right for me to collect. 'Great,' I said, thinking how impressive I'd look saving from the country's premier marksman.

I crouched between the posts as Jimmy ran up. The cameras whirred and a dozen pressmen got a perfect picture of me diving through the air while the ball sailed into my net on the opposite side! Fortunately, on that occasion there was no referee to prevent the retake.

Liverpool exacted revenge for our victory over them in the semi-final of 1962–63 by knocking us out of the FA Cup in the sixth round. We had beaten Blackburn Rovers, Plymouth Argyle and Middlesbrough, but for once our Indian sign over the mighty Reds didn't work. Having drawn 0–0 at Filbert Street in front of a crowd of 40,000 – another £5 for me – a Roger Hunt goal put paid to our hopes of another semi-final. At Anfield during the pre-match kickabout four practice balls disappeared into the Kop never to return. I declined to complain to the referee or the Liverpool officials. The Kop had only just forgiven me for the Ian St John photograph and the last thing I wanted was to get them on my back again.

We fared better in the League Cup, where a terrific run took us to yet another final. Once again we made a modest start, struggling to dispose of Peterborough United, Grimsby Town and Crystal Palace in the early rounds. At the time of the Palace tie, I was harbouring thoughts of a move should my wage negotiations not be resolved. But following our 2–1 victory over Palace, I found the press were batting for me: 'No one could ever accuse transfer-seeking goalkeeper Gordon Banks of playing to get away from Leicester City,' wrote Steven Richards in the *Daily Express*. 'His display for the League Cup holders in last night's fourth-round replay at Selhurst Park was one of his greatest for the club . . .'

As far as I was concerned my dissatisfaction was with Matt Gillies and the board, not the club. Deep down I never wanted to leave Leicester City, and always enjoyed a great relationship with both my team mates and the supporters. However unhappy I was with the terms on offer, it never affected my game.

Our performances in the early rounds of the League Cup had been uninspiring, to say the least, but all that changed in round five when we were involved in a tie at Coventry City that erupted like a volcano. A crowd of 28,000 turned up at Highfield Road to witness what turned out to be a sensational night for us. An own goal from the Coventry centre half and skipper, George Curtis, gave us an early lead. Minutes later I bent my thumb backwards in a challenge with George Hudson and spent five minutes on the sidelines receiving treatment. At the other end, almost every shot we had resulted in a goal. Left back Richie Norman helped himself to two, but blotted his copybook when he was put clean through by Mike Stringfellow and, in typical full-back fashion, with only the Coventry goalkeeper Bob Wesson to beat, blazed wide. Richie's miss wasn't costly; both Billy Hodgson and Mike String-fellow also helped themselves to a couple of goals and a fine effort from Davie Gibson saw us win by an amazing 8–1 scoreline.

We accounted for Plymouth Argyle over two legs in the semi-final, which took us through to a final against Chelsea. Although the League Cup final was still a two-legged affair, the competition had been given extra kudos when the Football League announced that this season's winners would play in the Fairs Cup (now the UEFA Cup) the following season.

This added incentive gave the final an extra edge and the first leg at Stamford Bridge was hotly contested. Chelsea gained the upper hand courtesy of a 3–2 scoreline, our goals coming from

Colin Appleton and Jimmy Goodfellow. Although we had approached the game with every intention of winning it, we were confident of overturning the deficit in front of our own fans. It wasn't to be. We laid siege to the Chelsea goal for much of the second leg, but their defence held firm and their goalkeeper, Peter Bonetti, was in inspired form. George Graham and Terry Venables were in that Chelsea team but their stars on the night were in defence. Marvin Hinton, Ron Harris, John Hollins, Johnny Boyle and Allan Young, whom Chelsea had signed on a free transfer from Arsenal, combined to form an impenetrable back line. For all our concerted efforts to break Chelsea down, the game ended goalless. Tommy Docherty's side had won 3–2 on aggregate. I was bitterly disappointed, as was everyone at the club. Not only had we failed to retain the League Cup, we had also missed out on a financially lucrative place in Europe.

Leicester City made a profit of £44,000 on the season. Although we hadn't made it into Europe, the club was presented with a great opportunity of making extra income and offering our loyal supporters a football treat when the FA offered us a prestigious friendly against one of the greatest club sides in the world. Santos of Brazil were on an eight-date tour of Europe. The opportunity of hosting a match against a team boasting six of the current Brazilian international side, including the world's greatest player, Pelé, was too good to turn down. That, however, was exactly what the Leicester City board did.

The World Club Cup was a two-legged affair between the winners of the European Cup and its South American equivalent, the Copa Libertadores. Santos first won the World Club Cup in 1962, beating Benfica 3–2 and 5–2. They had retained it the following year with a 7–6 aggregate win over AC Milan and were fresh from winning the Brazilian League Championship and the Copa do Brasil for a record fifth successive season. Though they boasted Pelé and a string of top internationals, Santos were not a rich club. Their ground, the imaginatively named Urbano Caldeira Vila Belmiro, had a capacity of only 25,000 (though major games were invariably switched to the Maracanã, where 152,000 had seen their game against AC Milan). The price of admission to matches in Brazil was very low, so clubs such as Santos toured to generate extra funds. They didn't come cheap: the fee they wanted for playing at Filbert Street was £7,500, and that was too much as far as the Leicester board was concerned.

Santos would have attracted at least 35,000 to Filbert Street. The profit margin on that was considered too small. What if it rained? People might not turn up! Santos were fixed up with a game at Fulham instead. The crowd at Craven Cottage? 42,000.

The Leicester board had been extremely short sighted in declining this friendly. More than that, though, it looked as though I was never going to have the chance to face Pelé.

The board also turned down a request from their former centre forward, Arthur Rowley, for a testimonial match. Arthur had just hung up his boots following a spell as player-manager with Shrewsbury Town, and his career total of 434 goals remains, to this day, an all-time record.

Arthur had played for Leicester before my arrival and his goal-scoring record for the club was second only to that of Arthur Chandler, who had played in the 1920s. Between 1950 and 1958, in 321 league and cup appearances, Arthur Rowley scored 265 goals for Leicester City. If Arthur Rowley wasn't deemed worthy of a 'thank you' testimonial game, who would be?

In 1998, during a week in which Manchester United announced profits in excess of £11 million, Arthur put his medals up for sale 'because they're just lying about'. He's in his seventies now, but in the minds and memories of those Leicester supporters fortunate enough to have seen Arthur play he remains eternally young and strong. For ever a hero.

The 1964–65 season ended with Bobby Moore elegantly ascending the steps to the Royal Box at Wembley to collect yet another cup. A year after West Ham United had beaten Second Division Preston North End to win the FA Cup, Bobby led the Hammers to a 2–0 victory over Munich 1860 to clinch the European Cup-Winners Cup. It was one of the best games of football ever to have been played at Wembley and West Ham's success was a tribute to their manager, Ron Greenwood, whose policy of purist football verged on the sublime. The West Ham goals came from Alan Sealey and Brian Dear, who were in the side only because of injuries to Peter Brabrook and Johnny Byrne. That Sealey and Dear fitted so seamlessly into the West Ham system was yet another tribute to Greenwood, whose belief in positive, stylish football ran through the East End club from first team to juniors. West Ham became the second English team, after Spurs in 1963, to win a major European competition. Their success fuelled the growing belief that English football was making great strides towards becoming a major force once again in Europe, if not the world. As Bobby said after the final, 'If our game continues to develop the way it has been doing these last three years, next year England will have a team capable of winning the World Cup.' His opinion was later to be echoed by a certain England manager.

The season also saw the retirement of Stanley Matthews, who in February, at the age of fifty, had played his last game for Stoke City, against Fulham. Stan enjoyed his final bow on 28 April when a packed Victoria Ground saw a Stan Matthews XI take on an International XI that included the likes of Alfredo di Stefano, Ferenc Puskas and Lev Yashin. It was incredible to think that Stan had first signed for Stoke thirty-five years earlier and had made his league debut in 1932. For him still to have been playing the equivalent of Premiership football at the age of fifty I still find remarkable, though, according to Stan, 'I made a mistake retiring at fifty. I still had another two good years left in me.'

Tragedy touched football with the death of the Spurs inside forward John White. I had played against John on numerous occasions, both for Leicester and for England, and considered him a good pal. He was a very gifted player who could split an opposing defence wide open with a single pass. He was killed by lightning while sheltering under a tree during a game of golf at the Crews Club in Enfield. His midfield partnership with Danny Blanchflower was the source of Tottenham's double success of 1961, and his tragic and untimely death saddened us all.

I spent a good part of the summer of '65 on tour with England. Having enjoyed a 1–0 success over Hungary at Wembley in May we set off on a continental tour that was to feature the first appearance of a fiery young red-haired winger from Blackpool, Alan Ball.

The tour began with a 1–1 draw against Yugoslavia in Belgrade. The day before the game we trained in the Belgrade stadium. After the training session Alan Ball couldn't find his trousers and had us all in stitches as he wandered around the stadium wearing nothing but a shirt and underpants, asking the Yugoslav officials in his high-pitched voice, 'Excuse me, has anyone seen my trousers?'

Nobby Stiles eventually owned up and produced the missing flannels. Bally took it all in good part and Nobby's prank didn't upset or faze him at all. The following day, on his England debut, Alan was our best player.

From Yugoslavia we travelled north to Nuremberg, where a Terry Paine goal gave us a 1–0 victory over a West German side ranked third in the world. That game was a benchmark for me, both in my career with England and as a goalkeeper. I felt sure of my positioning, handling, distribution and of the way I organized what was a resolute England back line of George Cohen, Ray Wilson, Jack Charlton and Bobby Moore. Those lads were outstanding and this was the game when I first realized I was becoming comfortable and familiar with their individual styles and idiosyncrasies. In short, we played as a highly effective unit. The days when England took to the pitch with a team of gifted but disparate individuals were over. Against West Germany we had shown that we had all the makings of a very good team.

We concluded what had been a very happy and successful tour with a 2–1 victory over Sweden in Gothenburg. Alan Ball, with his first goal for England, and John Connelly were our goalscorers on a mudheap of a pitch that during the long Swedish winter doubled up as an ice rink.

Prior to the game there was a scare about Nobby Stiles. Nobby, half-blind without his contact lenses, had forgotten to pack his lens lubricant. It was then that our trainer, Harold Shepherdson, demonstrated just how much attention he paid to detail by producing a small bottle of the stuff.

'I leave nothing to chance,' said Harold, accepting Nobby's thanks.

'You didn't have a spare pair of pants for Bally though, did you?' replied Nobby.

The World Cup was just a year away, and we had made great progress. The team was now beginning to have a settled look about it, and Alf seemed happy with the nucleus of the side. Myself, George Cohen, Ray Wilson, Jack Charlton, Bobby Moore and Alan Ball had figured in all the tour games, while Bobby Charlton and Jimmy Greaves had been absent only owing to injury. Of the players who featured on that tour only two, Everton's Derek Temple and Mick Jones of Sheffield United, would not be included in Alf's World Cup squad.

Even without Greaves and Charlton we had remained unbeaten, scoring a memorable victory in Germany, but still the press found something to moan about: 'Where was the class? Where was the free-flowing, fluent football that English supporters demand of their national team?' Stuart Shaw, writing in the popular football weekly the *Soccer Star*, described our performances on tour as being 'as intellectual as a rocket scientist throwing paper darts'. A lesser man might have been disconcerted by such negative remarks, but Alf Ramsey took no notice of them. On the contrary, our performances had instilled in him the belief that England would have the makings of world champions come 1966.

I didn't enjoy the best of starts to the 1965–66 season. While playing for Leicester in a pre-season friendly against Northampton Town I went down at the feet of Town's Joe Kiernan and broke my wrist. It was accidental, but the injury put me in plaster and I missed the first nine games of the season. Matt Gillies yet again proved himself to be one of the most astute managers in the First Division when it came to quality signings at bargain prices when he picked up Jackie Sinclair, a very skilful winger, from Dunfermline for just £25,000. Jackie was very quick and, like Mike Stringfellow, had a keen eye for goal. Naturally two-footed, he was happy to operate on either flank and did so to good effect during his two years at Leicester. With his boundless energy and ability to make and score goals he was very popular with City fans, but when Leicester's fortunes began to fade, he was snapped up by Newcastle United, with whom he went on to win a Fairs Cup winners' medal in the Geordies' victory over Ujpest Dozsa of Hungary in 1969.

Jackie Sinclair was a favourite of the City faithful, but the other Matt Gillies signing of summer '65 was even more popular. Derek Dougan is a footballing enigma. Quite simply, there has never been a player like him, nor one so forthright in his views and opinions on the game. After making a name for himself in the late fifties with Portsmouth, Blackburn Rovers and Aston Villa, Derek had dropped into the Third Division with Peterborough United. Like Trevor Ford before him, Derek had no qualms about voicing his opinions on football and its establishment figures. He was a radical and original thinker whose caustic wit and sharp brain made many a manager think twice about taking him on. The fact that he was playing his football in the Third Division was in all probability due to his reputation as a troublemaker. Why on earth Matt Gillies signed him, I don't know. What I do know is that Derek was a stylish and formidable player who, in his time at Leicester, channelled his undoubted intelligence on to the field of play to the great benefit of the team and the constant delight of the supporters.

We often hear today about players having 'cult status'. Derek Dougan was one of the originals. Many people thought his best days were behind him when he came to Filbert Street, but in his two years at Leicester and subsequent eight years at Wolverhampton Wanderers he was to play the best football of his career, maturing into an intelligent and unselfish striker of the highest calibre and scoring 222 league goals in a career that, in the early days certainly, had more than its share of ups and downs. He also represented Northern Ireland on forty-four occasions and would, in my opinion, have been the perfect manager for the national team. He was also, incidentally, one of the first players to shave his head, in the early sixties while he was at Aston Villa. It caused a sensation.

The Doog made his debut for Leicester in our 3–1 defeat at Liverpool on the opening day of the 1965–66 season, but gave ample evidence of his quality as a player. He was a windmill of a striker whose talent and swirling personality were to leave their mark not only at Leicester City but on football in general.

Following my injury I returned to the Leicester team in late September for a League Cup tie at Manchester City. It was to be an unhappy return, a 3–1 defeat putting an end to our hopes at the first time of asking. (Manchester City also put an end to our FA Cup aspirations that year.) Our league form was once again inconsistent. We enjoyed some memorable results, including a 5–1 win at St James's Park over an in-form Newcastle United and five-goal victories over West Ham, also away from home, and Fulham. Having been beaten 5–0 at home by Manchester United, we then went and won 2–1 at Old Trafford, a series of results which summed up perfectly our topsy-turvy season. In the end our final league placing of seventh was respectable enough, but the overall feeling among the Leicester players was that it should have been better. Matt Gillies had added to our ranks full back Peter Rodrigues, a £45,000 signing from Cardiff City, and the club's youth policy also saw David Nish and Rodney Fern elevated to the first team, but the consistency was never there.

Strange to say, but in that 5–0 home defeat by Manchester United we were by far the better side. Our tally of thirty-six corners and twenty-four shots on goal is an indication of just how much pressure we put on United that day. They had five efforts at goal and scored from every one! What United gave us, of course, was a lesson in finishing. It also made me realize how much I still had to learn about goalkeeping.

Goalkeeping can be a thankless task. Unlike outfield players, a single error of judgement on a keeper's part almost invariably leads to a goal for the opposition. Even when we get it right we're not always appreciated – a fingertip deflection over the bar often generating wild applause while the same shot easily saved as a result of correct positioning is accepted as unremarkable.

I always tried to make life as easy for myself as possible by being in the right place at the right time. The fans might not always have appreciated what I was trying to do, though thankfully one man did: Alf Ramsey.

10. The Class of '66

I was relieved to finish the 1965–66 season without having picked up an injury. I gave nothing less than 100 per cent effort and application during the run-in, but the impending World Cup was always at the back of my mind. Leicester finished the season on a high note, beating West Ham 2–1 in a highly entertaining game at Filbert Street. In the West Ham team that day was Bobby Moore, whom I was expecting to play alongside in the World Cup, together with Geoff Hurst and Martin Peters. Geoff had only a handful of caps and Martin was thought of as a squad player, albeit one with considerable potential. Little did I realize the crucial roles both were about to play in the destiny of the World Cup.

In April of that year Geoff had won only his second cap, against Scotland in a cracking Home International match. We'd prepared for the game by training at Ayr United's ground. On the morning of the match I was given a foretaste of what was to come when bidding farewell to one of the hotel porters. He had been attentive and helpful throughout our stay and good value for the five-bob tip I'd given him.

'Thanks for everything. Enjoy the game,' I said.

'Awa'n boil yer heid! I hope we pulverize yer!' he said, adding in the most polite of voices, 'Oh, 'n' thank ye for the gratuity, Mr Banks.'

Though there was still an hour and a half to go before kick-off, the roads leading to Hampden Park were a seething mass of tartan-clad humanity which erupted into life whenever they spotted our team coach. Some just leered, many jeered, but a good proportion hurled insults and crashed their fists against the bus. John Connelly was beginning to feel very uneasy but Bobby Moore allayed his fears.

'Don't worry about it,' Bobby told him, 'it's just the traditional Clydeside shipbuilders' welcome for the England team.'

In the sixties Glasgow shipbuilding was in its heyday. Ships could be seen lolling in cradles from Greenock to the very heart of Glasgow. These were the workplaces of Billy Connolly and the labour activist Jimmy Reid. Boiler-suit blue and testosterone driven.

As we probed our way towards Hampden it appeared that all those Clydeside workers were on their way to the match, as well as a good many of Glasgow's other artisans. They numbered in excess of 135,000 and at no time did I spot the friendly face of an England supporter.

There were few grounds in the world that could match Hampden for atmosphere and fanatical support on the day of a big game. And they didn't come any bigger than this for either the fans or the players. With so many Scots in the Leicester side, for England to lose would doom me to a whole season of merciless chaffing and ribbing. It wasn't just friendly banter, either. On one occasion Jimmy Walsh and I actually squared up to each other; Ian King and Davie Gibson had to step in and separate us.

The players were fervent, but the supporters verged on the rabid. As we disembarked from our team bus, fists were brandished and cans and bottles touted as we ran a gauntlet of abuse to the players' entrance.

'Ganna de ye lot the day, no mistakin', yer shandy-swiggin' southern bigheids!'

And that comment was from the doorman.

When the teams walked out on to the pitch at Hampden, the noise descending from the heaving terraces was deafening: 135,000 tartan-clad souls not only made the welkin ring with one collective tumultuous roar, they appeared to crack it from east to west. After the official presentations I took off, cap in hand, to one of the goals for the pre-match kickabout. It was like being greeted by 20,000 irate geese, such was the incessant hissing resounding all around me. When the game kicked off the din became louder than ever.

Alf Ramsey had opted for a 4–3–3 formation for this game, though he would later modify this to 4–4–2 for the World Cup. In front of me was a back line of George Cohen, Jack Charlton,

Bobby Moore and Keith Newton. The three-man midfield comprised Nobby Stiles, Bobby Charlton and John Connelly with Alan
Ball, Roger Hunt and Geoff Hurst in attack.

Once we had repelled the Scots' initial onslaught the game settled
down. Liverpool's Roger Hunt worked tirelessly, making angled
runs that pulled the Scottish defence all over the park and created
space for Bobby Charlton and John Connelly to exploit.

Hampden was the home of Queen's Park, who had the twin
distinctions of being the only senior club in the UK to retain pure
amateur status as well as being Scotland's oldest football club,
founded in 1867. I often used to wonder who on earth they played
against, if they were the first club. (That sort of question has always
intrigued me. I once read that Baker Street was the first ever station
on the London Underground. I thought, What was the point of
opening just one? Where could you go?) In fact, during their
formative years, Queen's Park played against English teams and
actually competed in the FA Cup, reaching the final twice, in 1884
and 1885, and losing to Blackburn Rovers on both occasions.
Queen's Park's average gate in the sixties was around 1,000. Now
it was packed to the gills with 130 times that number.

Hampden roared as Jim Baxter fed the ball to Willie Wallace
some twenty yards from my goal. The Hearts centre forward took
the ball on for a few yards before hitting a thunderous low drive,
the sheer pace of which took me by surprise. I managed to gather
the ball into my chest at the second attempt. As I lay there spitting
the dust and grime from my mouth I noticed a pair of blue-
stockinged legs inches from my face. I looked up to see Denis Law,
his hands grasping the white cuffs of his shirtsleeves and a menacing
smile on his face.

'And I'll be here every time. Be sure of that, Gordon, son,' he
said, displaying his Cheshire Cat grin to the full. I knew Denis was
playing mind games in the hope of putting a bit more pressure on
me, but I also knew he would be true to his word. Should I ever
slip up and spill the ball, he would be there to plant it in the back
of the net.

Such pressure never affected me. The bigger the occasion, the more at stake, the more I liked it and, it seemed, the better I played. As Alf Ramsey once told me, 'Thrive on pressure, Gordon. You get no juice out of an orange until you squeeze it.'

Though playing only his second game for England, Geoff Hurst was already showing the prowess he would become famous for on the international stage. He exuded confidence. Whenever Bobby Charlton was on the ball, Geoff was screaming for it to be played to him. Any striker prefers the ball to be played early, and Bobby was just the man for the job. After about fifteen minutes of frantic play, Bobby played the ball to Geoff some twenty-five yards from the Scottish goal. Before the Scots could close him down, Geoff let fly and the ball sailed past the flailing arms of the Scottish goalkeeper Bobby Ferguson. When the ball ballooned the net I had a good idea what it would be like to play at Hampden for Queen's Park. There was almost total silence. Though some eighty yards from Bobby Charlton, I heard him scream, 'It's there!' His voice was as piercing as that of a pub singer in Westminster Abbey.

Roger Hunt scored a second to put us in the driving seat, but this was Scotland against England, and the Scots would fight to the death. Roger added to his tally but Denis Law made good his promise, opening the account for the home side. Bobby Charlton once again put some daylight between the two sides when scoring with a typical netbuster, but still the Scots wouldn't roll over. Celtic's Jimmy Johnstone put them right back on track with a fine opportunist goal and in the final stages reduced the Scottish deficit even further. I thought I had all my angles and my positioning correct as Jimmy corkscrewed his way past Keith Newton and Jack Charlton, but Jimmy simply glanced up, saw where I was and deliberately sliced across the ball with the top of his boot. The ball curled away from me only to return to its original trajectory and into the far corner of the net. I wouldn't have thought it possible for any player under such pressure, running at speed and with only a marginal view of the goal, to have scored like that. It was a great goal from a player blessed with an abundance of natural skill.

With the deficit reduced to 4–3 and roared on by the massed ranks of their supporters, Scotland laid siege. With only a minute of the game remaining my heart skipped a beat when Jimmy Johnstone, who had given Keith Newton a torrid afternoon with his jinking runs, turned Keith yet again and set up Willie Wallace, whose forehead smacked the ball wide of my left arm and goalward. The sardine-packed terracing took to its toes. I was beaten, but there was the diminutive form of Nobby Stiles stretching up into the air as far as his limbs would allow to head the ball off the line.

'Goa-ohhhhhhhhh!' moaned 135,000 voices in unison.

Nobby saved the day for England. What's more, his last-minute clearance off the line had saved us all from a year of torture from our Scottish club mates. I could have hugged him for that alone.

It was my first senior success at international level over the Scots in four attempts, as it was Alf Ramsey's. The Scottish bubble had been pricked, and the bogey of Hampden, where England had not won since 1958, had been laid. The understanding between Bobby Charlton and Geoff Hurst had been remarkable in what was only their second game together. Jimmy Greaves had missed the game through injury, and his return could only strengthen our hand.

The victory also demonstrated to Alf Ramsey that England had strength in depth and good, workable options. The character and application we had shown in winning against what was a very good Scotland team galvanized the squad and reinforced our belief that we would do well in the World Cup. Alf liked his players to show mettle and to demonstrate that they would not be intimidated by even the most hostile atmosphere. Scotland at Hampden was a severe test of our credentials as an international side, and we had passed it with distinction.

There were two things that Alf wouldn't tolerate in his players: indiscipline and complacency. I'd hardly call myself a rebel – in fact I was always totally committed – but even I managed to find myself on the wrong side of Alf's disciplinary fence on one occasion in 1964.

It was just before we left for a game against Portugal in Lisbon. The game was scheduled for 17 May, little over a week after a long and strenuous domestic season. The England team had assembled immediately after the last league game of the season at our usual hotel in Lancaster Gate. We had a couple of days to kill before leaving for Portugal, and many of us were champing at the bit, but Alf's rules didn't permit us to leave the hotel. Jimmy Greaves and Bobby Moore knocked on my door to say that some of the lads were going for a quick pint. Did I fancy it? I didn't need asking twice.

Our group consisted of Jimmy, Bobby, Johnny Byrne, George Eastham, Ray Wilson, Bobby Charlton and myself. Jimmy said he knew a quiet pub just along the road and that's where we headed. Of course we were recognized immediately we walked through the door, but in those days the press didn't camp on our doorsteps round the clock so we felt confident our minor misdemeanour would go unreported.

Closing time came and went, but Jimmy knew 'a little club just down the road'. We fell into line behind Jimmy and soon found ourselves in a quiet corner of a cosy little den where we could continue our evening in pleasant conviviality. So convivial was it, in fact, that it was past one in the morning when the six of us sheepishly slipped away to our respective rooms, thinking we'd got away with it.

On entering my room I immediately knew I was in trouble. There, on my pillow, was my passport, Alf's message to me that my place on the trip to Portugal was far from assured. I was still gathering my thoughts when the door opened and in walked the others, all with passports in hand.

Alf didn't mention the incident until after our final training session in Lisbon. As the session came to an end he said, 'I believe there are seven amongst you who would like to remain behind for a chat with me. Is there not?

'If I had enough players here with me, not one of you would be getting a shirt against Portugal,' Alf told us. 'Consider this a shot across your bows. I will not tolerate the sort of thing that happened in London before we left. You are here to do a job – for your country – and so am I. Thank you, gentlemen. I look forward to the game against Portugal in the knowledge that what happened the other night will never be repeated.'

We all knew that our international careers would be finished should we overstep the mark again. And even though I played well in Lisbon, where we won 4–3, Alf still dropped me for the next game against the Republic of Ireland.

I don't believe I was ever complacent about my place in the England squad, but Alf never missed an opportunity to ensure that it stayed that way. After one game I was preparing to head back to Leicester when I saw him in the hotel car park. 'See you, Alf,' I said, waving goodbye. Alf nailed me with a cold, piercing stare. 'Will you?' he said.

It is well known that Alf had taken elocution lessons. I don't know why. Perhaps he felt that a plummy accent would help his cause when his name was being bandied about for the England job among the many Old Etonians on the FA. Alf was the sort of manager who knew he could never be 'one of the lads', and his accent helped to distance himself from the players. He had a brilliant footballing mind, though, was totally dedicated, occasionally taciturn, yet often witty and warm. His record as England manager speaks for itself. Of the 113 games he took charge of, England lost only 17. At times he appeared cold and distant, yet I know of no one who played under him who didn't have great affection for the man.

At times Alf appeared to be at pains to play down his humble background, although he wasn't ashamed of his roots, and certainly no snob. Perhaps he was worried that certain monied FA officials might look down on his Essex upbringing. Alf's father had a smallholding in Dagenham in the 1920s from which he sold hay and straw to dairies and the various companies who still made deliveries by horse and cart. Alf's first job was as a delivery boy for Dagenham Co-op in 1935, a job he held until he was called up for National Service.

It was while in the army that he first played for Southampton, the club he joined as a full back when his service days were over. In 1949 he was transferred to Spurs for what was then a record fee for a full back of £21,000. He won thirty-two caps for England and was a key member of the Spurs 'push-and-run' side that won the League Championship in 1952 under Arthur Rowe. Though he had only an elementary education at school, he was intelligent and an avid reader, although his attempts to appear better read than he was sometimes misfired.

Following one England training session the players were discussing with Alf who was the best club chairman. Jimmy Greaves hadn't said much, so Alf asked him if he had any thoughts on the matter.

'Not really,' said Jimmy. 'There's small choice in rotten apples.'

'I'm surprised at you, of all people, Jimmy,' said Alf. 'The English language is the most descriptive of all. Surely you can think of something more imaginative than, "there's small choice in rotten apples". English is the language of Shakespeare.'

'That is Shakespeare,' said Jimmy, much to Alf's embarrassment.

Alf was proud to be English, as we all were. He had an enormous influence on me as a player and as a person, and I can pay him no higher compliment than that. When he died of a stroke in 1999, the death certificate gave his occupation as 'Knight of the Realm, England Football Manager (Retired)'. To that I would have added, 'Gentleman, friend to all his players and the only England manager to have won the World Cup'.

Prior to that World Cup, England set off on a short tour of northern Europe. We began in Helsinki with an easy 3–0 victory over Finland, completely outclassing the Finns in a game that Alf used to give a run-out to a number of squad players, including the experienced Jimmy Armfield, Norman Hunter of Leeds, Ian Callaghan of Liverpool and a young, lithe, left-sided midfield player from West Ham, Martin Peters.

Alf saw the tour as a means of fine-tuning the side and giving every player in the twenty-two-man squad a final chance to show what he was capable of at international level. Alf rested me for the next two matches – a 6–1 victory over Norway in which Jimmy Greaves scored four, followed by a hard fought 2–0 win over Denmark – opting for Ron Springett of Sheffield Wednesday and Chelsea's Peter Bonetti. I returned for our final game in Katowice against Poland. When we disembarked from our plane we saw at first hand what life was like behind the Iron Curtain. The Katowice skyline was drab in the extreme, a mishmash of charcoal–grey blocks of flats, chemical works and winding gear. The people looked downtrodden and what few cars we saw seemed to belong to another age. Jimmy Greaves surveyed the sight, turned to Alf and said, 'OK, Alf, you've made your point. Now let's get back on the plane and bugger off home.'

Alf continued with Martin Peters for the game against Poland, but his inclusion was the only one that surprised the press. The team that took to the pitch against the Poles, Peters apart, was the one expected to open our World Cup campaign. Once again, Martin gave Alf much food for thought. Playing in a 4–3–3 formation, Martin ghosted about the pitch creating space not only for others, but for himself. Martin impressed me with his great sense of positioning and vision, the more so since he was only twenty-two years of age. A well-drilled shot from Roger Hunt gave us a 1–0 victory over Poland and brought the curtain down on a tour in which we had remained unbeaten. Since our participation in the 'Little World Cup' in Brazil we had played twenty-one internationals and lost only one (against Austria, a match I had missed through injury). The spirit and confidence in the England camp were sky high, prompting Alf to repeat publicly a sentiment he had expressed some months earlier – that England would win the World Cup.

Our World Cup preparations had gone extremely well, but the build-up to the tournament in England began with sensation, then farce. The World Cup itself, the Jules Rimet Trophy, had been on display at, of all places, a Stanley Gibbons stamp exhibition at the Central Hall in Westminster. One morning security staff approached the glass case in which the trophy was displayed and were dumbstruck to discover that it had been stolen. Shock waves reverberated around the world. The theft of the World Cup was a huge embarrassment, not only to the Football Association but to the whole country. The police immediately launched a nationwide investigation. Ports and airports were closed for a time as the search for the World Cup began. The story was headline news every day and, despite leaving no stone unturned, the police could uncover neither clue nor motive.

A week later Londoner Dave Corbett was walking his dog, Pickles, around Norwood in south London when the dog disappeared into the front garden of a house and began digging at the base of a hedge. Pickles uncovered a newspaper-wrapped parcel which his owner was astounded to find contained the stolen World Cup.

I can only imagine the relief that must have swept through the corridors of the FA and Scotland Yard. The recovery of the cup made even bigger headlines and the cartoonists of the time had a field day. The culprit was never discovered. I assume that efforts were made, but such was the relief at its recovery that, as far as I can recall, the investigation fizzled out. To this day the affair remains a mystery. It was not to be the last time that the Jules Rimet Trophy would find its way into the hands of someone other than the captain of a victorious international team, but that's a story for later.

The '66 tournament was the first World Cup to exploit fully its commercial potential. It was also the first to enjoy blanket live TV coverage worldwide, and this played no small part in its unprecedented commercial success. The tournament adopted a corporate logo: World Cup Willie, a cartoon lion in a Union Jack shirt and white shorts. Willie appeared on everything from button badges, sports bags, T-shirts and pennants to cereal boxes, ashtrays, soft-drink cans and cuddly toys. He even released a record which became a minor novelty hit. (Curiously, it sold very well in Japan, though Jimmy Greaves reckoned it only did so because the disc was the perfect size for Tokyo parking meters.)

In many ways the marketing of the 1966 World Cup set the scene for what was to come. The days of people counting out their coppers and asking for a pie would soon be committed to history as supporters dug deep to buy anything and everything from World Cup Willie duffel bags to jumpers and jerkins. The strangest souvenir I can recall was marketed by Daniel Schuster's Football Souvenirs of Sutton, Surrey. Schuster's produced a glass wellington boot with

World Cup Willie on the front, marketed as 'a real souvenir for your mantelshelf'. This five-inch high wellie was supposedly a liqueur glass. It appeared that the imagination of those who made and sold World Cup souvenirs under licence knew no bounds.

In 2002, thirty-two teams contested the World Cup finals in South Korea and Japan. In 1966 there were sixteen, divided into four groups of four. The group winners and runners-up proceeded to the quarter-finals, which were played then, as now, on a straight knock-out basis. England kicked off the tournament on 11 July and the final was less than three weeks later, on 30 July. They didn't drag it out in those days. Thirty-two matches concentrated into twenty days around which television had to fit their schedules. Television was playing an increasingly important role in spreading the gospel of football, but football's governing bodies were still very much in charge of the game and beholden to no one.

The tournament took place in four geographical zones and at eight grounds. The south-east zone used Wembley and, for France versus Uruguay, White City. The White City stadium was a strange choice as a World Cup venue, given that London boasted White Hart Lane and Highbury, two of the best stadiums in the country at the time, as well as the cavernous Stamford Bridge.

White City was known more as a greyhound stadium than a football ground. Its inclusion had much to do with the fact that it offered covered accommodation for 50,000 in a capacity of 60,000. Much of Highbury's terracing was open to the elements, as were the paddocks on the lower tiers of the East and West stands at White Hart Lane. Today, alongside the Westway A40 flyover where the White City stadium once stood, there are now houses and offices offering covered accommodation for all.

The Group Two matches were staged at Hillsborough and Villa Park. Group Three teams were at Goodison Park and Old Trafford while Group Four was staged at Roker Park, Sunderland, and Ayresome Park, Middlesbrough.

Few grounds met the minimum requirements for seating, so some clubs had to install temporary grandstands, though grand is hardly the word for the low rows of benches and view-restricting crush barriers that appeared almost overnight at Roker and Ayresome.

England matches, prime games such as the semi-finals and those involving Brazil apart, attendances for the 1966 World Cup were decent rather than staggering. Many matches were played in front of well below capacity crowds owing to a combination of admission prices almost three times those for league games (7s. 6d. (37½p) for children as opposed to 2s. 6d. at a league match) and the fact that many games took place at the same time. If an attractive game was on television for free, what was the point of watching a less-attractive one and paying for the privilege? For example, only 24,000 turned up at Old Trafford to see Hungary against Bulgaria when England's game against France was broadcast live on TV. Incredible as it may seem today, all four quarter-finals took place on the same day. Needless to say, the three venues at which England didn't play were far from full.

The draw of the host nation live on television was a lesson FIFA learned during 1966. In subsequent World Cups, not only did matches involving the hosts not clash with other group games, all group matches were given different kick-off times. The structure of the World Cup finals would never be the same after '66, when the power of television was seen for the first time.

England not only had home advantage, but had been drawn in Group One, and all our games were to be played at Wembley. Alf had originally picked a squad of forty players that, three weeks prior to the tournament, had been pared down to twenty-two. The unlucky eighteen were goalkeepers Tony Waiters (Blackpool) and Gordon West (Everton); full backs Chris Lawler (Liverpool), Paul Reaney (Leeds) and Keith Newton (Blackburn Rovers); half backs Marvin Hinton and John Hollins (both Chelsea) and Gordon Milne (Liverpool); forwards Joe Baker (Nottingham Forest), Barry Bridges (Chelsea), Gordon Harris (Burnley), John Kaye (West Bromwich Albion), Peter Osgood (Chelsea), Fred Pickering (Everton), Peter Thompson and Tommy Smith (Liverpool – yes, Tommy was a forward in those days), Derek Temple (Everton) and Terry Venables (Chelsea).

The final twenty-two comprised myself and two other goal-keepers, Ron Springett (Sheffield Wednesday) and Peter Bonetti (Chelsea); full backs Jimmy Armfield (Blackpool), Gerry Byrne (Liverpool), George Cohen (Fulham) and Ray Wilson (Everton); half backs Jack Charlton and Norman Hunter (both Leeds United), Ron Flowers (Wolves), Bobby Moore and Martin Peters (both West Ham United) and Nobby Stiles (Manchester United); forwards Alan Ball (Blackpool), Ian Callaghan (Liverpool), Bobby Charlton and John Connelly (both Manchester United); George Eastham (Arsenal), Jimmy Greaves (Spurs), Roger Hunt (Liverpool), Geoff Hurst (West Ham United) and Terry Paine (Southampton).

Alf's backroom staff was tiny compared with that in attendance for England games today. Apart from Alf himself it comprised Harold Shepherdson (Middlesbrough) our trainer, the assistant trainer Les Cocker (Leeds United), who also acted as our physio, and Wilf McGuinness (Manchester United), who helped Alf with the coaching. That was it, four people in total, though we did enjoy the services of a doctor for the duration of the tournament. (Don't knock the doc, he managed to get himself on the official photograph of the final squad, and not on the end of the back row either. The doc was pictured wearing an England tracksuit and seated left of centre, between Alf and Jimmy Armfield, with Alan Ball, Ian Callaghan and Nobby Stiles sitting on the ground at his feet!)

I felt that Alf's final twenty-two was as strong as it could be. With all due respect to those players who had just missed out, I don't think there was anyone missing from the squad who could have added greatly to it. Alf got it right, and not for the first or last time.

Alf was confident we could go on to win the World Cup, though not only certain members of the press but a number of people in football had their doubts. The Scotland manager of the time, John Prentice, was on record as saying that England wouldn't win. The Leeds manager, Don Revie, sat on the fence while Matt Busby of Manchester United was similarly indecisive. The Celtic manager, Jock Stein, was a little more positive in his assessment of our chances

but one of my boyhood heroes, the former Manchester City goalkeeper Bert Trautmann, gave us little chance. Neither did the Stoke
City manager, Tony Waddington.

The press were no more encouraging. The *Daily Sketch* was
typical, saying, 'We wish Alf and the boys all the luck in the world.
If we are to even reach the heady heights of the semi-finals, they
will need it,' while Robert Page writing in the *Soccer Star* said,
'England for the quarter-finals, the semi-finals at a pinch. But no
further I'm afraid. It will be a Brazil–West Germany final.' As a
nation, England certainly did not expect.

Buoyed by this tidal wave of optimism, we embarked on our
quest to win the World Cup with a game against Uruguay, the
first-ever winners of the World Cup back in 1930.

No opening ceremony of any great sporting occasion could have
been better stage-managed than the opening of the World Cup at
Wembley on 11 July 1966. The weather was perfect: blue skies and
a warm sunny evening. A cosmopolitan crowd packed the stadium
and Her Majesty the Queen was in attendance along with the Duke
of Edinburgh. The football world waited with bated breath for the
commencement of what had been dubbed the first modern World
Cup tournament. There was a great sense of anticipation and hopes
were high for a feast of cavalier football. The opening ceremony
began at 6.30 p.m. as Wembley thrilled to the massed bands of the
Guards. Across the planet, 500 million people, the world's largest
television audience, watched. In the wake of the Guards, youngsters
paraded the flags of the competing nations. Twenty-two boys (no
girls) represented each nation and wore the strip of their designated
country.

Once the parade massed on the pitch, the Queen, accompanied
by the Duke of Edinburgh, emerged to be greeted by a roar audible
from inside the England dressing room. Sir Stanley Rous, president
of FIFA, welcomed the Queen and called upon her to officially
open the tournament. That duty done, there was a fanfare of
trumpets, the signal for us to emerge from the tunnel alongside our
opponents, Uruguay. We walked out into the warm July evening
to a tempestuous roar from the terraces.

We were fit and raring to go, never had our spirit been higher, but the first ten minutes after Bobby Charlton had got the game under way were nightmarish. I stood unemployed in my penalty box watching players flitting eerily about the pitch. When Bobby kicked off, the atmosphere had been electric, but after only fifteen minutes I sensed that the game was going to be a damp squib and prove almost too much for the nerves of my team mates.

I think it's fair to say that, man for man, the Uruguayan players possessed superior technique. They had an outstanding striker in Penarol's Pedro Rocha, but the negative tactics they employed sent the carnival atmosphere of the opening ceremony evaporating fast into the cooling London night. The Uruguayans became a cloying cobweb of shifting pale blue shirts, hell bent on suffocation rather than inspiration. I reckon that throughout the first half I touched the ball no more than half a dozen times. More often than not, simply to field a wayward through ball. Riveting stuff it was not.

We tried – Lord knows we tried – but we just couldn't find a way through the Uruguayan blanket defence. Jimmy Greaves fizzed a shot inches wide of the post. Bobby Charlton hit a sumptuous volley into a thicket of legs, but that was about as near as either side came to scoring. During the last ten minutes the crowd that had roared us on to the pitch began to boo Uruguay for their delaying tactics. Their goalkeeper, Ladislao Mazurkiewiecz, at one point actually threw the ball off the pitch when a ball boy was trying to throw it on!

When the final whistle sounded, the Hungarian referee Istvan Zsolt signalled an end to play with an almost apologetic spread of his hands. On hearing the whistle blow, Jack Charlton, Alan Ball and George Cohen simply turned and ran towards the tunnel as if wanting to put it all behind them as quickly as possible. At least we hadn't lost, and I had kept a clean sheet (no great achievement, given that I'd been a spectator virtually throughout), but I left the pitch feeling very deflated. The Uruguayans, on the other hand, were ecstatic and ran around hugging each other as if the World Cup had already been won. The Wembley crowd let them know what they thought of their spoiling tactics and I walked back up the tunnel with the sound of jeers ringing in my ears. What a start!

Elsewhere in the first round of group matches, the goals everyone had been hoping for flowed. West Germany posted their intent with a 5–0 victory over Switzerland. Two of Germany's goals were scored by a 19-year-old who stole all the headlines that day with an assured performance against the Swiss. It was the first time that the vast majority of us had heard the name Franz Beckenbauer. Brazil too got off to a flyer. Goals from Pelé and Garrincha gave them a 2–0 victory over Bulgaria in front of over 47,000 at Goodison Park. Both Brazilian goals came from trademark 'banana' free kicks, but a superb match was marred by the rough treatment meted out to Pelé. He was man-marked, at times ruthlessly, by Bulgaria's Peter Zhechev and picked up an injury that put him out of Brazil's next game against Hungary. In Group Four, Russia gave ample evidence that they too would be a force to be reckoned with, beating North Korea 3–0 at Ayresome Park. After such a disappointing and turgid start, the '66 World Cup began to take on a life and identity of its own.

Following our game against Uruguay, we returned to our base in the Hendon Hall Hotel where, when not training at the Bank of England ground in Roehampton, we watched the tournament unfold on TV. Much of our preparation had taken place at the FA's coaching school at Lilleshall in Shropshire, but as all our group games were at Wembley it had been decided we would be London based. Hendon is hardly a backwater, but quite often I would join other players for a stroll down the high street and at no time did we attract attention from the press, or even from over-enthusiastic fans.

Thus out of the limelight, our base at Hendon had a very relaxed atmosphere. What spare time I had was spent reading newspapers or watching television in the TV lounge. At ten thirty every night Alf would come in. So regular was he, you could set your watch by him. He'd simply say, 'Goodnight, gentlemen,' and off to bed we would troop like a dutiful band of Boy Scouts.

After a day on the training pitch I was ready for bed at ten thirty anyway. Not that the television fare served up by the only three channels then available – BBC1, BBC2 and ITV – provided any incentive to stay awake. Those of a certain age might remember the BBC's early and disastrous football soap opera *United*. *United* followed the on- and off-pitch antics of the fictitious Brentwich United. The Brentwich players all had comic-book names such as Jimmy Stokes (played by George Layton), Curly Parker (Ben Howard) and Vic 'Hotshot' Clay (Warwick Sims).

Apparently (this was black and white television) they played in red and white stripes. For added realism, footage of Sunderland or Stoke City in action was cut into the matchday scenes. Such editing was rarely convincing and led to some odd and unintentionally humorous moments, such as when George Layton would suddenly turn into Sunderland's Charlie Hurley half-way down the tunnel. *United* had a curiosity value, but it never took off. Storylines such as 'Holiday time is over, so it is back to work for the players of Brentwich United' and 'Deirdre runs short of envelopes in the club office while Greg Harris is worried about being fit for Saturday' saw the series disappear after little over a year.

Against Uruguay Alf had opted for Blackburn's John Connelly on the left, more or less in the role of an orthodox winger. When he announced the team for our second match, against Mexico, however, Alf made a change to our formation that was to alter the whole course of the tournament.

11. Rattin Gets Ratty

Against Mexico, Alf Ramsey brought Martin Peters into the team on the left side of midfield in place of John Connelly. Alan Ball was also replaced, his position on the right being taken by South-ampton's wide man Terry Paine.

Martin was a midfield player rather than an orthodox winger like John Connelly. Replacing Alan Ball with Terry Paine was a balancing move: in dropping one winger, Alf had brought another one in on the other flank. Even at this stage of the proceedings, Alf obviously still thought he needed an orthodox winger in the team, and was still experimenting to find the best formation.

Prior to the Mexico game we enjoyed a day out at Pinewood film studios. I'm a big movie fan, so this was a cracking trip for me as well as a good ploy on the part of Alf to brighten our spirits after the disappointment of the match against Uruguay. As Alf said, 'Laughter is contagious.'

Earlier that day we had had a training session at Highbury during which Jack Charlton, Alf and I had a heated exchange about the best way to defend against Brazilian free kicks. (Jack wanted to put a defender between me and the wall, which I said would obstruct my line of vision). After forty-five minutes of fruitless disagreement Bobby Moore stepped in.

'Alf, if laughter is contagious, the three of you have just found the cure.'

Alf quickly wrapped things up, saying, 'Gordon is in charge of his own penalty area. The matter is closed.'

At Pinewood they were filming *You Only Live Twice* and we all met Mr Bond himself, Sean Connery. The stunts James Bond pulled off, however, were nothing compared with the one Ray Wilson managed during our visit to Pinewood, where a buffet lunch was supplemented by a copious amount of bottled beer. Alf immediately restricted everyone to one beer each. Ray Wilson somehow managed to consume about eight. As the afternoon wore on, Ray became increasingly loud and outrageous, asking Yul Brynner, who was to appear in Newcastle reprising his role in *The King and I*, 'What're they calling it up there, then? The King and Why Aye?'

We spent the rest of the day trying to keep Ray as far away from Alf as possible. If Alf had ever discovered the state Ray was in, he would probably have been dropped from the squad.

Mexico and France had played out a 1–1 draw in their opening game, which was a good result for us. It meant that we went into our game against Mexico with every team in the group level. Mexico were a useful side whose main strength was an organized and effective defence. Against England they used a sweeper, Jesus del Muro, who played his club football for Cruz Azul. Del Muro started the game playing behind a back four with 22-year-old Ignacio Calderón of Guadalajara in goal. For nearly forty minutes we foundered on Mexico's resolute back line. I remember thinking that it was going to take something special for us to breach their defence. No sooner had I thought this than Bobby Charlton conjured up a piece of football magic that was very special indeed.

Bobby received the ball deep in our half of the field and glided down the pitch like a thoroughbred racehorse with the Mexicans conceding midfield and falling back around their penalty area. Bobby kept the ball under immaculate control and, thirty yards out, without breaking stride and with hardly any backlift, hit a thunderbolt of a shot with his right foot. The ball cut through the air like a bullet and was still rising as it ballooned the back of Calderón's net. Wembley erupted and millions of people across England leapt from their armchairs. It was a tremendous goal in the true Bobby Charlton tradition. We were off the mark, and how!

All these years later, Bobby's goal against Mexico is still considered to be among football's all-time greatest, and rightly so. In the dressing room after the game, we heaped praise on Bobby for his marvellous effort.

'You're full of compliments for our kid,' laughed his brother

Jack. 'But don't forget it was me who made the two-yard pass that set him on his way!'

Ominously, in Group Two, Argentina were involved in a bad-tempered match with West Germany. Over 47,000 turned up at Villa Park expecting to see a vibrant encounter between two fancied teams. What they saw was a dull, defensive battle littered with fouls. Argentina's Jorge Albrecht received his marching orders following a reckless challenge, and many thought that several of his countrymen should have followed him. Argentina had beaten Spain 2–1 and knew that a draw against the Germans would be enough to get them to the quarter-finals. West Germany, whose attack had ravaged Switzerland, were choked by a ten-man Argentine defence well marshalled by their skipper, Antonio Rattin. The behaviour of the Argentinian players left much to be desired and their dirty tactics and petulance resulted in a warning from FIFA about their future conduct. As we were to find out, it went unheeded.

In Group Three Portugal coasted to a 3–0 victory over Bulgaria which ended the Bulgarians' hopes of further progression, while at Roker Park one blinding flash of genius from Igor Chislenko of Moscow Dynamo gave Russia a 1–0 win over Italy. Against Russia, Italy left out their 'golden boy' Gianni Rivera of AC Milan, and their leading goalscorer, Paolo Barison of Roma. The casual approach of the Italians suggested they believed they had some divine right of qualification. The Italians believed their defeat against Russia to be of little consequence, as their remaining tie was against North Korea, a team the star-studded Italians expected to beat easily.

The day before our victory over Mexico I joined my England team mates to watch what was without doubt one of the best games of the qualifying stage. That night, to the accompaniment of 52,000 wildly cheering fans at Goodison Park, I witnessed the demise of Brazil. Their conquerors were Hungary by three goals to one, and the Hungarian victory was well deserved.

The Brazilian team was a mixture of youth and experience, welded together by the great Pelé. Pelé, however, was injured and watched helplessly from the stands as his team was torn apart by a

13. During the big freeze of 1962–63. Displaying all the benefits of Ursula's numerous hot dinners, I collect the ball under pressure from Ray Crawford of Ipswich Town. Braziers filled with burning coke kept the frost at bay, but, as you can see from the pitch, not for long.

14. The 1963 FA Cup semi-final against Liverpool. I manage to punch clear from Liverpool's Ian St John. There was only one team in this game – Liverpool – and they lost 1–0.

15. A very nervous day for me. My first game for England and Alf Ramsey's second game in charge – against the old enemy, Scotland, in 1963. I'm pushing away a low shot from Willie Henderson. Scotland won 2–1, both their goals coming from Jim Baxter.

16. The flying Englishman. A free kick from John White has me at full stretch in my international debut against Scotland. On this occasion I managed to keep the Scots at bay, though that wasn't always the case in this game.

17. Davie Gibson, Ian King, myself and Frank McLintock show our relief at the end of the FA Cup semi-final against Liverpool. This was the moment when I was 'set up' by a photographic editor from a well-known newspaper.

18. Oh dear! In my second game for England I'm mesmerized by the swerve of Pepe's 'banana' free kick. Alf Ramsey was not best pleased. Off to my left in the upper stand at Wembley, one of the few Brazilian supporters present celebrates.

CHARLES BUCHAN'S

FOOTBALL

MONTHLY

The World's Greatest Soccer Magazine

JANUARY, 1964

2/-
OVERSEAS PRICE 2/6
FORCES OVERSEAS
2/-

GORDON BANKS
Leicester City
and England

19. When I was a teenager, *Charles Buchan's Football Monthly* was the football magazine. Unable to afford to attend matches on a regular basis, the only way to see my heroes was in the *Footy Monthly*. When I was featured on the cover of the January 1964 issue, one of my childhood dreams came true.

20. Taking a high cross against West Germany in the 1966 World Cup final, oddly enough under no pressure on this occasion. Looking on, from left to right, are George Cohen, Jack Charlton, Uwe Seeler, Martin Peters, Bobby Moore and Lothar Emmerich.

21. Glory seized from our grasp in the dying seconds of the 1966 World Cup final. Wolfgang Weber's equalizer should not have been allowed. Karl-Heinz Schnellinger handled the ball. You can see Bobby Moore appealing.

22. A golden memory of a truly golden day. I join Martin Peters, Geoff Hurst, Bobby Moore and Roger Hunt to parade the World Cup around at Wembley. Notice how we are too exhausted to run.

23. 'Give it here, Banksy.' Winning the World Cup is the most difficult thing a player can do in football. It had been a long hard road and once I got my hands on the trophy I wasn't going to give it up easily – not even to skipper Bobby Moore!

24. The boys of '66. There were no prima donnas, no cliques, no loners. We were a team in every sense of the word. Left to right, back row: Gerry Byrne (reserve), Harold Shepherdson (trainer), Jack Charlton, myself, Roger Hunt, Bobby Moore, Geoff Hurst, George Cohen, Bobby Charlton; front row: Nobby Stiles, Alan Ball, Martin Peters and Ray Wilson. Bobby Charlton looks as though he is about to be taken away as it has all become too much for him!

rampant Hungary who, in Ferenc Bene and Florian Albert, possessed players of lightning speed whose direct approach caused Brazil all manner of problems.

It was an exhilarating game, the speed and tempo of which laid bare the defects of the Brazilians. Sadly, old hands such as Bellini, Djalma Santos and even the great Garrincha had no answer to the pace of the Hungarians, while the younger members of the side – Jairzinho, Tostao and Alcindo – lacked the necessary experience.

When Portugal finally put paid to Brazil by the same scoreline in their next game, it came as no surprise. The press hailed it as the end of an era. With the benefit of hindsight, it wasn't. Brazil were merely a team in transition. They had too many players over the age of thirty and too many youngsters. The notable exception was Pelé, who at twenty-five, though yet to reach his prime, already had two World Cup winners' medals. Though substitutes were still not allowed, teams could name a non-playing reserve. For their games against Hungary and Portugal, the Brazilian reserve was Edu, who at sixteen was the youngest player in this World Cup. His inclusion was indicative of a Brazilian team in the throes of major change and whose sights were set on the future.

Pelé didn't fail in the '66 World Cup, he was kicked out of the competition. The great man returned against Portugal, but the treatment meted out to him by Oporto's João Morais was more brutal than that which had resulted in his injury against Bulgaria.

Pelé's disappearance after half an hour put an end to what the press said would be 'a contest to decide the world's greatest player' between him and Eusebio. Everywhere he went Pelé was surrounded by three Portuguese defenders who were none too subtle in dealing with him. The leniency with which referees viewed robust play in this era was evidenced after a scything tackle from Morais that made no contact with the ball and took Pelé out at the knee. The referee, George McCabe of England, simply awarded a free kick, as probably most referees would have done. Football was then a very physical game. Only in exceptional circumstances was a player sent off. The tackle from behind was an accepted part of the game, certainly by Europeans, and body-checking was part of the football culture of South America. Football may have been emerging as the beautiful game, but it still followed a very hard and sometimes cynical script.

Pelé may have been kicked out of the World Cup, but even if he had been fully fit Brazil wouldn't have won it. They were simply not up to the job. Portugal's approach against Brazil baffled me, quite simply because they were good enough to beat Brazil with their sheer footballing craft. In Eusebio they possessed the one player who could come anywhere near Pelé in terms of footballing brilliance. I suppose it was just colonial rivalry.

While everyone was digesting the fact of Brazil's elimination, the unbelievable news came that North Korea had beaten Italy 1–0 at Ayresome Park. Italy were out. The scale of the upset was comparable to the United States' defeat of England in 1950.

The swaggering Italians had, on the night, been a strangely dispirited bunch and the unknown Koreans seized their chance. The goal that clinched it was scored by Pak Doo Ik, who, as a result, found himself immortalized in football folklore. The Koreans had played as if they meant to win, the Italians as if they couldn't lose. North Korea's victory set Teesside alight. Middlesbrough had not produced the biggest crowds for the World Cup, but it had generated fantastic support for the Koreans, whom the Teessiders adopted as their second team.

North Korea joined Russia in qualifying for the quarter-finals from Group Four and were far from finished so far as shock scorelines were concerned. Italy flew home with their tails between their legs. When the Italian team landed at Genoa airport they were pelted with tomatoes and eggs, and their manager, Edmundo Fabbri, was immediately dismissed. Like Brazil, they too had to rebuild for the future.

In our final group game, two poacher's goals from Liverpool's Roger Hunt gave us a 2–0 victory over France. The win saw us top our group with two wins and one draw to our name. Most satisfactorily from my point of view, we hadn't yet conceded a goal.

Our success was tempered by two problems. First, Nobby Stiles had picked up a booking following a foul on Nantes' Jacques Simon; should he be booked again, he would be out of the tournament. Nobby's game was fiercely competitive, some said dirty, but I knew him well enough to say that he never deliberately hurt an opponent. Every team needed a hard-man ball-winner and Nobby fulfilled that role for us. They didn't come much smaller in stature or bigger in heart than Nobby. He was permanently hungry for the ball, which might explain why he was so deadly in the tackle.

There was only ten stone of him, but many opponents recoiled from engaging with him in the tackle as if they had been confronted by ten tons. Having won the ball, he rarely passed it more than a few yards, but that was all he was supposed to do: win the ball and give it to Bobby Charlton.

Alf Ramsey was under pressure to drop Nobby, both from certain quarters of the press and from certain FA officials. Needless to say, Alf paid no heed.

Our second problem to arise from our game against France was more serious. Jimmy Greaves was on the end of a very late challenge from Jean Bonnel that resulted in an ugly gash on his left shin requiring fourteen stitches. With our quarter-final against Argentina only three days away, we all knew that there was no way Jimmy was going to be fit.

We had qualified from our group along with second-placed Uruguay. West Germany and Argentina qualified from Group Two, Portugal and Hungary from Group Three, with Russia and the surprise package, North Korea, from Group Four.

Against France, Alf had once again opted for one orthodox winger by playing Ian Callaghan from Liverpool. With Jimmy Greaves injured, I knew Alf had to make a change for the team against Argentina, but had no idea he would alter things so dramatically. We had used three different line-ups in our three group games. For the Argentina game Alf made a monumental decision. He decided to ditch wingers completely and play two midfield players in wide positions – Alan Ball on the right and Martin Peters on the left. Alf also introduced Geoff Hurst as a replacement for the injured Jimmy G.

The 4–4–2 formation we had adhered to for some time went out of the window. We were now to play 4–3–3. I thought at the time that the decision to dispense with wingers was a good one. Alan Ball and Martin Peters were highly intelligent players. They worked tirelessly, dropped back and helped out in defence, were good when going forward and, particularly in the case of Martin Peters, could make quality crosses into the opposition penalty area. More importantly, those crosses were made early, before opponents had time to get organized in defence.

The pressure on Alf to leave Nobby Stiles out of the side for the Argentina game gathered momentum. Some FA officials thought Nobby's robust style would serve only to inflame further the team that had already received a warning from FIFA about their conduct. Alf, however, resisted all calls to drop Nobby. 'If Stiles has to go, then so do I,' Alf told the FA, and meant it. The anti-Stiles brigade quickly backed off. Once again Alf had shown that he would not be dictated to regarding team selection.

The idea that 4–3–3 was a new formation that revolutionized British football and sounded the death knell for wingers is only partly true. 4–3–3 was, in fact, nothing new, though it was new to England as an international team. The 4–3–3 formation, with midfield players or half backs fulfilling roles in both defence and attack as well as the middle of the park in preference to orthodox wingers, whose prime job was to attack, had been applied with some success in Italy. 4–3–3 was a combination of the old 'W' formation, in which a team played two full backs, three half backs and five forwards, and the 4–4–2 system Alf had used in previous England matches.

In Italy the 4–3–3 formation had been deployed with considerable success by both AC and Inter Milan. The Italians referred to 4–3–3 as *catenaccio*, which in English means 'door bolt' or 'chain'. The Italians played 4–3–3 as a very defensive and cautious system, whereby teams denied opponents scoring opportunities by defending the 'scoring space' and adopting man-to-man marking supported by a sweeper. It was a system that relied heavily on counter-attacks spearheaded by speedy strikers. 4–3–3 paid handsome dividends for Inter when they won the European Cup in

1964 and 1965. Though 4–3–3 brought success, the way Inter played resulted in some very sterile football. Once one of their counter-attacks had produced a goal, irrespective of how early in the game they had scored, Inter shut up shop, fell back into defence and relied on their *catenaccio* system to stifle all the efforts of their opponents to equalize.

The origins of 4–3–3 can be traced back to the 1930s when Switzerland, managed by the Austrian Karl Rappan, used the *verrou* system (*verrou* also means 'door bolt'). The Swiss side of the thirties adopted a rudimentary sweeper in defence and relied on breakaway goals. This system was truly innovatory at the time. Though bereft of world-class players, in the 1938 World Cup in France Switzerland beat a powerful German team 4–2, only to go out at the hands of the beaten finalists, Hungary.

The Italian sides of the early sixties improved the Swiss *verrou* system and Alf was to develop 4–3–3 even further. He wanted us to be more adventurous than the Italians. Rather than simply falling back to defend a one-goal lead, Alf wanted us to play the ball out quickly to Alan Ball or Martin Peters, who in turn would hit early balls in for Geoff Hurst.

'We shall not rely on defence. We will still take the game to the opposition,' said Alf.

The work rate of Bally and Martin Peters was to play a vital role in England's success using the 4–3–3 system. Both worked immensely hard to help out in defence and fulfil their roles as wide midfield players. If Alan played the ball in from the right, Martin would be there to support Geoff Hurst and Roger Hunt in attack. Conversely, when Martin crossed the ball from the left, Alan would be buzzing about the penalty area looking to pick up any pieces. As I have said, both Martin and Alan were very intelligent players. Martin had great vision and a very cultured left foot while Alan was blessed with electrifying speed and great tenacity. Possibly their best assets were their lungs, which must have been like sides of beef, so much ground did they cover.

Alf didn't need to spend countless hours with a blackboard explaining the system to the players. Although we hadn't played that way before, we all had a good grasp of how it worked, for we had all come across 4−3−3 when playing against continental teams. All Alf needed to do was to convey the finer points of how we would deploy it.

Alf conducted his team talks in the afternoons. At the Bank of England training ground at Roehampton we would train in the morning, break for lunch, then gather in the conference room for one of Alf's talks. After a hard training session, lunch was very welcome.

The first day we had lunch at Roehampton everyone was delighted. The menu was tomato soup, a sumptuous side of beef with all the trimmings followed by a delicious home-made apple pie drowned in creamy custard.

The only problem was, this menu was never to change. Come the seventh consecutive day we would have given a king's ransom for beans on toast or a salad. As Ray Wilson remarked, 'This chef's idea of a balanced meal is a Yorkshire pudding on your dinner plate, and one on your side plate.'

Following such a large lunch, a number of players struggled to keep awake during Alf's team talks. Jimmy Greaves introduced an added element of excitement to the occasion by running a book on how long Jack Charlton could stay awake. The stopwatch was started as soon as Alf began to speak and stopped the moment big Jack's eyes closed and his chin dropped on to his chest.

Alf's words of wisdom often fell upon deaf ears as half the squad's attention focused on big Jack. I won a few bob, as did Bobby Moore, Ray Wilson, George Eastham and, of course, Jimmy himself. On one occasion, Alf was midway through a sermon about Portugal when Jack momentarily nodded off, only to sit bolt upright again when startled by one of his own snores. Jimmy Greaves immediately blurted out, 'All bets are off!' much to the bewilderment of Alf. Needless to say, Alf soon twigged, and Jimmy's involuntary outburst put the kybosh on that little entertainment.

On 23 July, the day of the quarter-finals, the sun shone, the attendances were good and the explosions came.

The first excitement came at Goodison Park, where North Korea rocked world football on its heels by racing into a three-goal lead against Portugal. Goodison giggled in disbelief. The waves of incredulity sped through the ether to every television and radio as the nation struggled to come to terms with what was the most amazing scoreline of the World Cup. How could North Korea maintain this sort of form, especially against the much-fancied Portuguese? They couldn't. Eusebio took the game by the scruff of the neck and, slowly but surely, Portugal eroded North Korea's early advantage. At half time it was 3–2, and in the second half the doughty North Koreans felt the full force of Eusebio's brilliance. Bent on absolute destruction he tore into the North Korean defence. Come the final whistle, Portugal were winners by five goals to three. Eusebio helped himself to four goals, the other Portugal goal coming from Augusto.

Just by reaching the quarter-finals and giving Portugal one almighty shock, North Korea had achieved more than they could have ever hoped for when setting out from their homeland. In coming back to win the game from three goals down, Portugal had shown themselves to be as sound in character and temperament as in technique. As for Eusebio, his virtuoso performance saw him elevate himself to a status in world football that had hitherto been the sole preserve of Pelé.

While the drama of Goodison was unfolding, we were involved in drama of a very different kind in our game against Argentina. It was an afternoon when the passions, the ruthlessness and the national pride that had been grafted on to the pursuit of the World Cup surfaced in both majestic and disgraceful ostentation.

The game was only minutes old when Alan Ball was cynically felled by Silvio Marzolini. The tone of the match had been set. We took the game to Argentina, a signal for the body-checking and cynical fouls to gather momentum as the Argentines resorted to all manner of thuggery to keep us at bay.

We had what I thought were legitimate appeals for penalties turned down following fouls on Alan Ball and Geoff Hurst as we continued our onslaught on the Argentine goal. The German referee, Herr Kreitlein, was rapidly filling his notebook with Argentinian names and ten minutes before half time decided that the 'unofficial referee', the Argentine skipper Antonio Rattin who had vehemently disputed every booking, had to go.

Herr Kreitlein was a small and dapper man whose somewhat irritatingly authoritative manner served only to further the displeasure of the Argentinians, and of Rattin in particular. Having committed a series of fouls Rattin was called over by Kreitlein. The Argentinian skipper gazed down at the referee, his expression one of utter contempt. Herr Kreitlein spoke only a few words before Rattin spat forth a volley of invective. It was the last straw for the German, who turned to the team benches and raised his right arm to indicate that Rattin had to go.

As everybody knows, Rattin refused to leave the pitch. The game was held up for seven minutes as chaos reigned. I stood dumbfounded on the edge of my penalty box as I watched a heated argument develop between the match officials, the players, the Argentine management and FIFA delegates. At one point the South American players left the pitch en masse, as if to suggest it was a case of 'one off, all off'. Two police officers came on to the scene; the Wembley crowd rumbled ominously as volatile Argentinians and beleaguered FIFA officials faced each other down. Eventually Ken Aston, the referees' liaison officer, and Harry Cavan, FIFA's match delegate, managed to convince the Argentine manager Juan Carlos Lorenzo and his delegation of fellow countrymen that Herr Kreitlein's decision was irreversible. Rattin was off.

The match restarted with Rattin hurling insults from the sidelines. At this point drama descended into farce as Argentine players fell to the ground like bags of hammers every time one of our players came near them. Once on the ground they writhed around like electrocuted earthworms. It was pantomime stuff, but no one was laughing. Least of all Bobby Moore, who resisted the temptation to restore parity of numbers by not reacting to a slap in the face from Alberto Gonzalez.

The breakthrough we had been labouring for eventually arrived thirteen minutes from time. From wide on the left wing, Martin Peters crossed the ball into a space between the Argentine goalkeeper Antonio Roma and his defence. Geoff Hurst timed his run to perfection. He ghosted into the space, leapt high and, with a deft flick of his head, guided the ball past the static Roma and into the net. The two Hammers had combined to produce a Ron Greenwood special. The Wembley terraces exploded into a heaving mass of humanity. Hats were hurled, arms held aloft, as 90,000 people celebrated what was to be the winning goal.

Our joy at gaining a place in the semi-finals was tempered by Argentinian bitterness. Come the final whistle, all the vitriolic emotion of a team who believed they could have won the World Cup was once again unleashed upon the unfortunate Herr Kreitlein, who had to be escorted from the pitch by Ken Aston and a small posse of the Metropolitan's finest.

At this point Alf Ramsey did something that was very uncharacteristic. In the time-honoured tradition of international football, George Cohen offered to exchange shirts with the Argentinian number 11, Oscar Mas. The two players were in the process of doing just that when Alf intervened and put a stop to it. He was so obviously angered by the conduct of the Argentinians that he would allow no gesture of friendship or fraternization. The photograph of Alf tugging George Cohen away from Mas appeared in the world's press on the following day. As far as South American countries were concerned, of course, Alf was the bad guy. His reputation among them was to get even worse a few hours later when he said, 'The behaviour of some players in the competition reminds me of animals.' Though he never directly referred to the Argentinians as animals, the South American press, in particular that of Argentina, widely reported that he had in fact done so. The British papers picked up on this and took a similar line. Thus was the 'animals' myth created and Alf Ramsey, to my mind, very badly maligned.

For years to come this misinterpretation of Alf's possibly unwise post-match comment was to hang like a millstone round his neck whenever England came up against a South American team, not least during the 1970 World Cup in Mexico.

Alf took it all on the chin. Two aspects of his character that I admired were his grace and his dignity. Alf must have known he had been misquoted, but he steadfastly refused to involve himself in a slanging match with the press in order to clear his name. Nearly forty years on, I am delighted finally to have the opportunity to do so.

As for the match itself, Herr Kreitlein must shoulder some of the blame for the way it degenerated. He was quick to punish minor infringements while allowing more serious misdemeanours to go unchecked. When players feel they are not being protected by an official, they invariably take matters into their own hands and trouble escalates. Having said that, the Argentine players were, of course, the main culprits. Their whole attitude to the game, and the competition in general, left much to be desired. The tragedy of it all was that the Argentinians were very good footballers. In players such as Rattin, Oscar Mas, Ermindo Onega and Luis Artime they possessed footballers of real class. Their Achilles heel was their lack of discipline.

Following the game FIFA suspended Antonio Rattin for four international matches, and both Ermindo Onega and Roberto Ferreiro for three. The Argentinian FA was fined £83. 8s. 6d., this paltry and curious amount being the equivalent of 1,000 Swiss francs which, at the time, was the maximum fine FIFA could impose.

Ermindo Onega received his ban for ungentlemanly conduct (spitting in the face of an official) and Rattin for bringing the game into disrepute. Luis Artime and Jorge Solari were both cautioned during the game as were the Charlton brothers, Jackie and Bobby, the first and only time that ever happened. Argentina were also warned that unless they could guarantee the good behaviour of their players and officials, they could face a ban from the 1970 World Cup, although that would have been of no consequence since they didn't qualify.

Why did the Argentinians behave as they did? While their actions are certainly inexcusable, they may perhaps be explicable. It might be claimed that Rattin laboured under a misunderstanding. He had been booked for a foul on Bobby Charlton and was later to claim that at the time of his dismissal he had merely wanted to complain to Herr Kreitlein about some of our tackling. The referee spoke no Spanish, so Rattin needed an interpreter. According to him, he was in the process of asking for one when the referee gave him his marching orders.

In South America it was quite common for a team captain to discuss events with a referee, and even question his decisions. Rattin said he simply couldn't understand why Herr Kreitlein took exception to this. But Herr Kreitlein, of course, was a European.

I believe that the difference in footballing cultures was at the root of the trouble that day. Both sides followed the same set of rules, but those rules were interpreted very differently by each. Even now the difference remains noticeable, despite television's global coverage and the fact that many of South America's top players currently ply their trade in Europe, although it is far less marked today than it was during that notorious quarter-final.

The pressure on us eased somewhat on reaching the semis. We were the first England team ever to reach the last four and would now be ranked by FIFA among the top four sides in the world. It had been a good many years since England had been placed so highly and was indicative of the progress we had made under Alf's management.

If someone were to ask me which of all the games I played for England was the best in terms of pure football, I would have no hesitation in saying it was our semi-final against Portugal. Portugal were the bookies' favourites and understandably so. They had a number of world-class players at the peak of their powers, none more so than Eusebio, a player who combined exquisite grace with explosive power. The game took place the day after the other semi-final, in which West Germany had beaten Russia 2–1 at Goodison Park. The last time the Germans had reached the World Cup final had been in 1954, when Jules Rimet himself handed them the trophy that bore his name following their shock 3–2 defeat of Hungary. With their sights on a second World Cup success, the word coming back from the German camp was that they would sooner face us than Portugal in the final.

The West Germans may have wanted England to reach the final but, incredibly, this view was not shared by the entire nation. Following our victory over Argentina, Lord Lovat wrote a letter to *The Times* in which he excoriated England for leaving 'Argentinian players . . . jerking in agony on the pitch'. He also said that 'The Argentine were the better players and England have got through to the last four by a lucky disqualification and by crippling two Frenchmen earlier in the tournament'. I didn't have a clue who Lord Lovat was, or by what authority he was speaking, but I quickly came to the conclusion that he knew precious little about football. Happily, however, the unknowledgeable peer was in a tiny minority; the rest of the country and its press were firmly behind us.

Alf Ramsey decided to field an unchanged team against a Portuguese side that had already earned £1,000 bonus per man for reaching the semi-final. (Oddly, the Portuguese players would have received less – £500 each – for reaching the final, though a Lisbon bank had promised each player £750 if they won the tournament in addition to the £500 promised by the Portuguese FA.) Like my England team mates, I was simply on a £60 match fee, though the team had been promised a £22,000 bonus should we win the World Cup.

Portugal were, to my mind, the most complete footballing side in the World Cup. In Eusebio, the Black Panther, they had the star of the tournament. He was an exceptionally gifted player who was one of the best strikers of a ball I have ever come across. The name Eusebio equalled goals, and not of the bread and butter variety. His were invariably dramatic, always memorable and tended to overshadow the magnificent work he did in midfield.

For Eusebio was not just a goalscorer. In the mid-sixties his peerless skills kept Benfica among Europe's foremost clubs and made Portugal, who prior to his emergence had been no menace to anyone, one of the most feared teams on the international stage. Eusebio had dominated the tournament and had almost single-handedly taken Portugal into the last four. Like many great players, he wasn't tall, but he had very broad shoulders, exceptional upper-body strength and powerful legs that pumped him all over the pitch at remarkable speed. At full throttle he must have seemed like a blur to defenders. Of course that didn't bother Nobby Stiles, who had been assigned by Alf to mark him – without his glasses everybody was a blur to Nobby.

At the time I didn't wear goalkeeping gloves unless the conditions were very wet. Prior to leaving the dressing room I'd chew on two or three pieces of gum and then smear some saliva into the palms of my hands. This tacky goo gave me a better grip when handling the ball, and also a degree of control when palming it away during a diving save. Chewing gum also helped my concentration immensely. When the dressing-room buzzer signalled that we should make our way out to the Wembley tunnel, I asked Harold Shepherdson, our trainer, for some gum as usual. His slack-jawed expression told me all I needed to know: he didn't have any. I began to panic.

'I've got to have it, Harold,' I told him. 'You know how greasy a ball gets out there at night.'

The Wembley pitch consisted of lush, springy Cumberland turf which, when damp with dew, gave goalkeepers all manner of problems. The ball would literally shoot off the surface and even when volleyed would slip and slither in your hands like a bar of soap.

One of the lads, I think it was Jack Charlton, remembered there was a little newsagent's at the end of Wembley Way, opposite what is now the Hilton Hotel, that stayed open late at night.

'Gordon simply has to have it. Move it!' barked Alf, to poor Harold. Harold shot out of our dressing room like a squirrel with its tail on fire.

A few minutes later the teams were shoulder to shoulder in the tunnel, but there was still no sign of Harold.

'Delay the referee!' I heard Alf tell Bobby Moore, who, as captain, was at the head of the line.

As luck would have it, the band that had provided the pre-match entertainment hadn't cleared the pitch yet, anyway. Riddled with anxiety I peered through an exit door, outside which hundreds of ticketless supporters were milling about. In the distance was Harold, running for all he was worth across the Wembley car park, an arm raised in triumph. Those supporters must have wondered what on earth was going on. Looking back, I often imagine the face of the newsagent as the England trainer appeared in his shop desperate for chewing gum only minutes before the World Cup semi-final.

M. Schwinte, our French referee, blew his whistle and the teams began to walk up the tunnel just as a breathless Harold arrived at the gate. He was so winded that he couldn't speak. He just thrust the gum into my hand and collapsed against one of the gates. I quickly threw three pieces into my mouth and ran up the tunnel to take my place in line. The TV footage shows me chomping away like mad, with the commentator saying, 'And there is Gordon Banks, chewing his gum and looking very relaxed.' He didn't know the half of it.

Everybody made a telling contribution to what was a great game of football and a memorable night, though I must make special mention of Nobby Stiles, who stuck to Eusebio like bark to a tree, and Bobby Charlton, whose performance in midfield was sublime. The 90,000 crowd were solidly behind us and Wembley's circular roof was almost lifted by the continuous chant of 'Eng-land! Eng-land!'

The players warmed to the atmosphere. Alf Ramsey had told us that, when we came up against a team willing to come out and play fluent football, we would hit our true form. This was just such an occasion. The result was ninety minutes of pulsating football. The game came alive right from the kick-off, Nobby Stiles remaining deep to counteract the considerable threat of Eusebio. Nobby, ably supported by Bobby Moore and Alan Ball, denied Eusebio the room to display his talent and the great man was never able to tear us apart as he had so many others.

After thirty-one minutes the Portuguese goalkeeper, José Pereira, blocked a shot from Roger Hunt. The ball rebounded into the path of Bobby Charlton, who calmly stroked it across the lush turf and into the net. The Wembley terracing became a sea of Union Jacks; we had taken a mighty step towards the final.

During the second half Portugal asserted themselves and for a time our slender advantage looked very shaky. We defended manfully, however, none more so than Jack Charlton, who was embroiled in a titanic struggle for aerial superiority with the giant José Torres. With only twelve minutes remaining, a gloriously fluent piece of play produced a second goal. The ball moved from Bobby Moore to George Cohen, who hit a long pass down the right wing. Geoff Hurst and José Carlos battled for possession, with Geoff seizing control. He pulled the ball back across the edge of the penalty area and Bobby Charlton, racing in, hit one of his trademark thunderbolts.

Pereira had no chance. We had made a goal out of nothing, and the Portuguese players were the first to acknowledge it. A number of them even shook Bobby's hand as he ran back to the halfway line for the restart.

I thought we were home and dry, but I was mistaken. Portugal staged a grandstand finish and eight minutes from time were awarded a penalty. A cross from Antonio Simoes was met by the towering José Torres and, with our back line wrongfooted, Jack Charlton handled the ball. I knew nobody saved Eusebio penalty kicks, but I was determined to give it a try.

I had discussed Eusebio and his penalty taking in some detail with Alf during training. I'd made a mental note that he always seemed to hit the ball to the goalkeeper's right and made my mind up to go that way. As I prepared to face the penalty, however, I caught sight of Alan Ball, who was repeatedly pointing to my right with some agitation. When Eusebio placed the ball on the spot, Portugal's captain, Mario Coluna, clocked what Bally was up to, ran up to Eusebio and whispered something in his ear. Eusebio nodded.

This threw me into a quandary. Initially I'd had no doubt in my mind about which way to dive. On seeing Coluna whispering to Eusebio, however, I was convinced that the Portuguese skipper had told him to change the direction of his penalty. I decided to double bluff them, and dive to my left.

Eusebio hit the ball to my right. It was the first goal I had conceded in 443 minutes of World Cup football. I could have strangled Bally.

Portugal now had their tails up. Minutes from the end, Coluna latched on to a crossfield ball and hit a rasping drive that was heading for the roof of my net. Instinctively I took to the air. I only managed to get the fingertips of one hand to the ball, but that was enough to deflect it over the bar.

At the final whistle the Portuguese players were devastated, but to a man sporting in defeat. Eusebio was inconsolable and wept unashamedly. It had been a classic game and Otto Gloria, the Portuguese coach, summed up the thoughts of many when he said, 'Surely, this was the final tonight.'

Football may have been the winner that night, but it was England who were in the World Cup final.

12. Alf's Final Word

People say there is no room for sentiment in football. By and large they're right, but sometimes you just can't avoid it. The case of Jimmy Greaves and the World Cup final was, for me, one such occasion. Jimmy had been a key member of the England team for seven years, during which time he was his country's most prolific goalscorer, but Alf Ramsey – ever the pragmatist – decided to field the same side in the final that had done so well against Argentina and Portugal. Obviously I was delighted for Geoff Hurst, but I couldn't help feeling desperately sorry for Jimmy.

Of course, Alf's decision was the correct one and deep down I think Jimmy knew from the moment he was injured against France that his World Cup was effectively over. The Argentina game had been just three days later, with the semi-final three days after that, and Jimmy must have realized that missing both matches would put him out of contention for a place in the final, should we make it that far. Characteristically, when Alf announced the team Jimmy immediately wished Geoff Hurst the best of luck.

On the morning of the match a few of us went for a walk down Hendon High Street to stretch our legs. Even at 8.30 a.m. the place was buzzing and countless people came up to us to wish us luck.

I bought a paper, but back at the hotel my mind was so much on the game ahead that I couldn't take in a word. A crowd had gathered outside, and we left for Wembley with the cheers of over 2,000 people ringing in our ears. (Who said the English were quiet and reserved?) We all hoped against hope that we wouldn't let them down.

We were confident, but Alf Ramsey had ensured we weren't complacent. Alf had the knack of putting everything in perspective. He'd done his homework on West Germany and had made us aware of their strengths without putting us in awe of them. Since 1965 England had played twenty-two internationals and lost only once. As a team we were on a roll and really believed in ourselves. And so did Alf.

The dressing-room rituals took on extra significance that day. I must have tied my laces at least three times before I was happy that the knot was comfortably secured at the side of the boot and not across the lace holes, where I might be aware of it when kicking the ball. The strips of bandage that kept up my stockings had to be perfectly flat; my top tucked smoothly down into my shorts. I could have no distractions, even of the most minor sort. No irritations. No excuses for myself.

I warmed up with a series of stretching and bending exercises, then pummelled a ball against the wall of the warm-up room until my hands were accustomed to the feel of it. That done, I repeated the boots/stockings/shirt ritual.

Nobby Stiles headed for the toilet for the umpteenth time. Jack Charlton stood in front of a mirror applying Vaseline to his eyebrows. Ray Wilson dipped into Les Cocker's kit bag, found a little jar of Vicks VapoRub, smeared some around his nostrils and on the front of his red shirt. Bobby Moore sat impassively, his socks rolled to his ankles, as Harold Shepherdson rubbed copious amounts of liniment into his legs. Bobby Charlton and Geoff Hurst chatted while making last-minute adjustments to their boots. Nobby, back from the loo, sat with arms folded and legs outstretched. Martin Peters sipped tea from a thick white cup that belonged in a British Rail buffet. George Cohen, ready and willing, was immersed in the special-edition match-day programme. How could he read at a time like this? Roger Hunt sat like a zombie, elbows resting on his knees, hands clasped, his attention riveted on the floor. Suddenly he sat up, clapped his hands together and sniffed, then resumed his previous catatonic demeanour. Nobby passed me on his way to the loo again.

I was breathing deeply, trying to stay calm, as Alf said his piece, but my mind was roller coasting:

'Jack, be hard and competitive . . . Nobby, get a foot in . . . *Is that stud longer than the others? No, the floor's not flush* . . . Alan, work and work and work up and down that line; always be looking to play the ball in early . . . *That left tie-up seems a bit tight* . . . Long ball, short ball, it doesn't matter, Martin, as long as it's the right ball . . . Bobby, control the middle . . . *Must look for Bobby for an early throw out* . . . be aware of Seeler; he can get up high for a little fellow . . . *And I can get higher* . . . George and Raymond . . . *Raymond????* . . . When Gordon has the ball, go wide, give him the option . . . *Yes, be looking for them* . . . And –'

Burrrrrrrrrrrr!

We're off!

'Good luck to you all.'

'Best of luck . . . Best of luck . . . Best of luck . . . Good luck . . . Good luck . . . Come on. Come on! *Let's go!*'

Even though I'd planned to wear gloves, Harold Shepherdson still gave me chewing gum. It tasted really good in my dry and caked mouth and I spat into the palms of my hands anyway as I followed Alan Ball out of the liniment-scented warmth of the dressing room into the cool Wembley tunnel. The West German players were already in line, bobbing up and down, jiggling their arms and running on the spot, their studs on the concrete chattering away like eleven Volkswagens with tappet trouble. My opposite number Hans Tilkowski extended a hand. I wiped the gum-spit off on my jersey before tentatively responding, then chewed away like mad to conjure up a good gob of goo.

Standing in line, I noticed just how tidy Alan Ball's hair was. How red it was. How much shorter than me he was. The top of his scalp had tiny freckles on it. I wondered if he knew they were there.

Somewhere in the distance I heard a band playing. Then no band. From the head of the line came the shrill blast of a whistle. The teams set off up the slight incline towards the rectangle of light at the end of the tunnel. What a tunnel. How could it be so long? A sudden and deafening roar swept down towards me as the first players emerged. The rectangle of light grew bigger until I was in sunshine so bright that I had to squint. A cacophony of noise avalanched down from the undulating masses on the terraces. The volatile sound of Wembley in full cry.

I glanced up to where I thought my parents, my brothers, Ursula and our son Robert might be and raised an arm in that direction. They would think I had seen them. I imagined Ursula saying to Robert, 'There, Daddy has seen us among all these people. I told you he would.'

Flanked by Alan Ball and Roger Hunt I stood guardsmanlike as the bands played the national anthems. I didn't normally sing out with gusto, but I did on this occasion, happy to have some release from the nervous tension that had built up inside me.

Then a hurricane of hurrahs from the terraces. A sea of Union Jacks. The constant collective chant of 'Eng-land! Eng-land!'

Both sides fidgeted nervously as the presentations were made: Gordon Banks; George Cohen, Bobby Moore, Jack Charlton, Ray Wilson; Alan Ball, Nobby Stiles, Bobby Charlton, Martin Peters; Roger Hunt, Geoff Hurst. And the Germans: Hans Tilkowski; Horst Hottges, Willy Schulz, Wolfgang Weber, Karl-Heinz Schnellinger; Helmut Haller, Franz Beckenbauer, Wolfgang Overath, Siggy Held; Lothar Emmerich, Uwe Seeler.

We kicked off under gold-leaf sunshine, though previous heavy rain had made the pitch soft and greasy. In such conditions errors of judgement were inevitable, especially where the pace of the ball was a factor. But an error of a different kind gave West Germany the lead.

One of our prime strengths was our resolute back line, but it was an uncharacteristic mistake in defence that allowed West Germany to open the scoring after just thirteen minutes. Ray Wilson went up to meet a centre but his header lacked power and distance. The ball fell to Helmut Haller who, from my left, shot across the face of goal.

Although Haller's shot lacked pace, Jack Charlton's defensive position had left me momentarily unsighted. I saw the ball late. Before I could adjust my positioning it had passed me and crept into the corner of my net.

I was devastated. Having been on the losing side in two FA Cup finals at Wembley, I could see it happening all over again. But the game was still young and I knew we had plenty of time to assert ourselves. What's more, I was convinced that we would do so.

West Germany could have put up the shutters and defended their lead. To their credit, they instead continued to play with purpose and poise and it was clear to me that they were chasing a second goal.

Five minutes later we caught them napping. Wolfgang Overath fouled Bobby Moore on our left side. Bobby quickly got to his feet, looked up to see where Geoff Hurst was, then floated the free kick into the West German penalty area. Before the Germans had sensed the danger, Geoff ghosted into the penalty box unmarked and headed the equalizer. It was almost a carbon copy of Geoff's goal against Argentina. Wembley filled with noise and I skipped up and down punching the air with my fist at the joy of it all.

Level once again, both teams settled down to play competitive but entertaining football, much to the appreciation of the packed terraces. Nobody pulled out of a tackle, yet no one opted for brute force and ignorance, each team matching the other in technique and intelligence.

We took the game to the Germans only for them to come straight back at us. Alan Ball seemed to be the epitome of perpetual motion. Unflaggingly buzzing up and down our right channel he was having the game of his life and causing Schnellinger all manner of problems.

Deep into the second half it was Alan who won the corner that led to our second goal. Schnellinger looked glad of the rest but there was no respite for Alan, who raced over to take the corner himself. He swung the ball over for Geoff Hurst to hammer it towards Tilkowski's goal. Schulz lunged at the ball but didn't strike it cleanly. The ball ballooned into the air. As it dropped, Martin Peters stepped forward to rifle it into the net. There was a pleasing symmetry about the timing of the goal – having fallen behind after thirteen minutes, we were now in the lead with thirteen minutes left.

Those minutes ticked away, each one seeming like an hour. But we were going to win – I could sense it. Then, with the game in its dying embers, the Swiss referee Herr Dienst penalized Jack Charlton for a foul on Siggy Held.

It looked like a harsh decision to me and big Jack wasn't happy about it either. In his view, the foul should have been given the other way for backing in. Lothar Emmerich drove the free kick into my penalty box, which was a sea of red and white shirts. I thought I saw Schnellinger help the ball on with his hand. (Although I was too busy to notice it at the time, the linesman must have thought so too because he raised his flag briefly, then inexplicably lowered it again.) The ball bounded across the face of my goal towards the post with me in hot pursuit. Wolfgang Weber came sliding in. I saw that Ray Wilson had extended a leg to block the ball should it come low, so I threw myself with my arms outstretched above Ray's leg. One of us was bound to block Weber's effort.

Wolfgang Weber was a highly intelligent footballer. He was quick off the mark, but his mind was even quicker. As Weber slid on to meet the ball he glanced up, assessed the situation immediately and lifted the ball with the toe of his boot. Ray tackled fresh air, I grasped at nothing and the ball shot over both of us and into the net. The disappointment I felt was matched only by my disbelief.

For all Weber's skill, however, the goal should never have been allowed to stand. Although the referee failed to spot it in the goalmouth mêlée, I am quite certain that the ball was handled. As soon as Schnellinger's hand touched the ball both Bobby Moore and Martin Peters appealed, but Herr Dienst would have none of it. The goal stood. Seconds later, Herr Dienst did blow his whistle – to send us into extra time.

I felt as if the bottom had dropped out of my world. Glory had been snatched away when I had practically had it in my grasp. All manner of emotions swept through me. In a matter of moments I felt deep disappointment, anger, self-pity and, finally, determination: We hadn't lost. The game and the World Cup were still ours for the taking. I just had to play as well as I possibly could for another thirty minutes. That was all. I knew I could do that. On this day, of all days, I could do anything and hang the consequences.

If the boots were flying, I'd dive in. I was king and the penalty box was my domain. If I could keep a clean sheet, then any one of ten outfielders could win it for us.

It must have been even worse for Alf, watching from the bench. During the interval he took to the pitch and issued to us all the challenge of our lives: 'You have won the World Cup once,' he said, 'now you must go out and win it again.'

I looked across to Bobby Charlton, Nobby Stiles and Alan Ball. Their heads were nodding, their faces a mixture of strain and determination. Bobby Moore clapped his hands together.

'We're gonna do it, come on. We're gonna do it,' he told us.

On a stamina-sapping pitch such as Wembley's, the tempo of a game usually drops in extra time. Not in this game. I looked on in amazement, wondering how anyone could maintain such a pace. Alan Ball was everywhere, his appetite for the ball as ravenous as the jaws of hell. Bobby Charlton glided as if the match were only ten minutes old. Nobby Stiles made his previous performance in midfield look like a warm-up run. Roger Hunt criss-crossed Wembley like a pinball. Big Jack was imperious in defence and Bobby Moore . . . Well, Bobby was Bobby. In the frantic pace of the game he remained as cool as a snowbank, elegantly and seemingly without effort controlling our back line, though his sweat had stained his shirt as red as a Kansas schoolhouse.

Luckily I managed to hold on to everything the Germans threw at me – and Seeler, Held and Haller threw a lot. With ten minutes of extra time on the clock, Nobby Stiles put a long pass down our right wing. Who chased it? Alan Ball, of course. Alan hit a low ball into Geoff Hurst, who was some ten yards from Tilkowski's near post but facing the touchline. Geoff swivelled and hit a rising drive that crashed on to the underside of the crossbar and bounced almost vertically downwards before being headed away by Wolfgang Weber.

I didn't realize it at the time, but I was watching history in the making. Roger Hunt, following up, was in no doubt that the ball had crossed the line. The West German players were equally convinced that it had not. Encouraged by the Germans to take a second opinion, Herr Dienst walked over to the Russian linesman, Tofik Bakhramov. For what seemed like an age, the two conferred as an anxious silence descended on Wembley. German players stood hands on hips, Geoff Hurst was on tenterhooks and the crowd was treated to the rare sight of Alan Ball standing still. Eventually the referee turned and pointed to the centre spot. Wembley erupted once more. It was a goal.

And it *was* a goal. I am sure. True, I was standing at the other end of the pitch, but Roger Hunt's reaction and subsequent testimony have left me in no doubt as to the legitimacy of Geoff's effort. Roger was a prolific goalscorer, he alone was right there when the ball crashed down from the crossbar into the goalmouth. Believe me, if Roger Hunt had thought for one moment that the ball had not crossed the line, he would have knocked it in himself. He didn't, because he knew it was a goal.

Not only that, but the linesman, Bakhramov, was up with play and looking along the goal line. The two people best positioned to judge whether the ball had crossed the line both said that it had.

None the less, the debate concerning the legitimacy of England's third goal continues to this day. I can understand the Germans' prolonged efforts to prove their case (though no concrete proof has ever emerged), but I cannot for the life of me discern what motivates the many English people who assist them. Why have so many boffins from the Academy of Rear-End Speech wasted countless hours of computer time trying to show that the ball never crossed the line? It galls me that some of my countrymen should expend so much effort trying to disallow retrospectively the goal which to all intents and purposes won the World Cup for England. What's the point? And where's their patriotism? To the best of my knowledge, no Argentine has protested with such vehemence against Maradona's 'hand-of-God' goal against England in 1984, or tried to prove that Sol Campbell's disallowed effort for England against them in France '98 should have stood.

The devastating blow we had received seconds from the end of ninety minutes was almost repeated in the final minutes of extra time. With little over a minute of the game remaining, Siggy Held latched on to a pass from Emmerich and dispatched a fiery shot towards the left-hand corner of my net. Fortunately I'd taken up a good position and my angle was spot on. I hit the ground as though felled by a sniper's bullet and was grateful to clutch the ball to my chest. Moments later West Germany were back. Held nodded the ball across the face of goal and caught me wrong-footed. As I quickly attempted to readjust my balance I watched helplessly as Uwe Seeler's lunge missed the ball by the width of a bootlace. That, however, was only a prelude to the climax of what had been a cliffhanger of a game.

Once again the ball was delivered into my penalty area only for the imperious frame of Bobby Moore to chest it down and move upfield with customary ease. Bobby momentarily looked up, spotted Geoff Hurst some ten yards inside the German half and chipped the most exquisite pass in his direction. Bobby's limbs must have been terribly weary, but you'd never know it from the way he played that ball downfield. To this day I find it hard to believe that, so late in the game, Bobby could emerge from defence with such élan and retain the necessary vision to execute such a deft pass over such a distance.

Geoff took the ball on his chest. At first I thought he would saunter towards the corner flag to kill time, but suddenly his legs began to pump and, unimpeded by flagging German defenders, he took off towards Tilkowski's goal.

Famously, three supporters came on to the pitch thinking that the referee had blown for time. Who were those lads? Where are they now? Did they really think it was all over? Like the unknown soldier, their anonymous presence has seeped indelibly into history.

Hans Tilkowski did what he had to do. He came out to narrow the angle, but Geoff summoned what dregs of strength remained in his body and blasted the ball goalwards. The roof of the net ballooned and what followed was unforgettable.

I ran to the edge of my penalty area and punched the air in a display of complete and utter joy. Bobby Charlton dropped to his knees. Nobby Stiles and George Cohen unashamedly hugged one another. Alan Ball ran five paces before doing a cartwheel across the pitted emerald turf. Jack Charlton looked up to the heavens and appeared to say 'Thank you'. Roger Hunt leapt in the air, both hands outstretched above his head.

Seconds later, at the final whistle, Bobby Charlton cried like an innocent man suddenly released from jail. Nobby danced his famous toothless jig. Alan Ball ran and whooped around the pitch like a Commanche. Martin Peters saluted the crowd. Me? I felt as Christopher Columbus must have when realizing he hadn't sailed off the edge of the world. Jimmy Greaves came on to the pitch and hugged Nobby Stiles. Ron Flowers grasped me to his chest. Meanwhile, Alf Ramsey remained a model of dignity and grace, declining to gatecrash what he obviously regarded as the greatest moment in the lives of his players, although the success was as much his as ours.

Bobby Moore eventually led us up the thirty-nine steps to the Royal Box and the World Cup. Before shaking the hand of Her Majesty the Queen and receiving the trophy, Bobby had the good grace to wipe the palms of his hands on his shorts. A captain in every sense of the word.

England's dream of winning the World Cup had been realized and so too had mine. As I descended the steps from the Royal Box clutching the medal every player in the world yearns for, I couldn't believe the journey I had made. The road from Tinsley Rec to a World Cup final had been long and winding, but the difficulties I had faced along the way suddenly evaporated as my whole being was engulfed with euphoria.

The England post-match banquet was held at the Royal Garden Hotel in Kensington Gardens. The Prime Minister, Harold Wilson, called in to see us, then joined in the singing with the crowds outside. Speeches were made, wine and champagne flowed. Cars flying Union Jacks honked around London until the small hours of the morning. Alf Ramsey, the architect of our success, took the arm of his wife Vickie and travelled back to their home in Ipswich to 'make ourselves a decent cup of tea'.

It was all over, like the man said, but the memories will reside with me for ever.

Alf, later and deservedly Sir Alf Ramsey, was in a class of his own. Some managers are tactically aware. Some excel at coaching. Others are good at motivation and man management. Alf was superb at everything. That's what made him so special. That's what made him the manager who won the World Cup for England.

Always fair to his players and scrupulously honest, he was a man of unyielding integrity and absolute loyalty. Alf put his job on the line for Nobby Stiles after the game against France, as he would have done for any of us, and his loyalty was reciprocated. He was devoted to the team ethic, yet at pains to point out that no one was indispensable. He bore no grudges and he had no favourites. Alf's unrivalled knowledge of the game and the opposition were complemented by superb tactical acumen, yet his instructions to us were always clear and simple.

How best to sum him up? At the post-match banquet, the Secretary of the Football Association, Dennis Follows, introduced Alf as 'a great man'. When Alf took to his feet, he was at pains to correct that statement: 'There are no great men,' he said, 'only men.' Alf Ramsey may have been just a man, but he was one possessed of an extraordinary talent.

I have never understood why the FA didn't think fit to have an extra winner's medal struck and presented to him; why no statue in his honour was erected outside Wembley. Whatever the reason, it's a shame, it really is, for had it not been for Alf Ramsey we would never have won the World Cup.

Nobody plays in the World Cup just for the money. And just as well, too, in our case. We received a bonus of £22,000 from the FA which, to the unanimous agreement of the players, was divided equally among the squad. That gave us all £1,000, taxed at 40 per cent in those days, so we received £600 each for winning the World Cup.

By contrast, an enterprising street vendor who posed as a press photographer screen-printed some T-shirts with his ill-gotten frames and sold them outside Wembley before our games. He told us he made over £1,500.

The late Kenneth Wolstenholme, the commentator who famously said, 'Some people are on the pitch; they think it's all over. It is now!' had the good sense to copyright those words. Ken told me that over the years he made more money from the royalties than the entire team earned for winning the World Cup.

But this is just a footnote; a comment. It certainly isn't sour grapes. I and every other member of the team would have played for nothing. The glory of winning for England was paramount, and the joy we felt and still feel in knowing we had brought so much happiness to so many people is something that money could never buy.

13. The Leaving of Leicester

Winning the World Cup in 1966 was a watershed for English football. Things were never to be the same again. But although winning the World Cup certainly had a profound effect on our domestic game, other factors unrelated to football also played their part.

The consensus is that the success of Alf's 4–4–2 formation in the final brought to an end, almost overnight, the use of orthodox wingers in English football. The truth is somewhat different.

Prior to the '66 World Cup, many coaches had been asking wingers to play deeper, though still on the flanks. The success of Alf Ramsey's 4–4–2 and 4–3–3 systems served to make the four-man midfield more common. The difference after 1966 was that 4–3–3 and 4–4–2, variations of which had previously been common in the professional game, filtered down through semi-professional football to park teams.

If anything, our success in the World Cup served as a convenient benchmark for the myriad changes that were affecting not only football, but the whole of society at that time. Following England's historic 6–3 home defeat against Hungary in 1953 and the subsequent success of Real Madrid in the 1960 European Cup it had taken some time for English football to get its house back in order. The changes that began in the late fifties gathered momentum following Real's sublime performance at Hampden and finally bore fruit in the mid-sixties. Our success in the World Cup was not so much a new beginning as a grand finale to ten years of gradual modernization and change.

Change was also to be very much on my personal agenda when the 1966–67 season got under way. Winning the World Cup had spawned a sharp rise in league attendances. A crowd of nearly 50,000 saw Leicester City's opening-day defeat at Liverpool, and the healthy gates were to continue throughout the season. In 1965–66 just over 12 million people had watched matches in the First Division. In 1966–67 that figure increased by 2 million. The knock-on effect of our World Cup triumph was that English football was once again rated the best in Europe, if not the world, and the growth in attendances reflected that.

Manchester United, Tottenham Hotspur, Nottingham Forest, Leeds and Liverpool were locked in a battle for the Championship, though Leicester were never far behind. For much of the season we fluctuated between fifth and eighth which, considering the size of the club and its financial resources, was no mean achievement.

I was also performing well in goal. My development continued apace and at twenty-nine I was looking forward to at least six more years of top-flight football. So it came as something of a bombshell when Matt Gillies told me that my best days as a goalkeeper were behind me.

The portents had been there in March 1967 when Gillies suddenly – and in the eyes of the City supporters, controversially – sold Derek Dougan to Wolves for £50,000. The Doog was a cult figure at Filbert Street, as he would later become at Molineux. His contribution to the team had been significant and he was enjoying playing First Division football again. Wolves were in the Second Division, though on course for promotion. Derek wasn't keen to go, but when your club values your transfer fee above your contribution to the team, you might as well move on. As it was to turn out, Derek enjoyed the best days of his playing career with Wolves, forming a prolific scoring partnership with John Richards.

I suppose I should have seen it coming. Leicester had had no qualms about letting one icon go, and I was only too aware that in Peter Shilton the club possessed a reserve goalkeeper of considerable promise. Peter was only eighteen, but I had seen enough of him on the training ground and in reserve matches to know that he had all the makings of a great goalkeeper.

But surely I was safe. People kept telling me I was England's best, and we had just won the World Cup, after all. The French sports paper, *L'Équipe* had ranked me as the number one goalkeeper in the world. What's more, FIFA had published their best eleven from the '66 World Cup and I was in it. I firmly believed that my best days were ahead of me. About this I wasn't wrong. My mistake was to believe that Matt Gillies and the Leicester board were similarly foresighted.

It was a Tuesday morning in April. In our previous match we had fought a hard-earned goalless draw with a Leeds United side that needed points for their Championship challenge. I had played well in that game, so after training when Matt Gillies called me over for a chat, I had no idea what was to come.

'Gordon, the directors and I have been talking,' said Matt. 'Not to put too fine a point on it, we think your best days are behind you, and you should move on.'

I was speechless. Dumbfounded. Shell-shocked. It took a few moments for me to gather my thoughts. Even then all I could do was to ask Matt if he was serious.

'I think it's best for all concerned,' he said.

I drove home in a dream. I felt rejected, unwanted. I had that dreadful feeling of betrayal. It wasn't so much the sudden rejection, but the surprise of it. In two sentences, my world had been turned upside-down.

The next day Richie Norman told me that Peter Shilton had issued an ultimatum to the board: unless he played in the first team, he would leave the club. Richie was my best pal and I didn't doubt his word.

I would like to say that I hold nothing against Peter for stating his case in such explicit terms. I always knew that he would succeed me in the first team – I just didn't think it would be so soon. Even at eighteen, Peter had tremendous confidence in his own ability. He did what he had to do to further his career. What surprised me was the board's eagerness to comply.

It was the end of the road for me at Leicester City. I was placed on the transfer list priced the same as Derek Dougan: £50,000.

A number of clubs showed an interest. West Bromwich Albion, Manchester United, Liverpool and West Ham all made overtures. For reasons unknown, neither West Brom nor Manchester United followed up their initial approach. I quite fancied Liverpool and Bill Shankly had told me on a number of occasions that, should Leicester ever wish to sell me, he would be in for me like a shot, but when push came to shove, Shanks didn't take up the option.

This lack of interest on the part of the big clubs had, I believe, much to do with the fact that many managers still didn't fully appreciate the worth of a good goalkeeper. Bill later blamed his directors: 'I wanted to sign you, Gordon, but the board here wouldn't let me. They said it was too much money for a goal-keeper.' I never knew whether to believe him or not. Even in 1967 he was a legend at Anfield, and I think that if he had really wanted to sign me, he would have found a way.

For years the top clubs were happy to pay huge fees for outfield players, but never for a goalkeeper. In the late seventies and early eighties when Peter Shilton and Pat Jennings were seeking moves, Manchester United never came in for them, being content with Gary Bailey in goal. Now Gary, like his successors at United Jim Leighton and Les Sealey, was a fine keeper, but in all truthfulness never in the same class as Shilton, Jennings or Ray Clemence. Manchester United consistently tried and failed to repeat their First Division Championship success of 1967. I firmly believe that if they had invested in a top-class goalkeeper they wouldn't have had to wait twenty-six years to do so. The fact that their Premiership-winning side of 1992–93 included the excellent Peter Schmeichel in goal only reinforces my point.

With Liverpool's interest cooling, West Ham United seized the initiative. Ron Greenwood was keen to do business and from my point of view the prospect of linking up with my England colleagues Bobby Moore, Geoff Hurst and Martin Peters was very appealing. West Ham were a club only marginally bigger than Leicester, but I liked their football philosophy and their purist approach to how the game should be played. Ron Greenwood struck me as an honest, decent guy who was a man of his word. He was, and it was Ron's desire to keep his word that scuppered my proposed move to his club.

Earlier in the season Greenwood had enquired about the Kilmar-

25. England – World Champions. Need I say more?

26. I spent countless hours after normal training working hard to improve my technique as a goalkeeper. Here I am on duty with the England squad. The glove I'm wearing seems to be the sort you often see lying forlorn in a road.

27. Training with England. It looks as if I've been caught out by the speed of a break from the opposition – it must have been Alan Ball.

28. Alf Ramsey was the greatest manager I ever played for. His knowledge of the game, tactics and opponents was second to none. Here Alf offers his England charges the benefit of his profound knowledge and, as always, we are attentive listeners.

29. Leicester City's four home internationals. From left: Derek Dougan (Northern Ireland), myself, Davie Gibson (Scotland) and Peter Rodrigues (Wales).

30. Welcoming a young Peter Shilton to Filbert Street. Little did I know that my days at Leicester were numbered. Notice our training tops: Graham Cross reckoned they'd been knitted by Matt Gillies' mother.

31. It was difficult to adjust to the speed and flight of the ball in the high altitude of Mexico '70. Here I appear to be just about coping. In the background is Norman Hunter, who for all his fearsome reputation was booked only four times in his career (which, of course, may say much for the tolerance of referees in those days!).

32. The save that brought me global fame. As soon as the ball left Pelé's head I heard him shout '*Golo!*' But I had other ideas.

33. The ball balloons over the bar to safety. Bobby Moore said, 'You're getting old, Banksy. You used to hold on to them!'

34. The mark of a good goalkeeper is how few saves he is called on to make. Organizing your defence is the key to good goalkeeping. Here I'm telling Bobby Moore, no less, who he should be marking.

35. In action for England against Scotland in 1971. Also in the picture are Martin Chivers (number 10), Roy McFarland, Billy Bremner and Bobby Moore. England won 3–1.

36. George Best about to pounce and flick the ball away from me during the game at Windsor Park in 1971. To this day, George still insists his goal should have been allowed. I'm with the referee on this one.

nock goalkeeper Bobby Ferguson only to be told that he was not for sale. Kilmarnock, however, had promised Ron first refusal and Ron promised Kilmarnock that he would buy Ferguson at the drop of a hat. Just as Ron Greenwood and I were about to agree terms, someone dropped the hat. Bobby Ferguson was up for sale. Ron wouldn't go back on his word, and West Ham couldn't afford us both, so I was unexpectedly back on the market.

Initially I was disappointed. It would have been great to play in the same team as Bobby, Martin and Geoff every week, but like Mr Micawber I have always believed that 'something will turn up'. Two days later, it did.

Matt Gillies called me into his office one morning in April 1967 to tell me he had received a firm offer. As I hadn't asked for a transfer, he and the board would consider paying a loyalty bonus in recognition of my seven years' service at the club.

That sounded fine by me. Who had made the offer?

He told me it was Stoke City.

Stoke, a mid-table First Division side, were hardly the most fashionable club of the day, but I'd played against them often enough to know they were a good side with the potential to be even better. Having discussed the matter with Ursula, I told Matt that I was interested and he immediately arranged for the Stoke manager Tony Waddington to come to Filbert Street to discuss terms. I had no idea what wages Stoke City were offering, but as Leicester were the worst payers in the First Division, I didn't expect to take a drop.

Prior to meeting Tony, I had a discussion with Matt about my loyalty bonus. It didn't go well.

'Have you and the directors reached a decision?' I asked.

'We have.'

I settled back in my chair to await the good news.

'We've decided not to pay you a penny,' he said.

I was both stunned and livid and told him exactly what I thought of him and his board, but he wouldn't be swayed.

'There's to be no compensation payment and that's final,' Matt said firmly.

'Then the deal's off,' I told him. 'If it means me staying here and playing in the reserves, then so be it. You and the board can sing for that fifty grand.'

I left Matt's office in a dark mood and found Tony Waddington sitting in the main foyer.

'I'm sorry, Mr Waddington, but the deal's off,' I said, and proceeded to tell him why.

His face betrayed no emotion at the news. He simply stood up and said, 'Leave this to me,' before sweeping into Matt's office without knocking.

Five minutes later he marched out. 'Two grand all right?'

I told him that would be fine by me.

'Good!' he said. 'Then let's do the deal and get out of here.'

A couple of years later, during a pre-season tour of Holland, I got talking with Doc Crowe, a Stoke City director. I told Doc how happy I was at Stoke and the story of how my transfer would have fallen through if Tony Waddington hadn't persuaded Leicester to come up with the compensation payment.

'Did he hell,' said Doc. 'We paid you that!'

He went on to tell me how Tony Waddington had found Matt Gillies as awkward and intransigent as I had. Afraid that the deal would fall through, Tony had simply walked out of Matt's office and plucked the £2,000 figure out of the air, knowing that his own directors would back his judgement and that the board, already committed to paying Leicester £50,000, wouldn't balk at parting with an extra couple of thousand to secure the services of the current England goalkeeper.

That was typical of Tony Waddington; he was a great guy and one of the most underrated managers in football. Tony realized the importance of a good goalkeeper to a team and I'd like to think he believed that his board's money was well spent. Later he said that having me between the posts saved Stoke City twenty goals a season. Whether that was truth or flattery, it was nice of him to say it.

Some say that Tony was ahead of his time in recognizing the value of a good goalkeeper. To my mind it was more a case of other managers being behind the times. Whatever, I loved the man.

He always tried to sign gifted players who would entertain the supporters; always believed that football at its most inspirational and creative has a place in the best of all possible worlds.

His first priority was to his players, his second to the supporters who paid their hard-earned cash to watch us. He never forgot how important the role of football was in the lives of working people, as evidenced by his marvellous description of football as 'the working man's ballet'.

Ursula had lavished so much love and attention on our home in Kirkwood Road that it sold almost straight away. We found a house about ten miles from Stoke, just over the Cheshire border in Madeley Heath. The house, which had a mock Tudor frontage, was larger than our Leicester home and the area contained a substantial amount of woodland which evoked a feeling of country living. We settled straight away, and on my first day at Stoke City the warm reception I was given made me feel equally at home there, too.

I made my Stoke City debut at Chelsea on 22 April 1967. Chelsea won by the only goal of the game and, though disappointed not to have begun a new chapter in my career with a victory, I came off the Stamford Bridge pitch happy in the knowledge that I hadn't let myself or my team down. Tony Waddington seemingly agreed because he patted me on the back and said, 'Well done. Your best is yet to come, and it'll coincide with the best days this club has ever known.'

I made my home debut for Stoke against Leicester City. Needless to say, I was really on my mettle that day. Goals from Peter Dobing, Harry Burrows and young John Mahoney gave us a 3–1 win over my old team mates, who I have to say were generous in defeat.

Only two games of the season remained, against Arsenal and Manchester United. United had clinched the Championship the previous Wednesday evening by beating West Ham 6–1 at Upton Park and over 60,000 packed Old Trafford to see them crowned champions. Though missing the injured Denis Law, United were still formidable with Bobby Charlton, George Best and Nobby

Stiles at the top of their form. The pressure from United was nigh-on relentless, but I learned in this game that Stoke City had a resolute defence. Despite the pressure we held on for a goalless draw and a moral victory.

I could never have believed when I kept goal for Leicester City at Liverpool on the opening day that by the end of the season I would be playing for another Midlands club. You never know what's in store, though, and that's very true of football. England were the World Champions, but in April 1967 in a European Championship qualifying match, we slipped up in sensational style, much to the delight of our friends north of the Border.

Following the World Cup, England had drawn with Czechoslovakia and beaten both Northern Ireland and Wales. It was evident from those games that World Champions England were now the prize scalp on the international scene. All three teams raised their game and pulled out all the stops against us. But there was also an undercurrent of resentment flowing from certain nations, some quarters in South America even going so far as to suggest that the World Cup had been rigged to enable England to win it. I know FIFA have done some strange things, but to think they would (or could) manipulate a major tournament in this way is utter nonsense.

I suppose that behind this accusation was the fact that we had played all our games at Wembley. Whether this was by chance or design I can't say, although it is usually the case that the team from the host nation invariably play their group matches at the national stadium. In the 1958 World Cup Sweden played in Stockholm, and Chile in Santiago in 1962. Mexico played all their matches in the 1970 tournament at the Azteca stadium in Mexico City. To the best of my knowledge, no one has ever implied that those nations were favoured. And, of course, England didn't even *have* a national stadium by the time they qualified for 2002!

In '66 the winners of Group One had been designated to play their quarter-final tie at Wembley, the runners-up at Hillsborough in Sheffield. It so happened that we won Group One, so we played Argentina at Wembley. If we'd finished runners-up, we would have had to head north.

Whether out of jealousy or resentment, all manner of outlandish theories emerged as to why we had won the World Cup. But the simple truth is that we won it because we were the best side in the tournament and the world. The final was our forty-fourth match under Alf Ramsey and we had lost only six times. Over the same period of time, that record was unmatched by any other international team.

Conspiracy theorists apart, England as World Champions were there to be shot down, and in April 1967 Scotland came up with the firepower.

Neither players nor supporters need to be motivated for a clash between England and Scotland. It is the oldest fixture in the international calendar, one steeped in history, permeated by patriotism, fuelled by fervour and fanaticism and completely nerve-racking to play in. And if there weren't enough at stake, the game was both part of the Home International Championship and a qualifier for the European Championship.

England did not get off to the best of starts. Jack Charlton broke a toe in the early stages and, as substitutes were not allowed, he had to play on. Alf switched Jack up front, which affected the balance of the team. Minutes later we suffered another setback. Scotland's Billy Bremner caught Ray Wilson with a tackle that was later than a privatized train. Despite damaged ankle ligaments, he too carried on valiantly. Jimmy Greaves, back in the side, also picked up a knock which, though not as serious as Jack's or Ray's, definitely took the edge off his performance.

With England effectively down to nine men, we did well to give a very good Scotland team such a close game. No doubt any Scot reading this will say I'm just making excuses for our defeat, so let me say that, on the day, Scotland were the sharper and more incisive team and deserved their victory. In fact, they would have beaten any nine-man team in the world!

Seriously, though, the Scots were up for it from the start. They took to the pitch hyped-up but in control of their emotions. They exuded gritty determination and their will to win was plain for all to see. As both teams walked out on to the pitch, I knew we were in for one hell of a battle – *Denis Law was wearing shinpads!* In all the games I had played against Denis, this was a first. I remember thinking, If he's tooled up for battle, what can we expect from Billy Bremner, Tommy Gemmell, Eddie McCreadie and John Greig?

As far as the Scottish lads were concerned, this was their World Cup final and in no time at all we were made to realize just how much the match meant to them. They took the lead through Denis Law. Denis received the ball from Jim Baxter, turned in the space of a hearthrug and fired a shot to my right. I managed to parry the ball, but in a flash Denis was there to lash the rebound into the net. It was like Hogmanay, Burns Night and the resurrection of Harry Lauder all rolled into one as thousands of Scottish supporters wildly celebrated.

The game then developed into one of attack and counter-attack. Bremner, McCreadie and Gemmell snapped away at the heels of anyone in a white shirt. Bobby Charlton probed and prodded but found the Scottish defence as uncompromising as the truncheon of a Glasgow polis. Twelve minutes from time, Celtic's Bobby Lennox outwitted George Cohen on the byeline, cut inside and crashed the ball past me and into the net.

Almost from the restart a limping Jack Charlton pulled a goal back. I was hopeful we could get something out of the game, but fate had other ideas. Having evaded two tackles, Jim McCalliog bore down on my goal at an angle and I quickly came out to narrow it. I should have given more cover to my near post to force him across the penalty area. Instead McCalliog glanced up, saw the gap I'd left and struck the ball with venom between me and the near post. I was left to curse what I knew had been a silly mistake on my part while picking the ball out of the net.

We were far from done for, however. Geoff Hurst put us back in the game with a fine piece of opportunist finishing and in the closing minutes we laid siege to Ronnie Simpson's goal. At one point I thought we had scored the equalizer but Jimmy Greaves's effort was hacked off the line. The seconds ticked away, the Scottish players dug in and their supporters got behind them in no uncertain terms. Scotland defended like demons in and around their penalty area. They denied us space in the approaches to goal and began to frustrate us to the point of desperation. There was conflict, there was drama and in the end, when Herr Schulenburg from West Germany sounded his whistle, there was defeat for England.

It was bedlam. Scottish supporters poured on to the pitch, many producing penknives. They were no threat to us, however. Those Scottish lads had only one thing in mind – to take a chunk of the Wembley pitch back home as a souvenir of a famous victory over the World Champions. The famous turf was left pitted and scarred as dozens of ecstatic Scotsmen carved it to pieces. Legend now has it that there is a house in Bonnybridge with a Wembley penalty spot in the centre of its lawn. I believe it!

The despondency felt by the England players was in marked contrast to the euphoria of the Scottish team. Any thoughts I had of the Scottish players being gracious in victory were immediately dispelled by Denis Law at the post-match buffet.

'Gordon, tell me this,' said Denis. 'England are World Champions, but we've just beaten you. So does that mean we are the World Champions now?'

Denis and his team mates roared with laughter. To the side of him was a large bowl of mayonnaise, but I resisted the temptation.

I took all the ribbing in good part. They were worthy winners on the day and deserved to savour their moment of triumph.

As the England team coach left Wembley, our police motorcycle escort had to pull up at a crossroads. There was a pub on one corner from which spilled hundreds of Scottish supporters toasting their team's victory. They saw our coach and, perhaps befuddled by alcohol, took us for the Scotland team. Glasses were raised and bonnets thrown into the air. There were cries of 'Well done!' and 'Great performance!' Alan Ball stood up and waved and suddenly it dawned on them who we were. I'd never seen Alan Ball move so quickly. Pint glasses, pies and bottles crashed against the side of the coach. Our driver, throwing caution to the wind, put his foot down and shot across the intersection with a bevy of tartan-clad supporters in hot pursuit. Thank goodness we hadn't won.

It was a great time to be a Scottish football supporter. Though the national side's victory didn't make them World Champions, two months later Celtic became the first British team to be crowned European Champions following their superb victory over Inter Milan in Lisbon. The seat of power in the football world was back in Great Britain.

Between 1968 and 1970 Tony Waddington slowly but surely turned Stoke City from a middling First Division side into one capable of challenging for silverware.

Tony had taken over as manager in 1960 when Stoke were poorly placed in the Second Division and pulling crowds of around 9,000. His success came by blending youth and experience, a stratagem he adhered to throughout his seventeen-year spell as manager.

The Stoke City side of the late sixties was very much in the Waddington mould. Players such as Jackie Marsh, Alan Bloor, Eric Skeels, Tony Allen, Mike Pejic, Bill Bentley and Denis Smith were all products of Stoke's successful youth policy. The experience of the home-grown players was backed by a number of seasoned professionals of quality whom Tony had signed for modest fees.

Tony Waddington had the knack of persuading good players who were coming to the end of their careers that they had two or three more years at the top when their respective clubs thought otherwise. By and large he was right. Grateful for a few more years in top-flight football, the experienced pros Tony signed rarely let him down. He wasn't the most technically minded of managers, nor the best tactician, but he didn't have to be. Good, experienced players don't need to be told what to do. They know.

Full back Alex Elder had won a Championship medal and played in an FA Cup final for Burnley as well as winning forty caps for Northern Ireland. Willie Stevenson had won both the League Championship and the FA Cup with Liverpool. I had been in the same England Under-23 team as Peter Dobing who, in addition to playing for Manchester City, had played for Blackburn Rovers in the 1960 FA Cup final. Both Maurice Setters and David Herd had bags of First Division experience under their belts and had been in the Manchester United side that had beaten Leicester City in the 1963 FA Cup final. Roy Vernon (Blackburn and Everton) and Harry Burrows (Aston Villa) were also seasoned First Division players.

And then there was George Eastham. George was an exceptionally gifted player from the traditional school of inside forwards. He scored a lot of goals and he also created a lot for his colleagues. George was what we used to call a 'schemer'. A highly creative player with superb vision who could pass the ball inch-perfectly. His first club had been Newcastle United. From there he moved on to Arsenal, doing exceptionally well at Highbury and winning a place in the England team. (He was, of course, a member of the England squad of '66.)

To fine-tune the team, and provide balance between youth and experience, Stoke had Terry Conroy. Terry was a Republic of Ireland international. Naturally two-footed, he possessed incredible stamina, lightning pace and one of the best body swerves I ever saw. As Jackie Marsh once remarked after seeing Terry execute a sublime dummy on Arsenal's Ian Ure, 'TC, you not only sent Urey the wrong way, the crowd on that side of the ground had to pay again to get back in.'

The camaraderie in the Stoke dressing room was fantastic and hardly a day went by without me splitting my sides with laughter at the antics and comments of my team mates, although sometimes the joke was on me.

In London for a game against Chelsea, Terry Conroy, Jackie Marsh, George Eastham and I were killing time with a walk around the streets near our hotel. Terry spotted a pavement artist and we strolled over to view his work. We gazed down at a drawing of a bald head over which a few lines of yellow chalk had been scratched.

'It's Bobby Charlton,' said Terry, convulsing with laughter.

Another paving stone showed another balding head, this time with black chalk hair. The mouth was a black hole with just two white teeth in it.

'Nobby Stiles. Brilliant!' said Terry, warming to this artwork of the most primitive type.

We shuffled along the line of crude drawings of the England team, howling with laughter at each one. Eventually we came to a face with a crooked nose and a gormless expression surmounted by a manic shock of black hair.

'Who's this supposed to be?' I asked.

'Gordon Banks,' said the artist proudly.

That did it for Terry. He collapsed to his knees. Tears streamed from his eyes and he beat the pavement with his fists. Jackie and George clutched their stomachs and slid down the wrought-iron railings they had been leaning on for support.

I had to laugh myself. I didn't really have a choice.

One of the prerequisites of a good team player is the ability to take a joke. A football changing room is a testosterone-driven man's world. A petulant reaction to a practical joke only invites more of the same. In many respects, it's a test of character. If you're too sensitive to take a bit of playful ribbing, you're not the sort of player who can be depended on when the going gets tough on the pitch. Wallflowers are biennials, but their life expectancy in a football dressing room is much shorter.

You have to take the stick from both your team mates and the opposition. As a goalkeeper, I experienced plenty of the latter. In the sixties every First Division club seemed to have a barnstorming centre forward whose first job would be to test the mettle of the opposing goalkeeper. At the earliest opportunity the opposing number 9 would usually attempt to clatter me. You had to be up for that; it was part and parcel of the job at the time. Only by giving as good as you got could you win the mind games.

In 1969 against Sunderland, however, I definitely came off second best. Terry Conroy had given us the lead at Roker Park and we looked comfortable for two points. There were only fifteen minutes of the game remaining when Sunderland's Gordon Harris split our defence with a through ball. Their young centre forward, Malcolm Moore, gave chase and I came quickly off my line. It was touch and go who would reach the ball first, but I was determined that it would be me.

As Moore advanced I dived at his feet while he slid forward in a last-ditch attempt to get a toe on the ball. His knee whacked against my forehead and everything went black.

The next thing I remember is being prostrate on the ground with Stoke's trainer Frank Mountford wafting smelling salts under my nose. I told him I was all right, but Frank wasn't so sure. He called for a stretcher and I lay there listening to my team mates debating what best to do.

David Herd immediately rallied to the call. 'This lot won't put a single goal past me. Give me Gordon's top,' he said. Then everything went black again.

I woke up in Sunderland General Hospital suffering from acute concussion. When I eventually recovered my thoughts I noticed Frank Mountford sitting at the end of my bed.

'How'd we get on?' I asked. 'Herdy said they wouldn't put a single goal past him.'

'They didn't,' said Frank as he gathered my clothes together. 'They scored four!'

Goalkeeping. It isn't as easy as it looks.

In addition to physical strength you also need mental toughness. It's no good performing heroics for eighty-nine minutes if you lose concentration for a second and give away a silly goal. And you have to take bad luck and poor decisions in your stride.

Sometimes these last two combine disastrously, as in 1973 when high-riding Stoke City visited Anfield. Liverpool were in a great run of form and no team relished playing them on their home turf. The game was a thriller. We worked hard for each other and deserved the lead Jimmy Greenhoff gave us with a well-timed header just after the half hour. Roared on by the Kop, Liverpool laid siege to my goal, but for all their dominance had only an equalizer from Emlyn Hughes to show for their efforts.

The Liverpool players had been taken to the very limits of their skill and stamina by a Stoke City side whose commitment was absolute. A draw at Anfield in those days was considered a great achievement for a visiting team and we well deserved one, but events in injury time conspired to deny us what was rightfully ours.

With only seconds remaining Jackie Marsh clipped the heels of

Liverpool's Ian Callaghan. Callaghan kept the ball and the referee waved play on, but when Callaghan stumbled and went to ground a few yards further on he decided instead to award Liverpool a free kick just outside our penalty area.

We thought it was a bad decision but didn't protest. Callaghan hammered the free kick into a very congested penalty area. It took a deflection off Eric Skeels and I quickly adjusted my positioning to get behind the ball, only for it to deflect a second time off the calf of Kevin Keegan and into the net.

After pulling out all the stops for the best part of the game, a controversial refereeing decision and two cruel deflections all in the last thirty seconds meant that I left the pitch on the losing side.

The Stoke squad combined the products of a good youth policy, such as Alan Bloor, Eric Skeels and Denis Smith, with Tony Waddington's astute signings of experienced pros with a few good years left in them. The former were long-term prospects while the latter, naturally, came and went.

This curious mixture of stability and transience enabled the team to survive quite comfortably in Division One without ever threatening the elite band of clubs challenging for honours. But all that was to change in 1970.

At the start of the new decade the Stoke team had a much more settled look about it. The home-grown talent had matured and blossomed while the older players such as George Eastham and Harry Burrows were still good for a few years yet. Tony was still buying experienced pros, but in Jimmy Greenhoff and John Richie he had invested in two players who were in their prime rather than on their way out.

John Richie was in his second spell at Stoke and Tony Wadding-ton had signed him on both occasions. The first time had been in 1961, when John was a part-timer with Kettering Town. John quickly adapted to life as a full-time professional and his goals for Stoke led to an £80,000 move to Sheffield Wednesday in 1966. When Danny Williams took over as manager at Hillsborough, John found himself out of favour and Waddington had no hesitation in forking out £28,000 to bring him back home. What a bargain that turned out to be. John scored 176 goals for Stoke in 343 appearances. He played alongside Jimmy Greenhoff, signed from Birmingham City in 1968 for £100,000, to form a striking force that was to figure significantly in a renaissance that would see Stoke City challenging for the League Championship, FA Cup and League Cup.

The turning point for Stoke City came in 1970–71 and it followed another important stage in my own career, for that summer I played in another World Cup for England. It turned out to be a memorable tournament, one in which Brazil more than made amends for their lacklustre showing in 1966 by producing the greatest team performance in the history of international football. A World Cup in which I was, at last, able to pit my wits on the biggest stage in the world against the man I believed to be the greatest footballer in the world – Pelé.

14. Pelé and Me

It always gives me great pleasure to tell my grandchildren that I had a number one hit. The England squad recorded 'Back Home' prior to the 1970 World Cup in Mexico and the record-buying public liked it in sufficient numbers that it went to number one in May of that year. ('Back Home' spent a total of sixteen weeks in the charts and was replaced at number one by Christie with 'Yellow River'.)

Also in May, on the day the England squad left for Mexico, there was news of another kind from the pop world. The Beatles were splitting up. It was, said one DJ, 'the end of a glorious era'. Little did I realize, that statement would soon also be applied to English football.

England's pre-tournament schedule began with a game against Colombia in Bogotá. We had spent the previous two weeks in Mexico, gradually becoming acclimatized to the searing heat and thin air. The heat was stifling but initially it was the altitude I found particularly difficult to cope with.

We stayed at a hotel in Guadalajara with a lift that wasn't working. I carried my luggage up two flights of stairs and by the time I reached my room my lungs were heaving like forge bellows. The altitude also had an effect on the ball itself. It took me some time to grow accustomed to the quicker pace and swerve of the ball in the rarefied atmosphere. As a goalkeeper my problems were compounded by the sublime quality of the light. It was so bright that I often lost sight of the ball in the shadows cast by the stadium, or even by players. I was in little doubt that the conditions would have a huge bearing on my individual performance and that of the England team.

The Mexico acclimatization fortnight was tough graft. Alf and Harold Shepherdson pushed us to the limit in training. I felt that I was on top form and playing the best football of my career. During one of Alf's shot-stopping sessions, Bobby Charlton turned to me after I had saved yet another of his thunderbolts and said, 'Gordon, I've run out of ways to beat you.' Coming from a player of Bobby's prowess and stature, that was praise indeed. I felt really great. The confidence I had in my own ability was sky high and, looking back, my performances in 1970 were, I think, my best ever. As a goalkeeper, I could get no better.

After the session I discovered I had lost seven pounds during that day alone. By the end of the fortnight I weighed twelve and a half stone, the lightest I'd been since I was seventeen.

Alf had organized two warm-up matches against Colombia and Ecuador to get us used to playing at high altitude. Oddly, his opinion was not shared by the West Germans, who did not arrive in Mexico until shortly before the tournament began. I believe Alf was right to organize the trip, despite subsequent events. It wasn't his fault that it turned into a living nightmare.

From the moment I set eyes on it I didn't like Bogotá. We had been booked into the Tequendama Hotel which, I'd been told, was the best in Colombia and on a par with any top hotel in the world.

On the drive from the airport, however, I found myself struggling with my conscience. I had grown up poor, but had never seen poverty such as was evident on the streets of Colombia's capital. On the outskirts of the city were cardboard shanty towns where exhausted mothers clutched babies with distended stomachs and stick-like limbs. Knots of ragamuffin children were assembled at the roadside to watch us pass by. Their faces shocked me: seven- or eight-year-olds with the looks of old men and women. What clothes they wore were grime ridden and filthy. Many were shoeless. As our team coach flashed by we looked into rows of vacant, expressionless eyes.

The city itself was a muck heap. At one point we passed a dead horse lying at the side of the road. Three days later when we returned to the airport, it was still there. To us the place looked like a living hell.

Alf Ramsey had warned us about life in Bogotá. Under no

circumstances were we to eat anything that hadn't been prepared by our own appointed chef. We were to drink water only from freshly opened bottles. For our own safety, we were not to leave the hotel without permission. Little did he know, there was plenty of trouble lying in wait for us behind the hotel's opulent façade.

Our friendly against Colombia proved to be a useful workout. Bogotá is 8,500 feet above sea level, some 1,500 feet higher than Mexico City, and though the rarefied atmosphere did pose problems, we coped. Every one of us was at the top of his game and we were fitter than we had ever been in our lives. I made an encouraging start when I came off my line to save at the feet of García, arguably Colombia's one truly world-class player. Five minutes later I foiled García again, diving low to my right to gather a snap drive after he had turned Keith Newton. Having coped with Colombia's initial pressure, we took the game by the scruff of the neck and began to control it. In the end we ran out comfortable winners courtesy of two goals from the ever improving Martin Peters, and one each from Bobby Charlton and Alan Ball.

On the same day, Alf gave the rest of the squad a run-out under the guise of England 'B' against a team comprising Colombian squad members to ensure that every member of the squad had a game under their belts at altitude. A goal from Jeff Astle of West Bromwich Albion gave victory to a team that included Peter Bonetti, Norman Hunter, Nobby Stiles, Colin Bell, Jack Charlton and Allan Clarke. Every player had been keen to do well, irrespective of which team he played in, because at this juncture the squad comprised twenty-eight players and Alf would have to trim it down to twenty-two for Mexico. Press speculation was rife about who Alf would send home. But Alf was soon to have more pressing problems on his mind.

During our stay at El Tequendama a curious incident took place. Bobby Moore visited the Green Fire jewellery shop in the hotel lobby to buy a present for his wife Tina. Bobby was accompanied by Bobby Charlton, on the lookout for a gift for his wife Norma, together with Nobby Stiles and Liverpool's Peter Thompson.

Minutes after they left the jewellery shop, the manageress accused

Bobby Moore of stealing a $600 bracelet. The Colombian police were summoned. After a prolonged discussion Moore and Charlton put their signatures to formal statements and the matter seemed to be closed.

News of this odd incident rapidly spread through the squad, though none of us thought it was more than a simple misunderstanding which had been quickly cleared up. Alf impressed upon us all that we should not breathe a word of it to anyone, especially the press. As Alf told us, 'This sort of incident tends to get blown out of all proportion.'

Following our game against Colombia we travelled to Quito, where goals from Francis Lee and Brian Kidd gave us a 2–0 victory over Ecuador. Quito is over 9,000 feet above sea level and its air is so thin that even a modicum of physical effort leaves you panting. During the game the ball deviated in the air like a Shane Warne googly. By now I was getting used to the increased speed and swerve of the ball and felt pleased with the fact that I managed to hang on to every shot that came my way.

Again Alf organized a 'B' international for the remainder of the squad, this time against the Ecuadorian champions, Liga. Jeff Astle helped himself to a hat trick in this game and a goal from Emlyn Hughes gave our second string a handsome 4–1 victory.

The favourable results, though, were secondary to the experience gained from playing so far above sea level. We were all becoming acclimatized by now and at the end of what had been a very successful and convivial trip to Ecuador, our confidence was as high as the altitude.

The following day we set off for Mexico City and the World Cup. Our flight involved a long stopover at Bogotá. Rather than having us hanging around the airport for the best part of a day, Alf had arranged for us to return to El Tequendama for some relaxation.

That afternoon we watched *Shenandoah*, a 1965 Jimmy Stewart western, in the hotel's TV lounge. About halfway through the film, two suited Colombians came into the room and left with Bobby Moore. As the England captain, Bobby was often called away to give interviews or meet visiting officials from the British embassy, so we didn't think anything of it when he hadn't returned by the time we left for the airport.

Even Bobby's absence on the plane to Mexico didn't cause a stir. Alf Ramsey made no mention of it, none of the press corps questioned it and, as two FA officials were also absent, we simply assumed that Bobby was doing some TV interviews and would follow us on a later flight. It happened all the time.

That journey to Mexico City was the most eventful and chaotic flight I have undertaken in my life. For a start, we ran into an electrical storm near Panama City, where we were scheduled to stop for refuelling. The plane rolled and dipped, at one point dropping like a stone when we hit an air pocket. It was harrowing even for the most seasoned air travellers, of which Jeff Astle was not one.

Jeff was a nervous flyer at the best of times, and this was far from being the best of times. Though Nobby Stiles and I did our best to allay his fears, poor Jeff couldn't help himself and went into a panic attack.

'He needs a drink to calm his nerves,' said Nobby.

Alf had banned alcohol, but a couple of the lads managed to procure a few miniature vodkas from a stewardess. We surreptitiously administered the 'medicine' to Jeff, two or three doses of which calmed him down somewhat. Fifteen minutes later, the storm seemed as nothing compared to the earthquake Alf Ramsey had just triggered.

Alf stood to address the players and the accompanying press corps. What he said was simply unbelievable. Bobby Moore had been arrested in Bogotá accused of stealing a bracelet from the Green Fire jewellery shop. Bobby Charlton was his alleged accomplice. He might just as well have said that Mother Teresa had been arrested for child abuse, it was that outlandish and unbelievable.

Of course, we in the squad knew of the original allegations, but this was all news to the press corps. They were now privy to the biggest and most sensational story of the World Cup but, short of hijacking the pilot's radio, had no means of contacting their editors back in London. They flapped about like headless chickens.

By the time of the refuelling stop Jeff Astle's medicine had gone to his head. We kept him well out of Alf's way, and did our best to smarten him up, but we needn't have bothered. Alf Ramsey was a man prepossessed. He paced the airport like a caged lion, his face inscrutable but his mind obviously on the plight of his captain.

As soon as we entered the airport building the press boys ran to the telephones. It was just like the movies. They were in a real dilemma – stuck in a Panama transit lounge while the story of the year was breaking back in Bogotá. Some editors ordered their men to hire a car to take them back. They soon changed their minds when informed that Bogotá was some 2,000 miles away. As it happened, the World Cup coincided with the RAC London to Mexico Rally (which, can you believe it, Jimmy Greaves had entered), so several motoring correspondents suddenly and unexpectedly found themselves on their way to Colombia.

When we eventually arrived in Mexico City a veritable army of TV, radio and press journalists ambushed us, their cameras flashing away at anyone and everyone. Jeff Astle, having been administered a little more nerve tonic, was by now unsteady on his legs and looking as if he had not changed his clothes for a fortnight. Alf issued a complete denial of the allegations, of course, though he was far from his normal cool, calm self. Alf was rattled and he wasn't the only one.

The local press had a field day. The Mexican newspaper *Esto* had discovered that a Midlands brewery had sent a case of beer to Jeff Astle as a good luck gesture. (Apparently Jeff had mentioned in a magazine interview that he liked it and the brewery's marketing department thought, quite rightly as it turned out, that it would be good publicity.) In truth, Jeff drank hardly at all, but the *Esto* story alongside a photograph of a dishevelled Jeff passing through arrivals at Mexico City airport painted a very different picture.

Esto linked the two stories to come up with the headline, 'England Arrive – A Team of Thieves and Drunks'. Alf nearly had a coronary, but soon regained his composure. Holding the newspaper in his hand, he walked up to Jeff and uttered the words every England player dreaded: 'Jeffrey, a word please . . .'

The one person to keep his head throughout this whole sorry

affair was Bobby Moore himself. Whoever it was that tried to disrupt our preparations for Mexico chose the wrong man to stitch up in Bobby Moore. Bobby was unflappable. He took everything in his stride and never ever lost his cool. His personality and character were very strong and his unruffled self-belief enabled him to survive the attentions of the Colombian authorities. They found no chink in his armour and eventually dropped the ridiculous charges against him.

I shudder to think what might have happened if the allegations had been made against some other members of the squad. We weren't all possessed of Bobby's iron will, and I think the experience would have devastated many of us.

The case against Bobby began to look more and more fragile as the investigation conducted by the Colombian police progressed. Bobby was in danger of being imprisoned for the course of the investigation until the president of the Colombian Football Association, Alfonso Senior, suggested Bobby be placed in his custody. That was the first positive point. The British Prime Minister, Harold Wilson, also offered to intervene, but in the end such politicking proved unnecessary as the case fell apart by itself.

The manageress of the Green Fire jewellery shop, Clara Padilla, told the police that she had seen Bobby Moore slip a $3,000 dollar bracelet sporting a large diamond into the left-hand pocket of his England blazer. (You will recall that the bracelet was worth $600 a few pages back. Well, that's South American inflation for you!) The problem with this tale was that our blazers didn't have a left-hand pocket. Padilla then changed her story, saying she had not actually seen Bobby pocket the bracelet, but had acted on the word of another customer in the shop, one Alvaro Suarez. Señor Suarez said he had seen Bobby slip what was now a $6,000 dollar bracelet studded with diamonds and emeralds into 'a pocket somewhere on his person'. The Colombian police stated that, 'having subjected Suarez to further and more intense questioning' – one can only imagine what that might mean – he too changed his story. Now he 'thought he might have seen the England captain put something in his pocket'.

The manageress was backing down fast, putting the blame for the whole affair on Suarez. Then the police discovered that their new star witness was a close friend and business associate of Danilo Rojas, the owner of Green Fire. They also discovered that the shop, Rojas and Alvaro Suarez were all in financial difficulties.

When Bobby appeared in court the judge, Pedro Durado, immediately threw the case out. Bobby was mightily relieved, though he at no time betrayed the anxiety he must have felt. He left the court with the same dignity and grace he had maintained throughout.

'I have nothing against the Colombian police and authorities,' Bobby told the waiting reporters. 'Charges were brought against me; they simply acted on them and they did their job. Their job was to establish the truth and they achieved this. I was totally innocent of the allegations against me and that has been established. All I want to do now is join up with my fellow England players in Mexico and give my undivided attention to helping England retain the World Cup. Thank you, gentlemen.'

What a man!

When Bobby Moore arrived at our hotel, the entire England squad lined up outside to applaud him. He hadn't had a change of clothing for nearly a week, yet he looked as smart as if he were stepping out of a tailor's shop after a complete makeover. His clothes were completely unruffled, as was the man himself.

As a postscript to the affair, I later found out that a well-known film star had earlier been accused of the same offence at the same shop. Allegedly, a sizeable amount of money was paid by the star's 'people' to hush the matter up. Bobby Moore and Alf Ramsey provided less easy pickings.

The unlucky six players that Alf omitted from the squad were Ralph Coates (Burnley), Brian Kidd and David Sadler (Manchester United), Bob McNab (Arsenal), Peter Shilton (Leicester City) and Peter Thompson (Liverpool). Alf gave permission for Thompson and Sadler to remain with us under the strict instruction that neither should 'abuse their freedom'.

The squad tasked with retaining the World Cup for England was, to my mind, stronger than the one that had won it in 1966. We had greater quality in depth and more players at the peak of their powers. We all knew we had a mountain to climb, but to a man we firmly believed we could lift the World Cup again, and so too did Alf Ramsey.

That we were not the most popular side in the World Cup was brought home to me when we watched the opening ceremony at the Azteca stadium on television. As in 1966, each country was represented by twenty-two children. The poor Mexican kids representing England were roundly booed and jeered by the crowd. As Alan Mullery remarked at the time, 'If that's their response to children in England shirts, what sort of reception will the real thing get?'

We were soon to find out.

We were drawn in arguably the toughest group of the lot, Group C. We were up against Romania, Czechoslovakia and, of all teams, Brazil, who were coming into the World Cup on the back of an unbeaten run that stretched back over two years. Brazil had won all six of their qualification matches, scoring twenty-three goals in the process and conceding just two. The Brazilians were a major threat to us, but as two teams were to qualify from each group, we were very confident of progressing. In fact, for all the prowess and power of Brazil, Pelé et al., we believed we were good enough to beat them.

Our first match was on 2 June, in Guadalajara against Romania. The hostile reception the Mexican crowd gave us when we took to the pitch was no surprise to anyone. The local press had done their utmost to blacken our name and had even exhumed Alf's misquote of 1966 describing the Argentinians as animals. The fact that Alf had insisted we bring our own food, chef, even our own team bus and driver to Mexico seemed to antagonize the Central American press. They accused us of being pompous, aloof, rude, unfriendly and anti-social. In fact, all Alf had done was to set a sensible trend. In subsequent World Cups just about every team would take along their own chef to prepare meals to the strict dietary requirements laid down by the squad dietician.

Alf ignored his bad press, his mind was too occupied with matters of football to be bothered by such trivialities, but his indifference was interpreted as aloofness. Here our FA learned a valuable lesson. The next time England participated in the World Cup finals, in Spain in 1982, manager Ron Greenwood had an official PR officer on hand.

We failed to sparkle in our opening match against a physical and defensively minded Romanian team. The game was a poor advertisement for football, but we achieved our aim. We won, thanks to Geoff Hurst, who latched on to a super pass from Francis Lee to score the only goal of the game through the legs of the keeper Adamache. Romania had been tough and difficult opponents, but we knew that our second game, against Brazil, would be harder still.

The match was scheduled for 7 June, five days after our victory over Romania. The day before the game Alf made me tremble at the knees when he approached me and said, 'Gordon, a word please.'

A year earlier, almost to the day, Alf had beckoned me in similar fashion. That had been before the first game of our tour of Central and South America, against Mexico. The news Alf had given me that day was devastating. He quietly and sympathetically told me that he had just received word that my father had died. Dad had been very ill for some months. As a family we had tried to prepare ourselves for the worst, but Alf's words still came as a great shock to me. I was grief stricken. Alf offered comfort and condolence. The Mexico game was the furthest thing from my mind and he knew it. He told me there was no question about my returning for the funeral.

I caught the next available flight home and on the journey steeled myself to make my last farewell to Dad. He had been a tremendous source of strength and inspiration throughout my life. His passing hit me hard and by the time the plane eventually touched down at Heathrow I was emotionally drained. But I knew that I had made the correct decision to return home and be with my family, and with Dad for one last time.

A year later I was on tenterhooks, anxious to hear what Alf had to tell me but hoping against hope it wasn't more bad news. But it was something else entirely.

'Gordon, a gentleman is on the telephone for you,' said Alf. 'It is a call I think you should take.'

I was astonished to hear a plummy voice on the other end of the line informing me that he was an equerry from Buckingham Palace.

'Mr Banks, I have the considerable pleasure and duty to inform you that you have been provisionally proposed to receive the Order of the British Empire in the forthcoming honours list. This call is to establish that you are willing to accept the said award, and to determine if you are in a position to accept it personally at Buckingham Palace. The occasion will be most auspicious,' he added, as if I needed encouragement.

For a split second I thought it must be a wind-up. This was just the sort of thing Alan Ball, Nobby Stiles, Jack Charlton or Alan Mullery might do. But Alf Ramsey himself had summoned me. They'd never involve Alf in one of their pranks. Besides, I could never imagine Nobby or Big Jack coming up with a word like 'auspicious'.

I was floating on air. I wasn't just pleased, I was euphoric. I informed Mr Plummy that I would be delighted to receive such an honour and thanked him profusely. The equerry swore me to secrecy, so I couldn't share my pleasure and pride with my team mates. Why on earth had I been chose for an OBE? As is my way, in the end I decided not to question it too deeply and simply enjoyed the moment. My joy was tinged with one sad regret: that Dad hadn't lived to see it. Though in all probability he would not have shown it, I know Dad would have been as proud of me as I am of him.

A couple of days before our game against Brazil, Alf Ramsey made an uncharacteristic faux pas. Following a training session he gathered us all together and told us that the eleven who had finished the game against Romania would start against Brazil. Full back Keith Newton had not recovered from the injury he had picked up against the Romanians, which meant his Everton team mate, Tommy Wright, was to continue at right back. Chelsea's Peter Osgood had replaced Francis Lee and Ossy couldn't contain his joy at having been selected to face Brazil.

Later that day we had a team meeting and Alf began talking about the roles of Francis Lee and Bobby Charlton, only for a perplexed Franny to point out that he hadn't been selected.

'But of course you are in the side, Francis,' said Alf.

He had completely forgotten that Osgood had come on for Lee against Romania. Alf was very embarrassed and Peter very disappointed. But not half as disappointed as he was when Alf named our five substitutes and he wasn't even among them.

We were staying at the Hilton Hotel in Guadalajara and hardly got a wink of sleep on the night preceding the game. Hundreds of anti-English Mexicans held an all-night vigil in the street outside. They constantly chanted 'Bra-zil', honked car horns and bashed dustbin lids together. The England party had taken up the entire twelfth floor of the Hilton but the constant noise kept us awake all night. I was sharing a room with Alex Stepney of Manchester United. At one point a group of Mexicans gained access to our floor and banged on our door. I opened it just in time to see half a dozen Mexican youths being chased down the corridor by a furious Jack Charlton.

The hotel security staff and the local police usually maintained a heavy presence at the hotel. Oddly, on this night, they were conspicuous by their absence. The most anyone managed was two hours' sleep, but such was our motivation and state of mind, we couldn't wait to get out there and face the Brazilians.

In Brazil's opening match against a talented Czechoslovakian team, Pelé had orchestrated the proceedings from start to finish. Brazil won 4–1 and Pelé had been the focal point of every Brazilian move. I was left in no doubt. Pelé was the greatest footballer in the world. He combined effectiveness, vision and power with grace, beauty and style. Just to see him taking the ball on his chest was to witness athleticism of the highest order. When Pelé met the ball in the air, his first touch was wonderfully deft, on a par with the perfection he showed when taking the ball to feet. His shooting was both powerful and accurate and it was obvious he didn't give a jot which foot he used since both were equally deadly. Physically he was very strong. Off the mark he was like lightning. Even when running at full gallop, Pelé's co-ordination made him seem marvellously relaxed. For years I had been looking forward to the chance of playing against the great man in a major competition. Now the moment had come. But he was playing some of the best football of his career. Much as I wanted to face him, I had no idea how we would be able to contain him.

The teams that day were England: Gordon Banks (Stoke City); Tommy Wright (Everton), Bobby Moore (West Ham), Brian Labone (Everton), Terry Cooper (Leeds United); Alan Ball (Everton), Alan Mullery (Spurs), Bobby Charlton (Manchester United), Martin Peters (Spurs); Geoff Hurst (West Ham), Francis Lee (Manchester City); Brazil: Felix; Carlos Alberto, Brito, Piazza, Everaldo, Paulo Cesar, Clodoaldo, Rivelino, Jairzinho, Tostao, Pelé. On the bench for England were Peter Bonetti (Chelsea), Emlyn Hughes (Liverpool), Jeff Astle (West Bromwich Albion), Nobby Stiles (Manchester United) and Colin Bell (Manchester City).

When Alf received the Brazilian team sheet he noticed that their influential midfielder, Gerson, wasn't playing. Gerson had a thigh injury and had been replaced by Paulo Cesar. 'That's like replacing a Jaguar with a Mercedes,' Alan Mullery remarked on hearing the news.

Alf had reverted to 4–4–2 – a system the players liked and which was more suited to us as a squad, since it allowed squad players to slot in comfortably. Colin Bell for Bobby Charlton, Big Jack for Brian Labone, Nobby for Alan Mullery and so on.

At the team meeting Alf had emphasized the roles everyone was to play. In the centre of defence Brian Labone was to pick up and mark Tostao, while Bobby Moore would pick up the bits whilst sweeping around the back. Alan Mullery had one of the most difficult tasks. Mullers was to 'sit in' just in front of the back four and push up when we were on the attack. Hard work, especially as the temperature in the stadium was over 100°F. Bobby Charlton was going to anchor the midfield and be our playmaker, pushing on with Mullers when we were taking the game to Brazil. Alan Ball and Martin Peters were going to work up and down the flanks, with Franny Lee playing off Geoff Hurst up front, Geoff being our target man.

The onus was on our full backs, Tommy Wright and Terry Cooper, to overlap Bally and Martin Peters, receive the ball from midfield and provide the crosses for Geoff. That was the plan, anyway. By and large, it was to work very well.

A crowd of over 72,000 packed into the Guadalajara stadium. During the national anthems I studied the Brazilian line. They looked awesome. As physically strong as they were technically adept. The heat was so intense I was sweating buckets just standing in line. I remember wondering how Alan Mullery could possibly fulfil the role Alf had assigned him for a full ninety minutes.

The opening ten minutes were spent probing and prodding in an attempt to sound one another out. Tackles were few and far between. We were strolling players in the searing heat.

Franny Lee tried to find Hurst but Brito extended a leg and Brazil leisurely wandered upfield. Brito to Paulo Cesar to Clodoaldo to Pelé. Whack! Alan Mullery dumped the great man on the ground. Mullers held up the palms of his hands to the referee in recognition of his clumsy challenge and kept on the right side of officialdom by extending a hand to Pelé, which was ignored. Mullers smiled and rubbed the top of Pelé's head.

'You OK mate?'

'I am not your "mate",' replied Pelé.

'It's best that you are,' said Mullers, 'believe me, yer don't wanna make an enemy of me.'

Pelé simply shook his head and smiled to himself.

I watched from my privileged vantage point as the game unfolded and the Brazilians treated me to a sight I thought I would never see on a football pitch. A walking midfield. With the instep of his right boot, Carlos Alberto nonchalantly pushed the ball into the path of Tostao. Tostao to Rivelino to Pelé. I took to my toes, arms hanging at my sides like a gunslinger at high noon. Pelé turned, hit the ball out wide to the left only for Peters to spring forward and intercept. Peters to Ball to Charlton to the overlapping Wright.

'Go on, Tommy, son.'

Wright to Lee, who played the ball back. Bobby Charlton arrived from deep and at some speed. Thump! Bobby hammered the ball at head height to Hurst who had taken up a position on our right. It was as if Geoff was nodding 'good morning'. His head dropped, the ball smacked against his forehead and bounced once before reaching Franny Lee. Lee to Ball to Wright and back to Lee again. The Brazilians appeared to be completely unconcerned. They simply watched and waited. Not one man in a yellow shirt ran towards any England player who had the ball.

Geoff Hurst had drifted into the Brazilian penalty box, Piazza shadowing him. Franny Lee waved his foot over the ball then poked it two yards forward with his left boot before smacking it goalwards with his right.

The ball covered twenty yards in no time at all. Felix in the Brazilian goal had his angles spot on and didn't have to move an inch. He put his hands out in front of his head and gathered Franny's effort as if someone had thrown him a practice ball in training. He threw the ball out to Carlos Alberto who stroked it down the wing to Jairzinho.

Suddenly, the game exploded into life as Jairzinho took off like a rocket. We had been caught completely on the hop by his sudden burst of speed. Jairzinho raced towards Terry Cooper and passed him with a superb dummy. I took my eyes off him for a split second to glance around my penalty area. What I saw spelled trouble.

The rest you already know: Tostao free at my near post, Alan Mullery trying in vain to close down Pelé, Jairzinho's textbook centre and Pelé's perfect header.

Ninety-nine times out of a hundred Pelé's shout of '*Golo!*' would have been justified, but on that day I was equal to the task. Although I've tried to analyse that save as best I can in the opening pages of this book, it was really just about being in the right place at the right time – one of those rare occasions when years of hard work and practice combine in one perfect moment.

As Pelé positioned himself for the resulting corner he turned to me and smiled.

'Great save . . . mate!' he said.

That tremendous spirit of mutual respect between the teams was to prevail throughout the rest of the match. It was a fantastic game of football. We knew we could match Brazil in the possession stakes, and our passing was as good as theirs. We held the ball up well, which is essential in such heat. We adapted our style to the slower, more methodical pace of international football, which was very much the opposite of the hell-for-leather approach of our domestic game. At half time the non-playing members, on Alf's instructions, gave us ice-filled towels to drape around our necks to cool us down. It felt great, so I asked Peter Thompson to chop up some more ice and place it in a polythene bag for me. I intended to use it while play was in the Brazilian half.

The Brazilians were seven minutes late coming out for the second half. They'd done this sort of thing before, in a friendly in Rio de Janeiro in June 1969. That time Alf had gotten them out by threatening a mass walkoff, but in Mexico there was little we could do but endure the burning sun and wait.

Less than ten minutes into the second half I decided to make use of my polythene ice-pack. All I found was a bag of tepid water. In little over ten minutes, every chunk of ice had melted.

As if it weren't hot enough, Brazil contrived to turn up the heat still further. Bobby Moore, who was having the game of his life, came across to challenge Tostao. That left a gap in the centre of defence which Alan Mullery filled. Brian Labone was marking Pelé on his own. Martin Peters arrived to provide back-up to Brian, but as he did so Pelé jinked one way, then the other, and found the space to roll the ball into the path of Jairzinho. Terry Cooper was on to Jairzinho in a flash but lost his footing on the lush turf. Jairzinho sidestepped to his right and I came quickly off my line to narrow the angle. I was just beyond the left-hand angle of my six-yard box when Jairzinho stubbed the toe of his boot at the base of the ball. It lifted over my spreadeagled body and into the opposite corner of my net.

'Yeaaaaaaaah, *Go-olo!*' Jairzinho screamed.

He whirled away and all I could do was watch disconsolately as he jumped so high in the air it looked as if he were attempting to touch the roof of the stands.

We gave it everything we had. Bobby Moore was imperious, Alan Mullery indefatigable, Alan Ball unlucky when he cut in from the left and saw his shot cannon off the Brazilian crossbar with Felix well beaten.

Towards the end, I thought we would deservedly equalize. Jeff Astle had just come on as a substitute when he found Felix in no-man's land and the Brazilian goal at his mercy. Everaldo and Piazza had collided when going for the ball. Everaldo recovered first but played the ball across the face of goal and Jeff was on to it in a flash. As the leading goalscorer in the First Division, this sort of chance was normally meat and drink to him. But somehow Jeff scuffed his effort wide. Perhaps it was nerves, or perhaps he hadn't had time to adjust to the game. Whatever, the opportunity was gone, as was our chance of taking something from what had been an even and exhilarating game.

Following the final whistle, Pelé went across to Bobby Moore, grabbed his face in both hands and gave it an affectionate squeeze. They then hugged one another and exchanged shirts. I think that gesture by Pelé summed up the entire game, and in particular the performance of Bobby Moore. The victor saw fit to lavish praise on the vanquished, because Pelé knew that Bobby had been out-standing, and that Brazil's good fortune was our bad luck.

There had been little to choose between the teams, but there had been one telling difference. Finishing. Brazil had taken their best chance and we had missed ours. At that level of football the conse-quences of missing a chance can be catastrophic. To be fair to Jeff, we did have other good opportunities to score. That we didn't proved to be our downfall. None the less, we emerged proud in defeat.

That save from Pelé is considered by many to be the greatest I ever made. It is certainly a save I am very proud of, one that gave me a lot of satisfaction. As for being my best ever? Such opinions are always subjective. I believe the accolades are largely due to the fact that it was made in a very high-profile match in front of a global TV audience. The following day I made newspaper headlines across the world and had become a 'world class' goalkeeper. But these things don't happen overnight. I think Alf had it right when he told the football writer Bryon Butler, 'His performance today was a continuation, rather than the culmination, of the standards he set himself over the years.'

In my opinion, a save I made in 1971 during a home match for Stoke against Manchester City was better than the one I made in Guadalajara.

Wyn Davies was a superb header of the ball, a centre forward who leapt to a phenomenal height. The Stoke defenders Denis Smith and Alan Bloor had unwittingly blocked my line of sight. When the ball was played from the wing to the far post I thought it would go out for a goal kick, then suddenly Wyn was towering above the ball some eight yards from goal. The ball cannoned off his forehead and headed for the net to my left at head height. In such circumstances, with ground to make up, a goalkeeper has to think himself into the space. I took off immediately I saw Wyn and somehow made up the ground. I not only got my hands to the ball but managed to hold it while soaring through the air.

Any Stoke City player will tell you that was my best ever save. Ask Rodney Marsh, though, and he'll say it was a save I made from a Francis Lee header at Maine Road in 1972. Jimmy Greaves believes it was one I made at White Hart Lane when, from six yards, I was suddenly confronted with a sumptuous volley on the turn from Alan Gilzean. Diving to my left, I managed to hold the ball in my left hand before gathering it into my chest as I came back down to earth. The way Jimmy tells the story, on seeing me produce that save he turned to his team mate and said, 'If I were you, Gilly, I'd quit now. I've long since given up thinking of ways to try and beat him.'

My greatest ever save? From Pelé, Francis Lee, Wyn Davies or Alan Gilzean? That's the beauty of football: it's all about opinions, as the guy standing next to you in the pub would no doubt disagree!

★

Following the Brazil match Alf gave us permission to attend a
cocktail party at our hotel to which our families were also invited.
Ursula was at home with our children, but it was great to see Mam
and my Aunty Dorothy. I had some good news for them – my
impending OBE. Mam was, naturally, delighted. She also told me
how well I had played against Brazil. Well, I thought, she would,
wouldn't she? But then one of the lads produced a copy of the
Mexican newspaper *El Heraldo*. The Mexican press rarely had a
good word to say about England, but there was a photograph of
my save from Pelé under the heading 'El Magnifico'.

Bobby Moore saw me grinning at the headline and came over
to me. 'I think they're referring to the header,' he said.

This is family reading, so I won't tell you what my reply to that
was.

The Mexican press may have warmed to us a little, but the
Mexican public was still very hostile when we took to the pitch for
our final group game against Czechoslovakia. I had more trouble
with the crowd during this game than with the Czech forward line.
They pelted me with orange peel, apple cores and coins throughout
the first half. I complained to the referee, who brought the matter to
the attention of the FIFA officials present. The FIFA representative
asked the Mexican police to stand behind my goal. That changed
things drastically: the amount of orange peel and coins raining
down increased fivefold. I wouldn't be short of change for the
telephone after this game! We dominated the match, but it was no
classic. A 'Sniffer' Clarke penalty gave us a 1–0 victory, but that
was enough to see us qualify from our group, along with Brazil,
who in their final group match beat Romania 3–2.

Jack Charlton replaced Brian Labone in the centre of defence
against the Czechs. Towards the end of the match, the Czech full
back Dobias tried his luck from twenty-five yards. The ball swerved
through the thin air and what should have been a comfortable save
for me suddenly became a problem. I managed to get the fingertips
of my right hand to the deviating ball and push it upwards. I
immediately spun round and was astonished to see the ball return
from the crossbar and straight into my waiting hands.

'Brilliant!' said Big Jack, 'and what's gonna be yor next trick against them Jormans?'

Little did I realize, but my next trick was to be a disappearing act.

15. Message in a Bottle

To this day I'm not sure what happened, exactly. All manner of wild and crazy theories have been put forward, the most common being that I was nobbled. All I knew was that I was going to miss a match crucial to our prospects of retaining the World Cup. A game which, with hindsight, was a watershed for English international football.

Everything was going to plan. We had qualified for the quarter-finals and the spirit and confidence of the players were excellent. There were even wonderful moments of light relief, courtesy of our police outrider.

Every day we travelled to the training ground in the coach Alf had had brought over from England, and on every trip we were escorted by the same motorcyclist from Mexico's Finest. In his pristine khaki uniform, mirror shades and knee-high black leather boots he was an imposing figure. We dubbed him Alfredo.

At first Alfredo took his duty most seriously, ever on the lookout for anyone and anything that might disrupt our journey. After a few trips, however, Alfredo became bored with the routine of it all and began to demonstrate just how confident and competent he could be on two wheels.

We were on a country road that passed through the occasional village when I happened to glance up.

'Hey-up, look at this fella!' I said, alerting the others.

Alfredo was standing up on his bike with both arms outstretched. We all craned to watch his antics and gave him a cheer. Alfredo looked over his shoulder, acknowledged our appreciation with a nod of his head, then showed us what he was really capable of.

At about thirty-five miles an hour Alfredo turned round to face us, sat down on the handlebars and once again stretched out his arms like a circus tightrope walker. I couldn't believe what I was seeing and neither could the rest of the lads. A highway patrolman riding backwards? We all fell about laughing before giving him another round of applause. But Alfredo wasn't finished yet.

I stood slack jawed as he turned back to face the way he was going and momentarily sat on the pillion before easing himself back. He then leaned forward, gripped the handlebars firmly and executed an amazing handstand.

We all whooped with delight at his expert showmanship. I'd been a dispatch rider in my time with the Royal Signals, but I'd never seen anyone perform stunts like this.

Every day after that Alfredo entertained us with the sort of tricks you'd expect from Evel Knievel. But although he seemed to be a terrific guy, he was a wolf in sheep's clothing. We saw the ugly side of him one day when a badly parked pick-up truck blocked our way. After a heated exchange, the poor driver felt the wrong end of Alfredo's baton in a quite unnecessary show of force before being packed off with a torrent of abuse.

Concerned for the beaten truck driver, Alan Ball, Bobby Moore and I started for the door of the coach, but Alf sensibly barred our way.

Alfredo walked up to our coach and we began to protest.

'He should no park here,' said Alfredo. 'He show no respect for this uniform. You are not in England now, my friends, and I am not your London Bobbies. I deal him my way. He don't do it again.'

'I bet he don't,' said Bobby Moore.

Needless to say, our entertainer had lost his audience.

Alf had been meticulous about our healthcare: food, drink . . . even sunbathing was rationed to twenty minutes a day and only around the pool. The one player to get a really good tan was Bobby Moore. I couldn't work out why until David Sadler and Peter Thompson told me that they'd found him up on the roof of the hotel one day catching some illicit rays in a pair of skimpy shorts.

The quarter-final against West Germany was scheduled for Sunday 14 June in León. On the preceding Friday Alf allowed us a beer with our evening meal. I can't remember if the bottle I was served was opened in my presence or not, but I do know that half an hour after drinking it I felt very ill indeed.

I reported to Neil Phillips, our team doctor, who diagnosed a simple stomach upset and prescribed a good night's sleep. I wasn't especially worried – Peter Osgood had earlier been similarly affected and had recovered within twenty-four hours.

I spent most of that night in the loo. On Saturday morning I still felt rough, though well enough to make the 150-mile trip to León. The plan was for us to train on the pitch at the Guanajuato stadium in the afternoon, but on the journey I began to feel decidedly the worse for wear.

The lads were very chirpy. Some played cards, others read, a few just chatted among themselves or watched the scenery. I sat at the back of the coach praying for it to end. I was suffering from terrible stomach cramps and in imminent danger of letting go at either end. I was in a clammy sweat yet shivering with cold, despite the 100°F temperature.

Dr Phillips checked me over and gave me some anti-nausea pills. 'Give it half an hour,' he said, 'you'll feel a lot better,' but I didn't.

When we eventually arrived in León I went straight to bed, then straight to the loo. I stayed there – there was no point in coming out.

There was still the best part of twenty-four hours to go before the game, so it was decided that my situation would be reassessed the following morning. The press boys knew something was wrong, but Alf played things down: 'Gordon is just feeling a little off colour. We expect him to recover after a few hours' rest.'

The trouble was, I was being sick (or worse) so often that I got no rest at all. This was no 'normal' tummy upset. I felt as weak as a kitten. My limbs ached; my stomach cramped. I continued to sweat and shiver as I spent another night camped in the toilet. I felt sorry for my room mate Alex Stepney, but even sorrier for myself.

By Sunday morning I was feeling a little better. I couldn't face a cooked breakfast, but I did manage to keep down two slices of dry toast and some bottled water.

Alf asked me how I was feeling.

'A bit better.'

'Fit enough to play?'

'Well, I'll give it a go,' I said doubtfully.

Alf suggested a fitness test. I'd seen Alf's fitness tests before; they were quite rigorous workouts and I knew that if I passed, I'd be fine for the game against West Germany.

I got changed and went to meet Alf and Harold Shepherdson on the strip of lawn dotted with acacia trees that ran down the side of the hotel. My stomach still wasn't right and I was still feeling weak, but with over three hours to go before the game I felt that, if my improvement continued, I might be OK.

'Gordon, will you jog over to the far tree and back again, please?' said Alf.

I jogged in a leisurely manner to an acacia tree some twelve yards away and returned.

'How do you feel?' Alf asked.

'OK.'

The exercise was repeated.

'How are you now?'

'Still OK.'

'Excellent! Excellent! said Alf. 'Harold will now give you some ball work.'

Alf asked me to walk to a point about eight yards away. As best I could, I bounced up and down on my toes, did some arm stretching and then spat into the palms of my hands ready to stop a few shots.

Harold rolled a ball underarm across the lawn with so little force that it only just reached me. Bemused, I bent down, picked it up and threw it back to Alf.

'Good. Very good,' Alf said. 'Once more, Harold, if you would.'

Harold rolled the ball again, if anything even more softly than before. It had all but stopped moving when I bent down and picked it up.

'How d'you feel?' asked Alf.

'Fine,' I said, still waiting for the fitness test to begin.

'Splendid!' said Alf. 'You're playing.'

I couldn't believe it. What on earth was Alf playing at? I only hoped that he knew what he was doing. I lay down on my bed hoping to get some sleep but almost immediately the sickness gripped me again. I hoped this latest bout would be the bug's parting shot, but it wasn't to be.

The pre-match team meeting was held in Alf's bedroom, there being no conference room available. As Alf began speaking, I began groaning. The stomach cramps had returned with a vengeance. Great beads of sweat formed on my brow, then ran in rivulets down my face. As Alf spoke he kept glancing in my direction. Eventually he addressed me in person.

'Well?' Alf enquired.

I shook my head. 'Not well,' I replied.

Alex Stepney and Nobby Stiles helped me to my feet and I heard Alf tell Peter Bonetti that he was playing in place of me. Still groggy, I walked out of the team meeting and out of the World Cup.

The game kicked off at noon, when the sun was at its zenith, to accommodate the European TV audience. To play in such heat is unwise at the best of times. For me it would have been suicidal. The game was broadcast on Mexican television, but with a time delay, presumably to maximize ticket sales. Thus, when the game kicked off on the television in my room the teams at the stadium were well into the second half.

I was feeling dreadful but my spirits soared as I watched Alan Mullery give us a 1–0 lead at half time with his first goal for England. Five minutes into the second half joy turned to euphoria as I watched a low cross from Keith Newton converted at the far post by Martin Peters. I rubbed my hands with glee: 2–0! The lads were doing England and me proud.

About twenty-five minutes from time the door to my room opened and in shuffled Bobby Moore, Brian Labone, Alan Mullery and Alan Ball. Their faces were grim, but I knew straight away that this was another of their practical jokes – we were still leading on the telly.

'How many did we win by?' I asked.

'Lost 3–2, after extra time,' said Bobby glumly.

'Don't have me on,' I said, 'I'm not in the mood.'

Then Bobby Charlton came in and I froze. Tears were streaming down his face and I knew the awful truth. This was no wind-up.

I struggled out of bed, crossed the room and turned off the TV with us still leading 2–0. To this day that's how I remember the game. We are for ever 2–0 up. I still haven't seen the match in its entirety. I have never been able to bring myself to watch it.

A lot has been said about Alf's tactics that day, and about the performance of Peter Bonetti. Since I haven't watched the game, I can't really comment. In Peter's defence I can say that he was a first-class goalkeeper and that both Alf and I had every confidence in his ability. Obviously, being drafted in at such a late stage gave him no time to prepare mentally for what was the biggest game of his life, but only Peter himself can say with any certainty whether his performance suffered as a result.

What I do know for certain is that Alf was desperate for me to play against West Germany. The ridiculous fitness test apart, Alf is on record as saying, 'The one player I could not do without against West Germany was Gordon Banks.'

After the game the football writer Ken Jones, then of the *Mirror*, found Alf very morose and with a few drinks inside him – both extremely rare occurrences.

'It had to be *him*,' said Alf to the bottom of his glass. 'Of all the players to lose, Ken, it had to be him!'

I am flattered that Alf thought so highly of me, though whether my presence would have made any difference to the result is impossible to say.

Likewise, I can't say whether the offending bottle of beer had been tampered with.

It irks me when some people drag out conspiracy theories to explain a bad result. Following England's 1–0 defeat of Argentina in 2002 some Argentinian supporters alleged that England, FIFA and the referee had contrived to produce an English victory to compensate for Maradona's 'Hand of God' goal in 1986. That sort of rubbish belongs in a fifth-rate thriller movie.

Similarly, I can't believe that anyone could have been so determined to prevent me playing in 1970 that they poisoned me, even though I had eaten the same food as my team mates and drunk from the same case of beer. Still, stranger things have happened. I don't suppose we'll ever know for sure.

Everyone was devastated after the Germany game, no one more so than Peter Bonetti. Peter believed he had let everyone down, though nobody blamed him. The team had always adopted a 'one for all and all for one' philosophy, and that spirit of camaraderie ensured that defeat was accepted collectively. Of course, it didn't make it any easier to swallow as we packed our bags to return 'Back Home'.

In their semi-final West Germany lost 4−3 in extra time to Italy, who in turn lost 4−1 to Brazil in the final.

Brazil's performance in the World Cup final of 1970 was a master class. On that day Brazil firmly planted their flag on the summit of world football. Their success was a triumph for adventurous football of the most sublime quality. The day when the world's most attacking team came up against arguably the world's best defence. Samba soccer took on *catenaccio* and effortlessly swept it aside.

Brazil's triumph was also that of Pelé and of football in general. Following his bitter disappointment of 1966, Pelé had a World Cup swansong to remember. The 'beautiful game' had a beautiful final which produced arguably the most complete performance by the most complete football team in the history of international football.

It would be twelve years before England qualified for another World Cup. At the time, if anyone had told me that England were to spend the seventies and beyond watching from the wings and sliding down FIFA's international rankings, I would have laughed. As a new decade was finding its feet we had not only very good international players, but a number who were world class. How could anyone have foreseen such a rapid and catastrophic decline?

When we arrived home Alf gathered us together for one last chat.

'You've all done me proud and you've done yourselves proud,' he said. 'It has been an honour and a privilege to have you in my charge.'

He then shook every one of us by the hand and thanked us for our efforts before slipping quietly away.

Some of the older players saw this gesture as an epitaph to their international careers. With hindsight, perhaps Alf could see the writing on the wall, and intended it as his own.

16. The Agony and the Ecstasy

Sir Stanley Matthews believed that Stoke City, although never fielding what he classed as a great team, had two that were 'very good'. Those were the one pipped for the Championship on the last day of the season in 1947 and Tony Waddington's side of the early seventies.

I was lucky enough to be a member of the latter when Stoke suffered agonizing defeats in two FA Cup semi-finals and won the League Cup. Cruelly, I was to be denied a place in the side that went so very close to winning the First Division Championship in 1974 for the first time in the club's history, but more of that later.

When I joined Stoke City I believed they were a good side with the potential to be even better. By 1970–71 that potential had been realized under Tony Waddington and Stoke were competing for honours with the best.

We began the season modestly enough. A goalless draw on the opening day against Ipswich Town was followed by two victories and three draws in our next eight league matches. Then, on 26 September, we took on Arsenal at the Victoria Ground. The Gunners boasted the best defensive record in the First Division. They had made a habit of winning games 1–0, earning both their 'boring Arsenal' and 'lucky Arsenal' tags around this time. But though they may have lacked the flamboyance of Manchester United, the flair of Liverpool and the zest of Leeds United, in truth this Arsenal team, containing players such as Frank McLintock, John Radford, Ray Kennedy, George Graham and Charlie George, were a great side. And on that day we tore them to shreds.

We were on song and the normally resolute Gunners defence had no answer. Two goals from John Richie and one each from Terry Conroy, Jimmy Greenhoff and Alan Bloor gave us a convincing 5–0 victory and sent the statisticians searching their records for the last time anyone had gone nap against them.

Terry Conroy's was a marvellous goal. His stinging drive from all of twenty-five yards followed a six-man passing movement and was voted *Match of the Day*'s Goal of the Season. (By coincidence the Arsenal goalkeeper, Bob Wilson, was being sounded out as a potential presenter by the BBC and had been invited on to the programme for a tryout. Poor Bob, on his TV debut, had to pass comment on the five goals he had just conceded!)

Beating Arsenal boosted the confidence of the team immensely, though it was to be in the FA Cup rather than the League where we were to shine that season.

Stoke finished the campaign in mid-table, though we did enjoy some memorable results. Leeds United arrived at the Victoria Ground as leaders of the First Division, and in front of Alf Ramsey we sent them away with their tails between their legs, two goals from John Richie and one from Harry Burrows giving us a 3–0 victory. We also earned a fine goalless draw at Fortress Anfield at a time when few sides ever left with anything more than a cup of tea. Liverpool put us under almost constant pressure and I had to be at my best to deny John Toshack, Phil Boersma and Steve Heighway, all three of whom had me at full stretch.

The Kop gave me a terrific reception before the kick-off. When I acknowledged their applause with a wave they applauded even more. This type of sporting reception was very gratifying, and at most grounds I was given a rousing welcome by the home fans. This was, of course, due largely to my exploits for England, and Bobby Moore, Bobby Charlton and Geoff Hurst told me they too received similar approbation from opposing fans.

It riles me today when I see the likes of David Beckham singled out by the boo boys, even though these so-called 'fans' of football are in the minority. Such treatment is both unjust and unwarranted. To his credit, David has risen above it all with dignity, and is all the more appreciated by true lovers of the game as a result.

March 1971 saw Manchester United at the Victoria Ground. For all my efforts and those of my team mates, there was no stopping

George Best. In this game, George was simply scintillating and his wizardry caused us all manner of problems from start to finish. Wilf McGuinness had just been sacked as manager and Sir Matt Busby had returned to take temporary charge. Perhaps this inspired George, for the Victoria Ground lit up like a Catherine wheel as he displayed his considerable array of skills to the full, culminating in what I believe to be the best goal ever scored against me.

We were defending the Boothen End. George received the ball just outside our penalty area and jinked along our defensive line in search of an opening. Faced with Jackie Marsh and Alan Bloor, George dropped his left shoulder and dummied left, only to drag the ball back and move to his right. It was as if someone had just put a Chubby Checker record on the Tannoy. Jackie and Alan twisted their bodies this way and that as they frantically sought to block his way.

George appeared to be showing too much of the ball. Eric Skeels came charging in for the tackle, his left boot extended, while George danced joyously on his toes before making the ball do a disappearing act and watching Eric slide by. Denis Smith and Mike Pejic then offered themselves up for humiliation. George duly obliged, motioning towards them before curling his foot around the ball and dragging away to his left. A three-yard burst of speed and he was free. That left just yours truly between him and the goal.

I came rushing out to cut down the angle. A goalkeeper faced with a one-on-one situation has to keep his eyes on the ball, not the opponent. George's left boot flashed over the ball. I made to go down to my right when his right boot took the ball the opposite way. I immediately adjusted my position and prepared to spread-eagle myself at his feet. But with another drop of a shoulder, George veered away to my right. Unbalanced I rocked on my heels before flopping down unceremoniously on my backside in the muddy goalmouth like an unsteady toddler. George, as if out for a stroll in the park, leisurely rolled the ball into the net. For a brief moment there was silence, then the whole of the Victoria Ground burst into appreciative applause.

George didn't sprint over to the United supporters and strut like a peacock before them; didn't run to his team mates for a schoolgirl embrace, then push them aside and make them play kiss-chase. He simply walked back to the centre line, his arm half-raised in acknowledgement of the applause he so richly deserved.

I wouldn't have thought it possible for any player to bamboozle so many defenders in such a small space. That George did was a truly remarkable demonstration of his skills. He shook off five quality defenders the way a dog shakes water off its back before dumping me on my arse in the mud. Such golden memories are treasured for ever, even by those on the receiving end.

Stanley Matthews, who was at the game, summed it up in five words: 'Stoke one, George Best two.'

On the wall of my study is a sequential series of photographs that shows George's goal. I often look at them and wonder how he managed it and I still haven't worked it out. They are a constant reminder to me of how privileged I am to have played against a man of such breathtaking brilliance. As a footballer, he was a genius.

Two months later I was facing that genius again, this time for England against Northern Ireland at Windsor Park. The first half was a very tight affair, with neither side able to break the deadlock. I'd just saved from Middlesbrough's Eric McMordie and was preparing to kick the ball upfield.

George positioned himself in front of me to try to put me off, as forwards often used to do. I veered around him and threw the ball up to kick. As I tossed it, George struck like a viper. He suddenly raised a boot and managed to flick the ball away from me. The ball, still airborne, headed for the goalmouth and we jostled each other like two schoolboys on sports day as both of us raced to reach it first. George leaned forward, extended his neck and managed to head the ball into the net. Windsor Park erupted, first with cheers and then with catcalls as the referee awarded a free kick against George for dangerous play. George was furious.

For days this audacious piece of opportunism fuelled much debate on television and in the papers, but the consensus of opinion was that the referee had been right to disallow the goal. In the end England won the match with a goal from Allan Clarke, but all anyone ever remembers of that game is George's lightning reaction to a ball tossed eighteen inches in the air. Whenever I meet George nowadays I often have cause to remind him of the perfect timing he used to demonstrate – he's a hopeless timekeeper and invariably turns up late!

The 1970–71 season saw Stoke City embark on a thrilling FA Cup run that was to end in heartache and controversy.

It began with a 2–1 success over Millwall. We then dispatched Huddersfield Town, though only after two replays. In round five we beat Ipswich Town after a replay, and then met Hull City at snowswept Boothferry Park where the home side gave us one almighty scare.

A crowd of 42,000 packed the second-division side's ground to see Hull race into a 2–0 lead, both goals coming from Ken Wagstaff. Terry Conroy gave us hope when scoring right on half time, and two second-half goals from John Richie crowned a remarkable comeback. But Hull wouldn't lie down. In the last ten minutes they piled on the pressure. It was backs-to-the-wall stuff and I had to be at my best to deny Chris Chilton and Ken Houghton. When the referee finally blew after six minutes of injury time it was a blessed relief to us all.

The semi-finals pitched us against Arsenal at Hillsborough. The Stoke fans were gripped by cup fever and our allocation of 27,500 tickets sold out in four hours. Arsenal were on course for a league and cup double and came into the match on the back of a run that had seen them win fourteen of their last sixteen games.

But we didn't fear them. After all, we'd beaten them 5–0 back in September. Tony Waddington told us to take the game to Arsenal from the start. To hustle and harass in midfield and destroy their rhythm. That was just fine by us. The cavalier football we were known for quickly, if somewhat fortunately, produced dividends when an attempted clearance from Peter Storey ricocheted off Denis Smith's body and into the Arsenal net for a freak goal.

After half an hour we doubled our lead when a Charlie George back pass was pounced on by John Richie.

Though Arsenal were a team never beaten until the final whistle, I really did think we were going to do it. Then, just after half time, Peter Storey pulled a goal back and the jitters set in. Perhaps owing to a lack of big-match experience among many of the side, we began to panic. We didn't display the calm authority required to play the ball out of defence. We conceded possession too often and Arsenal were not the sort of side to give it back again without a fight.

None the less, we weathered the storm and with the game deep into injury time it looked as if we were Wembley bound. With a final throw of the dice, George Armstrong played the ball into my penalty area. In jumping to collect it I was bundled over by a marauding yellow shirt. I thought the referee, Pat Partridge from Middlesbrough, would award us a free kick for the foul, but I looked up to see him pointing to the corner flag. We protested, of course, but when has player power ever changed a referee's mind once made up?

When the corner came across, my old Leicester team mate Frank McLintock headed it goalwards. I was left stranded. John Mahoney did a passable impression of me by diving full-length and tipping the ball to safety with his hand. It was all John could do, and you didn't get sent off for it in those days. Peter Storey's mishit penalty threw me completely and Arsenal had their draw.

Again, inexperience had a lot to do with the result of the replay. Only Jimmy Greenhoff and I had played in an FA Cup final, and I was the only current England international at the club, though Terry Conroy was a regular with the Republic of Ireland. Many of my team mates were devastated to concede an equalizer resulting from a disputed corner so late in the game. Arsenal, meanwhile, had been thrown a lifeline.

They grasped it like a drowning man. At Villa Park we never came anywhere near to repeating the sterling performance we had given at Hillsborough. Arsenal won 2–0 and were, in truth, by far the better side.

★

The following season we again reached the FA Cup semi-final. Again our opponents were Arsenal. Again the match went to a replay and, incredibly, once more a terrible mistake on the part of an official was to rob us of glory.

Having dispensed with my old club Chesterfield in round three, we then beat Tranmere Rovers and, for the second year running, Hull City, before being drawn away to Manchester United in the sixth round.

The 54,000 at Old Trafford saw a United team that included George Best, Denis Law, Willie Morgan and three members of the England squad of 1970: Bobby Charlton, Alex Stepney and David Sadler. Jimmy Greenhoff put us in front and we somehow weathered the resultant United pressure. Minutes from time, however, a piece of magic from George Best (who else?) gave United a replay.

A capacity crowd of just over 49,000 at the Victoria Ground witnessed a thrilling second encounter between the sides. That man Best (again) gave United a lead on seventy minutes that our centre half Denis Smith cancelled out four minutes later.

This was a personal triumph for Denis, who is listed in the *Guinness Book of Records* as being Britain's most-injured professional footballer. Denis was a one-club man and in seventeen years at Stoke City broke his leg five times, his nose on four occasions and his ankle and collar bones once. He also sustained a chipped spine, six broken fingers and received over 100 facial stitches. When Denis finally hung up his boots in 1982, Terry Conroy – who nicknamed him 'Lucky' – said, 'If Lucky had carried on playing for another season, BUPA would have gone bust.'

It says much for Denis's character, fortitude and combative spirit that, when he wasn't in A&E, he was a super centre half, one who never held back in a tackle. He was a rock in that Stoke City defence and is unfortunate not to have a few England caps to display in his cabinet alongside his plaster casts.

Just before our replay against Manchester United, the injury-prone Denis put his back out in training. It was so painful and debilitating that he was immediately declared unfit for the tie. Like the trooper he was, however, Denis still wanted to come along and cheer us on. As he was getting out of his car on the evening of the game, he bent forward and, amazingly, his spine righted itself. Denis immediately marched into Tony Waddington's office and declared himself fit.

Denis's equalizer took the game into extra time. I somehow managed to keep out efforts from George Best and Bobby Charlton before Terry Conroy sealed what had been an amazing night for Stoke, and for Denis Smith in particular, by hitting a great half-volley past Alex Stepney to take us into the semi-finals.

Hillsborough again. Arsenal again. George Armstrong gave them the lead two minutes after half time. On this occasion, however, we didn't capitulate as we had at Villa Park the previous season and concerted pressure on the Arsenal goal produced a deserved equalizer on sixty-five minutes.

Bob Wilson had earlier been injured when collecting a cross and the forward John Radford had replaced him in goal. We immediately put him under severe pressure with high balls and our second such effort produced the equalizer. Peter Dobing drove a centre into the Arsenal penalty area. John hesitated and Peter Simpson, under pressure from Denis Smith, headed into his own goal. It was just what we needed. We took the game to Arsenal and only some desperate defending on their part, and the width of a post, denied us the winner.

'History repeats itself,' said the eminent historian A. J. P. Taylor, 'and that's its biggest failing.' Having been denied victory over Arsenal in controversial circumstances in the previous year's semi-final, no one expected that another error of judgement by a match official would once again wreck our chances of reaching Wembley. That, however, is exactly what happened in the replay at Goodison Park.

Geoff Barnett in goal for the injured Bob Wilson was the only team change that night. In the opening exchanges, Alan Ball fizzed for Arsenal. George Graham also gave us problems but Denis Smith and Alan Bloor kept a tight rein on John Radford and Charlie George, and we rode out Arsenal's initial pressure and began to exert a little of our own.

On twenty minutes Jimmy Greenhoff burst into the Arsenal penalty area and was sent sprawling by the outstretched leg of Frank McLintock. Jimmy picked himself up, dusted himself down, took the penalty and nearly ripped the net off its hooks.

Arsenal had a reputation for coming back more times than the postman, and they got back into this game in controversial circumstances. On fifty-five minutes George Armstrong cut in from the left with Peter Dobing at his side. Both players were jostling for possession. Arms were flailing, shoulders leaning in. Suddenly George fell over and I was horrified to see the referee, Keith Walker, point to the penalty spot. To my mind, it had been six of one and half a dozen of the other. Charlie George stepped up to take the kick and pinged the ball to my left. Arsenal were level.

We thought ourselves hard done by, but ten minutes later worse was to follow. Following a spell of pressure from Stoke, Frank McLintock played a long ball out of defence. John Radford was well offside when Frank played the ball but, hearing no whistle from the referee, John did the professional thing and kept on coming. I came off my line but John swept away to my left and planted the ball firmly into the back of the net. The referee had been caught out by the swiftness of the Arsenal counter-attack and, like most of the Stoke team, had not been up with play when Radford received the ball.

Well, that's what linesmen are supposed to be there for, and Mr Walker decided to consult his. The linesman had been well placed, and we were all confident that the correct decision would soon be forthcoming. The pair exchanged a few words and I was stunned when the referee then turned and pointed to the centre circle. Goal to Arsenal.

If we were angry before, we were livid now. I sprinted up to the referee while Jackie Marsh and a posse of Stoke players besieged the linesman. For a moment there was chaos. The Stoke supporters were incensed, the Arsenal fans ecstatic. Press cameras popped and flashed and Jackie Marsh subjected the beleaguered official to a verbal tirade that would have made a navvy blush. As ever, it was all to no avail. The goal stood and we exited the FA Cup in cruel circumstances for the second successive season.

Our dressing room was like a morgue. Jackie summed it up for everyone when he said, 'I'd rather us be beaten 4–0 and know we had lost fair and square than go out like that.'

The TV highlights conclusively proved that Radford had been offside when receiving the ball. The programme also explained why his goal had been allowed.

To avoid a colour clash, both teams had worn their second strips. Arsenal wore yellow shirts and blue shorts, Stoke played in all white. When the ball had been played up to John Radford, the linesman had apparently mistaken an Everton steward in a white coat on the far side of the pitch for a Stoke City player.

It proved to be a very costly mistake for Stoke City, one that generated not only bitter disappointment but bitter feelings. After the match the football reporter John Bean asked Jackie Marsh what had been the game's turning point. 'When the linesman turned up,' replied Jackie.

Consolation for the Potters and their marvellous supporters came in the League Cup, though our route to Wembley was far from easy. Including the final, it took us twelve matches to win it – a League Cup record. Our semi-final against West Ham remains the longest League Cup tie ever. It involved four matches; the first took place on 8 December and the tie was not concluded until 26 January.

Our League Cup campaign began modestly with a 2–1 win over Southport, a game I missed through injury. Few teams win a trophy without enjoying a slice of luck and we had ours in the following round at Oxford United. We could easily have gone out of the competition that night. Oxford dominated the match for long periods but we managed to come away with a 1–1 draw and comfortably won the return at the Victoria Ground.

There then followed three epic ties against Manchester United. Having drawn both at Old Trafford and Stoke, we faced United for a third time. They arrived at the Victoria Ground as leaders of the First Division and struck the first blow after thirty-seven minutes when George Best hit a screaming right-foot drive into the top corner of my net. United, and George Best in particular, were rampant, but in the second half the experienced George Eastham proved his worth to Stoke by taking control of the midfield.

United had been running us ragged, but George started to put his foot on the ball and slow the pace of the game. With George orchestrating matters from the middle of the park we slowly took control. Peter Dobing returned the scores to parity on seventy minutes. Then, with only two minutes remaining, John Richie leapt above every United defender to head home a George Eastham corner.

Over 33,000 turned up at Eastville to see us beat Bristol Rovers 4–2 in the fifth round and set up a tasty semi-final clash against West Ham United and my good pals Bobby Moore and Geoff Hurst.

Things didn't go to plan in the first leg at Stoke. A penalty from Geoff Hurst and a goal from Clyde Best overturned the lead Peter Dobing had given us. We believed we could turn the tie round at Upton Park though, and our implicit belief in our own ability was not misplaced.

West Ham were a superb footballing side, but we felt we had the measure of them. The second leg was an epic. John Richie scored deep into the second half to send the tie into extra time with an aggregate score of 2–2. There wasn't a cigarette paper's width between the two teams and with three minutes of extra time remaining, a replay looked almost certain. Then again, nothing is certain in football.

I managed to parry a shot from Geoff Hurst. When the ball ran loose an almighty goalmouth scramble ensued, the ball becoming a pinball as the West Ham players fired one shot after another only for it to cannon back repeatedly from a thicket of legs. I decided to seize the initiative.

I had drummed into my defenders that, if I shouted 'keeper's', they would leave the ball regardless. The ball skidded across the mud towards Mike Pejic, who was standing in front of me. 'Keeper's!' I shouted. Mike seemed not to have heard me, for he shaped to clear. I relaxed, only to see Mike lift his foot to let the ball go. I scrambled madly for the loose ball, fumbled it, snatched at it and watched it squirm away from me. Harry Redknapp came across in front of me and I put my hand around his midriff and yanked him to one side. In my view, Harry was obstructing me, but Keith Walker, the referee, didn't see it my way and awarded a penalty. I was furious, not with the ref but with Mike Pejic.

Up stepped my old mate Geoff Hurst. As he ran up to take the kick, an eerie silence descended on Upton Park. Geoff usually relied on sheer power when taking penalties and it looked as though he was really going to hit this one. When Geoff had scored from a penalty in the first leg, he'd taken a long run-up and hit the ball to my right. I got a hand to it, but couldn't keep it out. Now Geoff was again taking the same sort of run-up.

I thought, 'He's not going to change here. I'll gamble,' and hurled myself to the right as he thumped it at shoulder height to that side.

I was flying through the air with both arms pointing skywards. Geoff had hit the ball so hard that I couldn't afford to have 'soft' hands. I tensed the muscles in my arm and wrist and, to my great relief, watched the ball ricochet up off my hand and over the bar.

My team mates could hardly believe their eyes. They ran up to me en masse to shower congratulations. We were still in the League Cup.

A press photographer captured that save from behind the goal. It's one of my favourite photographs, and often turns up in books about football (including this one), though I haven't got a copy myself. It's very atmospheric, with the floodlighting piercing the gloom from above. Geoff and I are all action while three Stoke defenders stand hands on hips in resigned immobility. The pitch looks like a ploughed field and my jersey is caked in mud. I like the photograph, not only because it encapsulates how British football used to be, but also because it captures both the drama and the atmosphere of the occasion.

And on the packed terraces, not a single replica shirt is to be seen.

Over the years football photography has changed almost as much as the sport itself. Most of today's press reports are accompanied by a shot of two players in competition for the ball in pin-sharp detail. Telephoto lenses are wonderful, but the close-cropped images they produce exclude the bigger picture entirely. This narrow focus on the individual at the expense of the panoramic is an apt symbol of the way the game is today.

That shot of my penalty save is both imaginative and evocative. British football in winter was a leathery, muddy, kipper-lunged occasion, a social glue to hold us together through the dark days. The photograph captures that world perfectly.

It took another two games for Stoke City finally to beat West Ham and create club history by reaching Wembley for the first time. Our opponents there were Chelsea. They were the bookies' favourites, but our confidence was sky high. Chelsea were stylish and swaggering. In Alan Hudson, Charlie Cooke, Peter Houseman and Peter Osgood they boasted players with as much flair as their flared trousers. Dave Sexton's side were far from being simply a collection of footballing Liberaces, however. Dave Webb, Paddy Mulligan and Ron Harris provided them with steel and backbone. They were a formidable team, but on the big day they were not quite formidable enough.

Terry Conroy gave us the lead with a choice header following a cross from George Eastham. Following his goal, Terry appeared to go off into a dream. I'd seen this sort of thing happen before – a good player makes a great start to a big game, scores, then thinks that his afternoon's work is over.

Seeing Terry start to coast, I shouted to Jackie Marsh to get upfield and snap him out of his stupor. A few well-chosen words from Jackie did the trick and Terry was soon back to his old self, hustling and harassing the Chelsea defence, making darting runs across our front line and tracking back with John Dempsey when Chelsea pushed forward.

With the half-time interval approaching, Chelsea put themselves back into the game. Alan Bloor uncharacteristically failed to clear his lines and the ball found its way to the feet of Peter Osgood. Peter stumbled as he was about to shoot, which threw me completely. I hesitated for a moment and Peter, lying on the ground, hooked the ball past me. We went into half time level.

Both sides battled to gain the upper hand in the second half. Things were evenly balanced but the deadlock was broken after seventy-three minutes, thankfully by us. Terry Conroy beat Ron Harris and his far-post cross found John Richie, who cushioned the ball back into the path of the onrushing Jimmy Greenhoff. Jimmy hit one of his trademark volleys, Peter Bonetti parried and there was the oldest player on the pitch, George Eastham, to prod the ball home. That breakthrough proved to be decisive. We won 2–1.

George, at 35 years and 161 days, became the oldest recipient of a League Cup winner's medal, while the win gave me my second such gong and not a little satisfaction. My belief on joining Stoke that they would win honours had proved well founded. Happily I joined my team mates and the population of Stoke in celebrating our success to the full.

When a team from the provinces wins a major trophy for the first time, the players and supporters go overboard. For days the city of Stoke took on a carnival atmosphere. Production in the potteries and coal mines of North Staffordshire suddenly rose dramatically. The council gave us a civic banquet and over a quarter of a million people thronged the streets to see us parade the Cup. The Lord Mayor, Arthur Cholerton, was in the process of twinning Stoke with a town in Germany. At the civic banquet Mr Cholerton told us that his German counterpart had asked him, 'Where is Stoke?' 'It's where the League Cup is,' replied Cholerton.

Our success closed a marathon season. We played a total of sixty-seven league and cup matches in 1971–72, not to mention friendlies and internationals. Our full back Jackie Marsh played sixty-five games that season, plus four friendlies. Did I mention our rotation system? When you collapsed from exhaustion, you got a game off!

To cap what had been a great season for me, I had the honour
of being voted the football writers' Footballer of the Year. I was
very proud to be the first goalkeeper to receive this prestigious title
since my boyhood hero, Bert Trautmann, in 1956. I was delighted
not just from a personal point of view, but also because the award
acknowledged the importance of goalkeeping in general. As if to
emphasize the point, Tottenham's Pat Jennings won it the following
season.

When we were together in the England squad I was forever 'selling'
Stoke City to Geoff Hurst. I firmly believed Stoke had a team good
enough to win the First Division title. I kept telling Geoff that if
he wanted to top up his collection of trophies with a Championship
medal he could do worse than take a trip to the Potteries. When
West Ham decided to sell Geoff, I made sure that Tony Waddington
knew about it.

Geoff signed for Stoke City in August 1972 and immediately
made his presence felt in a team with high hopes of challenging the
likes of Liverpool, Leeds and Arsenal for the Championship. On
21 October we travelled to Anfield, where we lost 2–1. Just another
game, I thought. In fact, it was to be my last in English football.

The following day I went to the Victoria Ground for treatment
on a minor injury sustained against Liverpool. Driving home, I
came up behind a slower car. The road was flanked by trees and
dipped before taking a sharp turn to the right. Not exactly the best
place to overtake, but I was keen to be home with Ursula and her
Sunday dinner. I pulled out to pass and suddenly found myself on
a collision course with an oncoming vehicle. I slammed my foot
on the brake as a prickle of adrenalin rushed across my forehead. There was an almighty bang. There was the sound of glass
shattering. Then there was nothing.

I've never liked the smell of hospitals. That stuffy, clinical fug was
the first thing I sensed when I awoke from a deep, drug-induced
sleep. I tried to open my eyes but nothing happened. It was as if
someone had glued down my eyelids. I broke out in a cold sweat.

I started to panic. A cool, clean, gentle hand held mine. Another hand eased me forward, then guided me back on to a tower of crisp pillows.

The nurse gave me a welcome cup of tea. She told me I had been in the operating theatre. That I'd had surgery on my eyes.

'How bad is it?' I asked.

'You can't see out of your left eye because it's so swollen. But that should clear up in a day or two,' she said.

'And my other eye?'

'The surgeon will explain when he comes to see you,' she said. 'You've had a very delicate operation.'

It seemed an eternity before the surgeon eventually arrived. 'The operation went well, Gordon,' he said. 'It lasted three hours. I had to do a lot of repair work; fragments of the windscreen perforated your right eye. I'm afraid there has been damage to the retina.'

It took all the courage I had to ask him the inevitable question. 'Am I going to lose it?'

'It will be a couple of weeks before I know for sure. With damage like this there can be all manner of complications.'

'But am I going to lose my eye?' I asked again.

'I'm afraid I couldn't put the chances at better than evens.'

Three days later the swelling on my left eye had gone down enough for me to see. I asked for a mirror. I was not a pretty sight. When a nurse arrived to change my dressing, the full extent of my injuries was revealed in gory detail. I had more than 200 stitches running from my face to my scalp. I was later to discover that the surgeon had also inserted over 100 micro-stitches inside the socket of my right eye and around the periphery of the retina. I had no idea what a surgeon earned, but in my book it could never be enough.

I can't put into words the extent to which the love and support of Ursula, our children and the rest of our family helped me through the most harrowing and desperate days of my life. Nor can I praise highly enough my surgeon or the doctors, nurses and other members of the North Staffordshire Hospital who gave me such tender care. Even today the kindness and love I felt from everybody brings a lump to my throat.

As the days passed I made a concerted effort to come to terms with my disability. At first I thought I could simply carry on as before. Then I leaned over to pick up a cup of tea from my bedside table and was shocked to grasp thin air. That's when the reality of my situation really hit home. I prayed that when the dressing was removed I would still be able to see through my right eye. I remember thinking, If I can't even get the angle right to pick up a cup of tea, how will I ever judge the flight of a football again? Football was all I knew. How could I provide for my family if I didn't have that?

My accident was big news. Tony Waddington held frequent press conferences, but still every day Ursula opened the curtains of our home in Madeley Heath to see a knot of photographers camped at the end of the drive.

Tony turned up at our home one day to find thirty pressmen blocking his way and Ursula in tears. The pressure was getting too much for her. Tony pleaded with them to give my family a break, and offered to act as spokesman and provide regular bulletins. Most understood, although one photographer was to overstep the mark.

The doctors at the North Staffs decided that my left eye had recovered sufficiently for me to watch a little television. I was in a private room with no TV, so a set was sent for. It duly arrived, carried by a man wearing a doctor's white coat. He placed the television on a table and then, to my utter astonishment, produced a camera from the folds of his coat.

'It's like trying to get into Fort Knox, trying to get in here,' he said cheerfully. 'I had to slip the TV engineer a tenner. Just one shot of you, Gordon? We'll make it worth your while.'

I don't swear as a rule, but rules are made to be broken and I told that photographer in no uncertain terms where he could insert his camera and his money.

When the real TV engineer arrived I was ready to administer another tongue-lashing, but it transpired that the photographer hadn't bribed the engineer at all, just conned him into believing that he was a close personal friend of mine.

When the surgeon eventually removed the dressing I thought my prayers had been answered. I could see out of my right eye, even though everything was a blur and when people were close to me they became shadowy dark shapes. My hopes and spirits soared, especially when the surgeon told me there was a 50–50 chance that my vision would continue to improve with time. On the downside, there was an equal chance of it deteriorating, but I didn't want to think about that.

I was discharged from hospital with a brand-new eyepatch. My kids called me Captain Pugwash. I took things easy and thanked God that I had survived the crash to be with my family. After six weeks of rest and love I was feeling good, and told Tony Wadding-ton my recovery was such that I was ready for a little light training.

Just to be back at the ground and among the lads gave me a tremendous lift. I was very hopeful of a full recovery, and perhaps even a successful comeback.

Time passed and everything was going well. On my previous visit the eye surgeon had been both impressed and pleased with the progress I had made. The sight in my right eye had improved sufficiently for me to read the calendar hanging on his wall and count the bulbs in his chandelier, though I still had to wear the eyepatch to guard against infection.

I was sitting in our living room looking out at the garden when I decided to lift my patch to see whether the improvement was continuing. I did so and was immediately gripped by fear. Some-thing was very wrong. I closed my left eye and the world went black. I was half blind.

The surgeon informed me that there was nothing more he could do. The edifice of hope I'd erected during the weeks since the crash came tumbling around my ears. Once again I struggled to come to terms with my predicament. I had overcome some enor-mous obstacles during my career in football, but now I was up against the biggest and most difficult challenge of my life. I called on every drop of strength, fortitude and resolve I could muster, and told Ursula that I wasn't going to wallow in a trough of self-pity. That not only was I going to come to terms with my situation, I was going to fight it.

'God's been good,' I said to her. 'I'm still here, and so are you, Robert, Wendy and Julia. That's the most important thing. As for the football – I'm going to play again.'

17. Striking Back

I received literally thousands of letters from well-wishers. Many were from people who had suffered similar injuries; one, from a little girl who sent me a wonderful drawing of herself which I still have, was especially touching. I was deeply moved by every single letter, but owing to their sheer number – one day twelve sackloads arrived – I simply couldn't reply to each one in person. I know that three decades have passed, but I'd like to take this opportunity of thanking everyone who sent me messages of sympathy and support. Your letters and cards were a great source of strength to both me and my family, and I will be forever grateful to you all for your heartfelt words of encouragement.

Tony Waddington allowed me a six-month period of adjustment. I commenced with light training and gradually built up my programme over the months. My eyesight was checked periodically and I underwent numerous tests to see how I coped with the speed, flight and direction of the ball. After the six months were up, Tony asked the $64-million question: 'Can you play on?'

It was the question I'd been asking myself for weeks. It had lain there at the forefront of my thoughts, ticking away like a time-bomb. I could avoid answering it no longer.

'Tony, you've been a great boss,' I told him. 'You've always been honest with me and I've got to be honest with you. I think you know as well as I do what the answer is.'

Tony slowly nodded his head. 'I've seen you in training. Personally speaking, I think you could still do us a job,' he said.

'I could,' I told him, 'but not the job that I used to do. I don't want that, Tony. If I can't meet the standards I set for myself, I'm going to have to call it a day.'

It was the summer of 1973. My career as a football league goalkeeper was over. Tony gave me a job as coach to Stoke's youth team, with a brief to offer specialist coaching to young goalkeepers.

The first day I gathered my young charges together I was dumb-founded. Of all the apprentices on the club's books, there was not a single goalkeeper! The lad who wore the jersey was a part-timer who trained two evenings a week.

The club were very supportive and granted me a testimonial. It was a great night. All my former England colleagues turned up to play, along with several stars from around the world. I was treated to the unique sight of Bobby Charlton running out of the tunnel alongside Eusebio, both wearing the red and white stripes of Stoke City.

Seeing Bobby Charlton and Eusebio playing for Stoke was not the only surprise I had that year. I travelled to London thinking I was about to do some promotional work for a company. The meeting was to take place in the lounge bar of a well-known hotel. For some minutes I hung about wondering where the representatives of the company were. I was suddenly aware of a man at my shoulder. I turned and was surprised to see Eamonn Andrews holding the Big Red Book in his hand.

'Tonight, Gordon Banks,' he said, 'this is your life!'

I was whisked away in a daze to a television studio were Ursula, Robert, Wendy, Julia, my mum and other members of my family were waiting to spill the beans.

One by one their disembodied voices sounded behind the scenes before revealing themselves to me and the nation. Members of my immediate family were followed by close friends, staff from the North Staffs Hospital, Tony Waddington, my former Stoke City team mates, Alf Ramsey, ex-England colleagues, old school chums and two guys I couldn't place and still can't. Just when I thought one of my best pals had more important things to do, a voice from behind the screen said, 'You're getting old, Banksy. You used to hold on to them.'

Good old Bobby. I should have known he'd never let me down.

I was happy coaching, but gnawing away at me was a desire to be playing again. In 1976 the opportunity came. I received a call from a representative of Fort Lauderdale Strikers asking if I would like to play for them in the NASL, the recently formed North American Soccer League. Although itching to get back between the sticks, I needed some time to think about it, but as I discussed the matter with my family and Tony Waddington it became increasingly clear that there was only one answer: Florida here I come. Tony, who agreed wholeheartedly with my decision, even promised me that there would always be a job for me at Stoke as a coach as long as he was manager.

The NASL had been founded in 1968 when the United Soccer Association and the National Professional Soccer League of America merged. The NASL sold franchises throughout the USA and Canada, giving rise to such teams as Atlanta Chiefs, Vancouver Whitecaps, Tulsa Roughnecks, Kansas City Spurs, Chicago Sting, Tampa Bay Rowdies, New York Cosmos, Los Angeles Aztecs and, of course, Fort Lauderdale Strikers.

Soccer was a minor sport in America, played in the main by children and college students. It received hardly any coverage in the newspapers, or on TV. In order for the NASL to compete against baseball, American football, basketball and ice hockey, the teams' home-grown players and international journeymen were bolstered by major stars from Europe and South America who were nearing the end of their careers.

The money was good, the level of football wasn't bad and the lifestyle was amazing. Such working conditions attracted the likes of Pelé, Carlos Alberto, Luigi Riva, Dino Zoff, Gianni Rivera, Giacinto Facchetti, Eusebio, Gerd Muller, Franz Beckenbauer, Uwe Seeler, Johann Cruyff and Teofilo Cubillas. The sizeable British contingent included at various times Bobby Moore, George Best, George Graham, Rodney Marsh, Tony Waiters, Trevor Hockey and Charlie Cooke.

The NASL boasted some world-class players, but I'd been told that many of the games were little more than keenly contested exhibition matches. Though I knew I now had no place in the competitive maelstrom of English league football, I thought the comparatively relaxed nature of the American version would be ideal for me. In truth, the standard of football in the NASL was higher than I had been led to believe. It was certainly on a par with the upper reaches of what is now the Nationwide First Division. A good standard indeed.

I flew out to Fort Lauderdale but, before putting pen to paper, the club insisted I undergo a medical. At the clinic a white-coated doctor took a series of X-rays, then gave me a thorough examination. The X-rays were developed before he'd finished. He slotted them into a lightbox and tutted.

'Mr Banks, what's this I can see in your right knee?'

'That's a metal pin I had inserted some time ago in England,' I said.

'Uh-huh. Right. I see. Um . . . there also appears to be some sort of plate in your right elbow.'

'When I was a young player, I shattered my elbow. The metal plate is to strengthen it and aid movement.'

More um-ing and ah-ing. He seemed to reach a decision.

'Mr Banks, could you stand upright, then bend and touch your toes for me?'

'I'm afraid I can't. I get very stiff knees. Although I can get down to a ball OK, I can't bend and touch my toes.'

That foxed him. He gave me a funny look and made a note on his pad.

'OK, Mr Banks,' he said, 'let's try something else. Place your left hand over your right eye. Now, can you read the top and second line on that eyechart for me.'

'Read it? I know him. He played for Czechoslovakia.'

He didn't even smile. 'Just read the top and second lines, please,' he said.

I did as I was asked. He was delighted. At last he had found something I could do.

'Good! Now can you place your right hand over your left eye and read the same two lines.'

'Ah, well, there we have a problem,' I told him. 'I have no sight whatsoever in that eye.'

The doctor looked at me sternly. 'Mr Banks, are you on the level? You're telling me that you can only see out of one eye?'

37. Doing some pre-season training of my own around the lanes of Cheshire in 1972.

38. My favourite photograph. Saving Geoff Hurst's penalty in the 1972 League Cup semi-final second leg at a very atmospheric Upton Park. The poses struck by my Stoke team-mates suggest they were expecting Geoff to score!

39. I celebrate Stoke City's victory over West Ham in the semi-final of the League Cup in 1972. This was our fourth meeting, at Old Trafford, and the longest League Cup tie ever.

40. I check that the laces of John Dempsey's boots are correctly tied during the League Cup final of 1972 between Stoke City and Chelsea.

41. A great day for Stoke City and George Eastham. After our epic win against Chelsea in 1972 I congratulate the scorer of Stoke's winning goal. At 35 years and 161 days old, George remains the oldest recipient of a League Cup winner's medal.

42. My son Robert puts me through my paces at our home in Madeley Heath. I even worked out the angle and my positioning for this one.

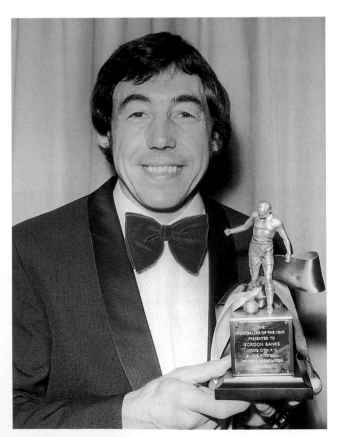

43. A great moment for me. Receiving my Footballer of the Year award in 1972. I was the first goalkeeper to win it since my boyhood hero Bert Trautmann in 1956. The following year, Pat Jennings won.

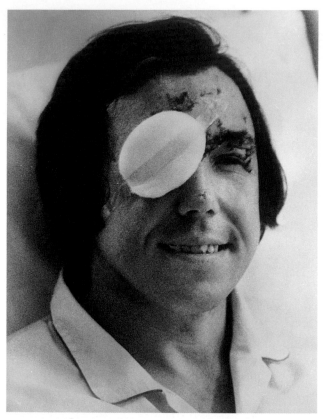

44. Still managing a smile after my near-fatal car crash in 1972. I wouldn't let my disability beat me. Encouraged by my family and literally thousands of well-wishers, I was to make a comeback in America.

45. My Ford Consul after the crash in October 1972 which resulted in me losing the sight in my right eye.

46. Ursula and Wendy sift through thousands of letters from well-wishers received after my accident.

47. *This is Your Life*. Left to right, front: my brothers Michael and David, Ursula, Wendy, Julia, me, Tony Waddington (on my left shoulder), Robert, Geoff Hurst and Bobby Moore.

48. In action for Fort Lauderdale Strikers. Following the loss of my eye, the decision to play again had been the most difficult of my life. Here, George Graham (8) decides to test out the strength of my ribcage.

49. *Below*: With my good friend George Best in the colours of the Strikers. George scored what I believe to be the best-ever goal against me. Quite simply, he was a football genius.

50. Pelé visits Wembley prior to England's last game there against Germany in the qualifying group for the 2002 World Cup. I was coaching some youngsters when my old friend turned up. I think the love and respect Pelé and I have for one another are obvious.

51. Working on the book with friend and collaborator Les Scott.

'Yes, but apart from that and the knees and the elbow, I'm fine.'

'Sir, what position do you hope to play for the Strikers?' he asked.

'Er, I'm the goalkeeper,' I said sheepishly.

I took to life in Florida, and American soccer, straight away. In England I had been used to playing on Christmas-pudding pitches. Every pitch in the NASL was like a bowling green. Though I loved North Staffordshire (and still do), my route to work there passed pottery banks, a murky canal and grimy factories, usually beneath a sky the colour of a non-stick frying pan. When I drove to the Strikers stadium I did so down avenues of trees like candelabra and past delis where the Danish pastries in the windows were displayed like art. The sun, which always seemed to be shining, had the intensity of gold leaf and felt like a warm hand caressing your face.

I've never been a great fan of driving for driving's sake, but I enjoyed cruising around Fort Lauderdale just for fun. I'd drive around the downtown district past the myriad parks and promenades, then along the north shore of the New River that snakes through the city. I'd take in the shops, galleries and sidewalk cafés on Las Olas Boulevard, then drive over the arching intracoastal bridge that leads to the ocean.

My apartment was spacious, light and airy. My building fronted a billiard-table lawn that drifted down to the sidewalk, passing on the way a large eucalyptus tree around which it flowed like a cool green tide around a rock. It looked as if Jackson Pollock's palette had been tipped over the flower beds, so diverse were their colours. The streets were free of litter, the service in the shops, restaurants and cafés was faultless and the amenities of the city first class. The quality of life there was so much better than I had ever experienced. I loved it.

I also loved the football, though it was a world away from what I had been used to. There were six points for a win, for a start. Should a match end level, it was decided by a series of one-on-one confrontations between striker and goalkeeper, the winners of which were awarded four points. Teams also received a bonus point for every goal scored, up to a maximum of three. Owing to the sheer size of the USA, teams didn't play on an alternating home and away basis. Instead we went 'on the road' for three games, then played three at home.

The mechanics of the NASL took no getting used to, but the pomp and circumstance that preceded every game was something else. The phrase 'over the top' doesn't come near to describing the pre-match hoopla.

At one end of the Fort Lauderdale stadium stood a set of metal gates that would have done justice to Solomon's temple. They led to an open compound, at the rear of which towered mock-Corinthian columns. Before a home game the team assembled there prior to being introduced individually to the crowd. The match announcer made every player sound as if he were a gladiator. He hyped up each and every one of us to the limit, stringing out his vowels like a wrestling referee.

'Laaaaaay-deeeeeees an' genel-merrrrrrrn. Let's hear it foooooooor, the he-row of the Stri-kuuuuuuurs deeeeeee-fey-yance, the worn 'n' ownleeeeeea – Go-or-or-dain Bang-kssssss!'

That was my cue to leave the compound and sprint through the gates to be fêted by the adoring masses.

It took a good twenty minutes just to get the teams out on to the pitch. I was always first out, and felt like a lemon standing there on my own, so I'd embark on a series of stretching and bending exercises followed by some short sprints, making out that I was fine-tuning my body for the battle ahead. Russell Crowe, eat your heart out!

But all this was as nothing compared with the fuss that was made when a new signing was introduced. We were away at Las Vegas Quicksilvers, who included Eusebio in their ranks. As we took the pitch the home side were introducing their latest signing, the former Wales, Birmingham City and Sheffield United midfielder Trevor Hockey. As I ran out I couldn't help laughing. Trevor rolled past me in a tank saluting to the crowd, wearing army fatigues and sporting a helmet. As the tank rumbled by I said, 'You look a right plonker, Trev.'

The smile was soon wiped off my face when the tank turned and passed me again as I walked towards my penalty area. With no warning, it fired its cannon. It was as if a bomb had gone off beside my ear. Instinctively I hunched my shoulders and ducked. I glanced up to see Trevor turn round and look in my direction, a wide-eyed look of surprise on his face.

'I think I may have embarrassed myself, Gordon,' said Trevor.

To this day I'm not sure to which context he was referring.

We had a decent side at Fort Lauderdale. It included Norman Piper, who had given sterling service to Portsmouth and Plymouth Argyle. Norman played wide on the wing and was a really good player. He got through a lot of work in a game, which was no mean feat in the conditions. Although all our home games were played in the cooler evenings, the biggest problem we had was adjusting to the humidity. That could be a killer, especially in the last twenty minutes of a game. Norman, however, just kept on going. He liked to run at opponents and, as they tired in the later stages, not only scored but created a lot of late goals for us.

Unless you include me, the Strikers didn't boast any real stars until the arrival of George Best. In the main, the team comprised good solid pros from clubs in the lower English divisions. Maurice Whittle joined us from Rochdale, where he had been used to playing in front of crowds of 3,000. I remember Maurice standing open-mouthed at New York Cosmos, where a crowd approaching 70,000 had turned up to see Pelé and Franz Beckenbauer display their skills. Not only did the NASL offer the likes of Maurice an opportunity to make some decent money from the game, it also offered them the chance to play against some of the giants of world football. You wouldn't get that at Spotland.

The team spirit was first class and, as in football dressing rooms the world over, practical jokes were rife. We had a young player called Tony Whelan, who had played for Manchester United reserves. Following a home friendly against Torino the team assembled at the airport with our manager, Ron Newman, ready to go on the road again. A bunch of us were sitting playing cards when I noticed Tony walking towards us. I nudged some of the other lads.

'They were terrific watches Torino gave us as keepsakes, weren't they?' I said to Norman Piper as Tony approached.

The lads all agreed enthusiastically.

Tony's ears pricked up. 'What watches are these?' he asked.

'Cartier,' I said. 'We all got one from the Italian manager.'

'He never gave me one,' said Tony, obviously miffed.

'Then you'd better have a word with Ron Newman,' I suggested, 'he's obviously pocketed yours.'

We doubled up with laughter as we watched Tony taking Ron to task about the 'missing' watch, and a bemused Ron protesting with increasing vehemence that he didn't have a clue what Tony was on about. They argued for fully five minutes before the penny dropped and they turned as one to see our card school rolling on the floor in disarray.

Ron Newman had played the majority of his football in the lower divisions of the Football League. He was a good NASL manager, not least because he lapped up the hype of the American game. The NASL was at that time divided into two conferences – Pacific and Atlantic – each of which had two divisions. The top teams from each division met in end-of-season play-offs. We were leading the Eastern Division of the Atlantic Conference as we set off for those three away matches, but we won one, and lost two, though we did pick up some bonus points in the second defeat, which went to a shoot-out.

Those two defeats saw the Strikers slip to third and the local media believed our chance of winning the title had gone. As we took to the pitch for our next home game, against Tampa Bay Rowdies, I was surprised to see a table in the centre of the pitch with a coffin on it. Once the introductions were over, a man with a microphone walked onto the field and headed for the coffin. What on earth was going on? He made a short speech about how, according to the media, we were dead and buried. Suddenly the lid of the coffin flew open and up popped Ron Newman like a jack-in-the-box. He grabbed the microphone and announced loudly, 'But, as you can see, the Strikers ain't dead yet, folks!'

The stadium erupted as the Strikers fans lapped up Ron's piece of showmanship. I can understand why they did. I mean, who wouldn't pay good money to see Sir Alex Ferguson do that at Old Trafford?

My decision to resume playing had not been an easy one. I was confident I could do a good job for the Strikers, but at the back of my mind was the fear that I would make a fool of myself. After all, how many one-eyed goalkeepers have *you* come across? Thankfully, nothing could have been further from the truth. I coped well with the flight and speed of the ball. My reactions were good and I was pleased with my general level of fitness. The only problem I had was the drastic reduction of my peripheral vision. I found I had to make a half-turn to bring players on my right into my field of view. This didn't seem to hamper my performance, though. On the contrary, I think I did pretty well. In 26 games that season the Strikers conceded 29 goals – the fewest in the NASL. Not only did this help us to win matches, it also denied our opponents bonus points for goals scored.

To my great delight, we won our division, though we were beaten by New York Cosmos in the play-offs. To cap what for me had been a great comeback and a marvellous swansong to my career, I was voted NASL Goalkeeper of the Year. That award gave me as much if not more satisfaction than many I'd picked up in England.

Having had a great time with the Strikers I decided to hang up my boots for good. I had overcome what had undoubtedly been the greatest challenge in my life. I had played football again and at a very good standard. My disability had not beaten me.

I returned to England in 1979 to discover that I was unemployed. Tony Waddington had resigned from Stoke in 1977 after seventeen years as manager, and my coaching job had gone with him. I wasn't out of work for long, however. The Port Vale manager, Dennis Butler, offered me a coaching role at Vale Park. When Dennis

resigned a few months later, my old Stoke City team mate Alan
Bloor took over. So I was back working alongside Alan, who took
on as his assistant the former Wolves player Graham Hawkins.

One of the problems with coaching is that you can only teach
those who are willing to learn. One day I gathered the first team
squad together to make a point on attack. Our centre forward was
Bernie Wright, a burly and somewhat surly striker who had been
at Birmingham City, Walsall, Everton and Bradford City before
joining Vale for £9,000 in 1978.

I'd noticed Bernie wasn't helping his midfield the way he
should and pointed this out to him, but he was having none of it.
He wouldn't follow my instructions, and became intransigent,
belligerent, and in the end quite rude.

I was very annoyed. I had been employed as the coach, yet here
was a player who didn't value my ideas and what I had to say about
the game. I suppose that sort of attitude is something a coach must
learn to cope with, but it certainly wasn't my idea of job satisfaction.
A few days later Alan resigned, and I left Port Vale with him.

On the whole I enjoyed coaching, but I was hankering to be a
manager. I applied for two vacant jobs, at Lincoln City and Rotherham United, and was offered an interview for both. In the meantime
I received a telephone call from the chairman of Telford United
of the Alliance Premier League, the equivalent of the Vauxhall
Conference today. The Telford chairman offered me the manager's
job. I politely declined, hoping that one of my forthcoming
interviews would land me a job in the Football League.

Big mistake. The Lincoln job went to Graham Taylor and
Rotherham United appointed Ian Porterfield as their new team
boss. A few days later, however, the Telford chairman was back on
the phone. With ten or so games to go to the end of the season,
Telford were in danger of relegation to the Southern League. All
he wanted me to do was keep them up. This time I accepted his
offer.

Telford United were a team of part-time professionals who
trained two evenings a week. Before accepting my new managerial
position I watched the players train in midweek and play on the

following Saturday. It was obvious that Telford were not a good side. I knew I would have my work cut out, but I accepted the challenge. Telford may not have had a good team, but I knew a man who did.

Bangor City had previously won the Alliance League, but at the time were experiencing financial difficulties. My thinking was simple: if Bangor had won this league, then they must have good players. And if they're strapped for cash, they might be willing to sell some.

I drove to Bangor's Ferrar Road ground to see them in action and was impressed by their goalkeeper and centre half. Having been given a budget to work to, I approached the Bangor chairman, Mr Roberts, and asked him how much he wanted for the pair.

'Fifteen hundred pounds . . .' said Mr Roberts.

'It's a deal,' I said.

'. . . But you're going to have to take our centre forward as well.'

I had seen the Bangor centre forward in action, and he hadn't impressed me.

'I'm not so keen on him,' I said.

'I'm afraid they're a job lot,' said Mr Roberts. 'They travel down from Cheshire together for games, and he has the car.'

What could I do? I signed the centre forward as well. The goalkeeper and centre half did a great job for Telford United and, car pooling be praised, so too did the centre forward. He scored a hatful of goals for us and by the end of the season Telford United were comfortably clear of the relegation zone.

The following year we enjoyed a good pre-season. I signed John Ruggerio from Stoke City, organized friendlies against Stoke and Wolves and followed up with a satisfactory if unspectacular start to the season.

We were in mid-table in November when I took a sabbatical in order to undergo an operation. I asked the former Blackpool and Stoke City player Jackie Mudie to take temporary charge of team affairs while I was away, satisfied that the team would be in good hands.

Unfortunately, during Jackie's temporary period holding the

reins, Telford lost an FA Trophy match to a team from a lower league. I returned to the club in December and was asked by the chairman to attend a meeting at the offices of the travel agents he owned.

'I'm sorry, but we are relieving you of your duties as manager of this club,' he informed me.

I was shocked. My sacking hit me hard. For a time it knocked for six all the passion and enthusiasm I had for the game. I had high hopes of taking Telford United on to bigger and better things, but had been given no time to achieve my aim. Time is the most important asset a manager can be granted, and to my mind, I had been denied it.

I was still under contract, but the club were in no position to pay me off. I was rather naive about such matters at the time, and had no idea what my legal position was. So when a few days later the Telford chairman called me to say that my contract terms would be satisfied if they offered me another position on the staff, I had no reason not to believe him. The position they offered me was raffle-ticket seller in a concession booth the club leased at a local supermarket! I don't know who was more surprised – me at this ridiculous offer or the chairman when, out of sheer bloody mindedness, I accepted it.

I sold draw tickets from that little kiosk for nigh on six weeks, as much as anything so that the locals could see just how shabbily their football club had treated me. Talk about hero to zero! Many ex-supporters agreed:

'A member of the England team that won the World Cup, the greatest goalkeeper there has ever been, selling draw tickets from this hovel? It's a bloody disgrace!'

The groundswell of dissent grew, and gave me the strength not to walk away from the money I was entitled to. Eventually public opinion in Telford swayed matters my way; well, half way at least. The chairman called me into his office and pushed a cheque across the desktop. The amount was about 50 per cent of what I was entitled to, but my point had been made. I accepted it and walked out of his office and football management. Ironically, the team I had largely assembled went on to enjoy considerable success in their league and performed a number of giantkilling acts in the FA Cup.

With a short and not so sweet career in football management behind me, I turned to the world of business. A Leicester motor dealer had plans to start up a corporate hospitality company and asked if I would run it for him. Ursula and I moved back to the Leicester area. We bought a house at Quorn and I settled down to running a business. The business wasn't mine, but it traded off my name. I fronted the company for ten enjoyable years, though it wasn't all plain sailing.

One day my secretary received a telephone call asking for centre court tickets for Wimbledon. No problem there. Then the caller said that his clients were two very rich Saudi businessmen who also wanted a couple of escort girls.

'Er, I'll have to get back to you on that,' she said, confused.

I told her to ring him back and tell him that we weren't in the escort business, which she duly did.

The following Sunday a well-known red-top newspaper carried a sensational story under a banner headline. I don't remember the exact wording, but you know the sort of thing: 'Strawberries and Sex on Centre Court'. I do remember the accompanying photograph, though – the manager of a rival company walking down one of the aisles at Wimbledon with two escort girls in tow, presumably searching for two non-existent Saudi clients.

Sound business principles saved me from an embarrassing situation that time, but on another occasion I wasn't so lucky.

As everyone knows, tickets for an FA Cup final are like gold dust. There are never enough to satisfy the needs of genuine supporters, and corporate hospitality companies have equal difficulty in meeting demand. So when I was offered a bunch of tickets for the 1987 final by a tout, I snapped them up.

A few weeks after the match I was up before the FA being asked to explain how tickets allocated to players from a leading club had found their way into the hands of my clients. Though I explained that they had been acquired through a third party, the FA were adamant that the buck stopped with me. I'd broken their rules and would have to face the consequences.

In truth, I'd been silly to buy those tickets. I didn't really have a leg to stand on. All I could do was plead guilty and await my punishment.

The FA banned me from receiving FA Cup final tickets for seven years. I think they wanted to make an example of me as a warning to others.

I was, by this time, working on the pools panel, a job I still do. Following the news of my ban I turned up one Friday evening at the London hotel that served as our base to find that the two other panel members, Roger Hunt and Tony Green, had framed a pair of Wembley tickets, which they presented to me with much fanfare.

The parent company of Gordon Banks Corporate Hospitality, which had been in poor shape anyway, went down the pan shortly afterwards, taking a lot of my savings with it. I had invested in the finance arm of the motor dealership and lost the lot. To my eternal gratitude, Leicester City offered me a testimonial game to help me out. It was a wonderful gesture on the part of the club, and one that touched me greatly. I had a great night and it was fantastic to see so many familiar faces again. We talked about the old days and I was amazed to find that, although we had all given up the game long ago, in the ensuing years we had all become better players!

I have now worked for the pools panel for some fifteen years. It still currently comprises Roger, Tony Green and myself, together with an adjudicator. In my early days it also included former referee Arthur Ellis and ex-Scotland goalkeeper Ronnie Simpson.

When I first joined we used to meet in the Waldorf Hotel in London. The food at the Waldorf was first-rate, although none of us was quite as impressed with it as Arthur. Every week he used to bring a doggie-bag – well, doggie-briefcase, actually, or a jacket with extra-deep pockets – in which he took home with him anything that remained uneaten.

'He's a walking Fortnum and Mason,' said Roger Hunt one Saturday. Arthur's philosophy was definitely 'waste not, want not'.

One day Arthur told us that he was thinking of buying a grandfather clock. 'You'll be having the pendulum taken out, then, Arthur,' I suggested. 'You'll not want the shadow it casts wearing a hole in your wallpaper!'

For a time the adjudicator of the pools panel was Lord Bath. He was a very friendly man who took his responsibilities as seriously as we did. We all became very good friends, and when Arthur's wife died Lord Bath attended the funeral in Yorkshire with the rest of us.

After the service Arthur laid on a buffet at his home. Lord Bath, who had travelled by train, asked Arthur if he could call a cab to take him to the station.

'I'm not having you travelling in a taxi, milord,' said Arthur. 'I'll sort you out for transport.'

Lord Bath thanked Arthur for his kindness. Ten minutes later Arthur was back.

'When you're ready, sir,' said Arthur, and led him out to the Co-op's hearse idling at the kerbside.

'It's all paid for. The driver has to pass the station, so he might as well drop you off on the way,' said Arthur to the speechless lord.

As I said, waste not, want not.

I really enjoy my work with the pools panel. We sit every weekend to judge the outcome of matches both here and in Australia. To accommodate the demands of television, many games are switched late from Saturday to Sunday or Monday, so there's usually something for us to do even when the weather doesn't disrupt the fixture list.

On occasions, the conclusions we arrive at can apparently have repercussions far beyond their pools-points value. In 1993 we debated the outcome of a postponed game between Tranmere Rovers and Sunderland. Our verdict was a win for Tranmere. The following day the Sunderland manager Malcolm Crosby was sacked! Pure coincidence, of course, but the papers couldn't resist saying that Crosby had become the only manager ever to be dismissed for losing a postponed game.

In addition to my work with the pools panel, I am still involved with the 1966 World Cup team. We often reunite for charity work, and also work together on cruise ships, regaling the holidaymakers with tales of the old days and offering our opinions on the current game. I do a little after-dinner speaking and I have become involved with a number of charities. One of these is the children's hospice at the North Staffs Hospital, a cause very dear to my heart. I've been very lucky myself, and it's nice to be able to give something back.

Not only do I have a wonderful family and a fantastic career behind me, but I've also survived a number of threats to my health. I've had two tumours removed, the first and most serious some fifteen years ago. I had become aware of a lump in my stomach, but as it caused me no pain or discomfort I thought little of it. Ursula, however, suggested that I should see a consultant 'just to be on the safe side'. I'm glad she did.

The consultant examined my X-rays and told me I had a large tumour that would have to come out. Even then the seriousness of the situation didn't register immediately. I took out my diary and began looking for some free dates.

'What on earth are you doing, Mr Banks? Good God, man, this has to be dealt with straight away,' he said. 'Go straight home and pack a bag.'

The stomach tumour was the size of a melon. The surgeon said it was one of the largest he'd ever seen.

'It's a beauty! Throughout Britain and the USA, only thirty-two have been found bigger than this,' he informed me with some pride.

I have to admit, I didn't share his enthusiasm. When the time came for me to leave hospital, the consultant presented me with a photograph of the tumour 'as a keepsake'. Needless to say, that's one snap that stays in the drawer when relatives or friends come round for dinner.

My sudden exit from the Leicester business community wasn't without its compensations. Our children had grown up and settled in North Staffordshire and Warrington. In order to be nearer to them, Ursula and I moved back to Cheshire. We now live in a village just over the Staffordshire border, some ten miles from Stoke. We're much closer as a family and we're very happy.

In recognition of the efforts of the Stoke team of 1972 in winning the League Cup, in 2002 the club gave every member of that side a ticket for life at Stoke City and I was made president of the club in succession to the late Sir Stanley Matthews. I'm a regular at their new Britannia Stadium, and my son Robert and I also watch Leicester City whenever we can. I also make the occasional nostalgic trip to Chesterfield. I'm not the sort of guy who will ever forget his roots and Chesterfield were, after all, the club that gave me my chance in league football.

In addition, I also watch as many televised matches as I can. As you might have gathered, I'm still football mad. In my view, the standard of football today is no better or worse than when I played. But, my word, it's certainly different . . .

18. The Changing Game

Football has indeed undergone many changes, some for the better, others not so. Compared to my day, the game is now quicker, players are fitter and teams better organized, irrespective of the level at which they play.

There is one change, however, that has received little attention, despite being fundamental to the sport – the ball itself.

When I started my career at Chesterfield, the ball most often used was a Webber Premier. This was a leather-panelled caseball, an improvement on the lace-up Tomlinson 'T' and Tugite balls used in the thirties, forties and early fifties. The Webber Premier had more leather panels, so kept its shape irrespective of how wet conditions were. It was advertised as waterproof, but had to be rubbed with Chelsea dubbin to make it so, and even then would soak up some moisture in the rain. Inside the leather casing was a valve bladder, which also added to the weight. The official weight of a football in the fifties was set at 16 ounces (454g). On very wet days the moisture and mud could make it significantly heavier.

The Webber made life for a goalkeeper relatively easy owing to the simple fact that, when struck, it travelled true. The Webber never deviated in the air; all I had to do was anticipate correctly and more often than not I would make the save.

In the sixties the Webber was replaced by the Mitre Permawhite Super, an altogether lighter (and whiter) ball. Its panels were laminated leather, which did away with the need for dubbin. The Mitre and its competitor made by Stuart Surridge were very good balls, but the big difference from a goalkeeper's point of view was that both deviated slightly in the air. Not by a lot, but by enough to make a save that little bit harder.

The ball in general use as I write is much less heavy than the Mitre; the one introduced in the 2002 World Cup is lighter still.

When struck with force it deviates in flight, both swerving and dipping. This is a nightmare for goalkeepers, and often makes them look incompetent, even foolish, when attempting to make a save.

When Rivelino swerved a Brazilian free kick round the wall in the altitude of Mexico '70, the world gasped. Goals like that are knocked in every Saturday up and down the country these days, and not because all those players possess Rivelino's skill. Today's ball may well make for more spectacular football and enable David Beckham to hit superb forty-yard crosses and passes, but it stacks the odds against the poor goalkeeper.

Take Tomas Sorenson, for example, the Danish keeper on the wrong end of a 3–0 scoreline against England in the second round of the 2002 World Cup. True, he didn't have the best of matches, but the light ball and the very wet conditions played their part in that. When Rio Ferdinand headed the ball at him in a downpour, Sorenson fumbled it over the line. That lightweight laminated ball in such conditions must have been like a bar of soap. Despite three attempts, he just couldn't get a firm hold. When Emile Heskey's first-time shot from twenty yards gave England their third goal one commentator remarked, 'You have to ask questions of the goalkeeper,' but Heskey's low, hard shot swerved one way then the other before bouncing on the sodden turf just in front of the diving Sorenson. Then, instead of rising a few inches as you might expect, it skidded low under his body. What may have looked like a straightforward save to the commentator was anything but.

In the same match a Danish player cut in from the right and hit a stinging shot towards David Seaman's far post. David does not have the nickname 'Safe Hands' for nothing. He had got his angles and positioning spot on and the fierce shot was straight at him, yet, rather than gather the ball into his midriff, Seaman beat it away with both hands. Why did he do that? Because he couldn't be confident of taking the ball cleanly.

Seaman did exactly the right thing. The ball was travelling at considerable speed and he was obviously wary of the fact that it might deviate in the air at the last minute. The conditions were very wet, so rather than risk a fumble he made a blocking save. 'A great save from Seaman,' said the TV commentator. It was, but the commentator never picked up on the fact that the England goalkeeper had consciously decided to block rather than try to hold the shot.

After the game a reporter asked Seaman about the quality of his opposite number's performance. All he said was, 'Well, conditions were very difficult out there.' They were and he knew it. I should imagine that at the back of his mind was a large dose of 'There but for the grace of God . . .'

The innovatory light ball also played a role in the downfall of England in World Cup 2002. David Seaman cannot be blamed for conceding what proved to be Brazil's winning goal in the quarter-final. Video footage from behind Ronaldinho clearly showed the ball heading beyond the left-hand post before curving so much that it ended up in the right-hand corner of the goal.

When defending an angled free kick from thirty yards out a goalkeeper has to anticipate the ball's trajectory. A free kick flighted from that distance is usually aimed at a point just beyond the six-yard box, where opposing forwards can run on to it. When the ball was struck David Seaman had to come off his line and gamble that he would reach the ball before the Brazilian forwards. Consequently he took three paces forward, which was the correct thing to do. He was simply caught out by the way the ball arced so severely in the air. As soon as the ball left Ronaldinho's boot, David Seaman was sunk. He had played the percentages and lost.

To add to Seaman's problems, Paul Scholes had, quite rightly, positioned himself in front of Ronaldinho as he ran to take the kick. However, as the Brazilian struck the ball Scholes moved just a little, perhaps blocking Seaman's view for a vital split second. A goalkeeper must be able to judge the pace of the ball in order to determine its probable flight, and I don't think David could see it at the point of contact. He may have been unsighted for a split second only, but, as he and England found to their cost, such margins can be crucial.

Both Seaman and Scholes are blameless: it was just one of those things. A goalkeeper has only brief moments in which to weigh up his options and act, and circumstances conspired to make Seaman's usually solid judgement go awry. That can happen even to the best goalkeepers, of which he is undoubtedly one.

Following the game Seaman was inconsolable, but his performance after conceding that goal was an object lesson for any would-be goalkeeper. If you feel you have made an error, you have to push it to the back of your mind for the rest of the game. This takes mental fortitude, and Seaman has plenty. A lesser player might have let that goal play on his mind, and could have let in two or three more as a result. Not Seaman. He contained his emotions until the final whistle. Such an attitude is the mark of a top-class keeper.

After such a poor start England did well even to qualify for the 2002 World Cup. Credit must be given to Sven-Göran Eriksson and his players for that. England beat Argentina but, generally speaking, the fancied teams beat themselves. Neither France, Argentina nor Italy played anything like as well as they could have.

The World Cup door was open for England, but we tripped over the doorstep. Brazil were a talented team, but not a great one. England were certainly capable of beating them. That we didn't was a result of too many mediocre performances on the day.

When asked to define a great player Sir Matt Busby said, 'The great players have great games in the great games. When it really matters, they perform.' And that sums it up. It's no good saying, 'If we played them tomorrow we could beat them.' It's today that counts.

In May 1966 the top five teams in the FIFA rankings were Portugal, Brazil, England, West Germany and Argentina. In July England beat three of them within the space of seven days to win the World Cup. We didn't have it easy. As both Pelé and Gerd Muller have said, winning the World Cup is the hardest thing to do in football. With FIFA's top-ranked teams out of the competition, England had a great chance to do just that in 2002. That they didn't take that chance might haunt those players for the rest of their lives. Football is a team sport, and it was the team that failed against Brazil – not David Seaman.

Nevertheless, I remain very hopeful for the future. We have

some excellent young players who should be even better players by 2006. Most of those who competed in 2002 will be part of the England set-up for some time to come. As long as they maintain their development and, just as important, their desire to win the World Cup, England can go all the way in Germany 2006. Should that happen, no one will be more delighted than the Class of '66.

I think the decision to introduce a very light ball for the 2002 World Cup was crazy. It was a completely new phenomenon for the players, all of whom had to spend time adjusting their game. But it was the goalkeepers I really felt for as time and again I watched the ball deviate two or even three times in the air.

Of course we all want to see more goals, but spare a thought for the man between the posts who has put in years of specialist training only to find that a hard job has become even harder overnight.

If FIFA want to create more goals, rather than introducing a balloon for a ball they should have concentrated their attention elsewhere. On shirt pulling, for example. I've lost count of how many times I have seen a player bearing down on goal or running to meet a cross who has been pulled back by his shirt. Such fouls have prevented many a certain goal. Clamp down on foul play and gamesmanship and there would be no need to manufacture goals by doctoring the ball.

At a time when the importance and value of the man in the number 1 shirt has finally been realized, FIFA are turning the art of great goalkeeping into a lottery.

I've said it before and I'll say it again – few sides win the Premiership unless their goalkeeper has enjoyed an exceptional season. When Blackburn Rovers won it in 1995, their goalkeeper Tim Flowers had a super campaign. Likewise, Manchester United in the nineties had the outstanding Peter Schmeichel, and the well-documented errors of Fabien Barthez were at least part of the reason for their failure to retain their title in 2001–2, when David Seaman's return to top form underpinned their usurpation by an excellent Arsenal side.

Another major difference in today's game is the quality of the pitches. Rarely these days does the reserve team of a Premiership club play on the home pitch – most have made arrangements with clubs in lower leagues to use their grounds for second team games. Along with the reduced wear and tear, drainage has also become far more efficient. When I played, midwinter pitches often resembled quagmires and the ball picked up mud as well as moisture, making it very heavy to kick and well-nigh impossible to swerve or bend. I'm a great admirer of David Beckham, but today's surfaces and the lightweight ball do give him an advantage. When pinging a cross into the goalmouth with the inside of his right boot, the ball curls away from the goalkeeper. This is very difficult to defend, although, credit to Beckham, he has practised his art to near perfection and his teams have scored a good many goals as a result.

David is a great player, but he is also fortunate to be playing at a time when conditions are so complementary to his undoubted talents. On pudding-like pitches and with a heavy ball he might have been merely a good one. As I said, football today is no better or worse than when I played – simply different.

I love the modern game. I like the way it is played, more often than not, in a cavalier and entertaining manner. Foreign players have exerted a positive influence, especially in the Premiership, but I do worry that their sheer number is impeding the development of home-grown players. Cream will always rise to the top – young players such as Danny Mills, Ashley Cole, Joe Cole, Steven Gerrard and Michael Owen are living proof of that – but the influx of foreign imports in the lower divisions gives me real cause for concern. In the Nationwide League, players from eastern Europe are often imported simply because they are happy with a wage below that of a domestic player. Such journeymen do a job, but are invariably a short-term solution. Wages apart, many managers know that they have only two, maybe three years to bring success to a club. Once again, the short-term solution is to buy a foreign player since it can take anything up to four years before an exciting academy player makes the first team. Four years of investment in time, expertise and money. Compare that with a cheap foreign import – especially one who arrives free on a 'Bosman'.

We don't have football grounds any more – they're all 'stadiums'.

The Taylor Report was long overdue, and it took the nightmares of Hillsborough, Bradford and Brussels before football took a long hard look at how it treated its paying customers. Facilities have been much improved, and I'm all for that. The improvements have also helped to rid the game of the criminal element, often erroneously referred to as 'football' hooligans, who besmirched its name in the past. There are real signs that football is once again becoming a family game.

'A little is lost and a little is gained in every day', to quote William Wordsworth. The same can be said of developments in football. Let me say now, though, that I wouldn't go back to how it was. Having been cannon fodder in a world war, many people in the late forties were treated as little more than terrace fodder by those who ran the game at the time. That attitude largely prevailed until the tragedy of Hillsborough.

Having said that, I can't help grieving for what has been lost. On the terraces, everyone had their favourite spot and stood there season in, season out, as did those around them. Going to a game was like a social occasion, an unchanging feature in an uncertain life. Now, unless you're a season-ticket holder, you end up sitting in a different position for every match. There is no sense of community any more.

At many stadiums today the fans are far from the action. Gone are the days when you could stand so close to the pitch that you could smell the manager's aftershave. The Victoria Ground was a typical example. Very little that happened on the pitch escaped the attention of the supporters. They felt very close to the players and vice versa. Someone standing by the tunnel entrance could sniff the liniment wafting up from the players' legs as they ran out; they could hear me calling to my full backs; the grunts of two players competing for the ball. The old grounds did not boast the architecture of the Reebok, the Stadium of Light or the redeveloped Elland Road – they were simply bear-pits where attention was focused on the action taking place a few yards away.

There is still brilliance, drama and excitement on the pitch, of course, but fans are now distanced from the action. The clubs and authorities appear to have compensated by encouraging supporters to become part of something bigger than just the match. Going to a game has been turned into an 'experience' – 'Welcome to Footieworld'. Again, this isn't necessarily a bad thing – just a great deal different from what I grew up with.

But the newest and biggest kid on the block is Profit – and he's at the root of everything. If you have shelled out £50 for a replica shirt, have the club's credit card and have paid extra simply to have a concourse that offers you exclusive use of a bar, the stadium needs to be something special!

When I played there was an intimacy between players and fans that is absent today. On Saturdays they would be less than five yards from my back. When I extended a hand to block the ball they heard the impact. We shopped in the same supermarkets, drank in the same pubs. Before every match we were besieged by autograph hunters and were happy to sign. But few supporters get within touching distance of the leading Premiership players, whose arrival at the ground is usually glimpsed only from behind metal crush barriers. Super-stardom has its benefits, but it also has its price, and an important aspect of contact between player and supporter is now for ever gone.

I may be in my mid-sixties, but that's not where I'm living. I don't yearn for a return to the 'good old days'. But there are times when I miss the simplicity of how football used to be. (I remember Matt Busby once being asked whether the game-plan approach of Manchester United in 1968 was a sign that football was becoming too complicated. 'Our game plan is this,' said Matt. 'When we have the ball we are all attackers. When the opposition has the ball, we are all defenders. Now what's complicated about that?')

I miss the little things: the frisson of anticipation at half time as the stewards hung up the scores from the other matches around the country, for example. Players today keep one eye on the electronic scoreboard to see how their rivals are faring. Believe me, from a player's point of view it is better not to know. Better just to play to the best of your ability and discover your fate at the final whistle. It's much simpler that way.

After the TV boom of the nineties, many clubs are now experiencing the bust. The collapse of OnDigital has affected many Nationwide League clubs. The Premiership is healthy, but the Nationwide is looking more and more like the symptoms on a medicine bottle.

I believe that football has become a fashion victim. In the nineties many people who didn't really care less about the game suddenly became supporters. Football was sexy; the new rock 'n' roll. Many professional people realized that to support a club offered social advantages. There's nothing wrong in that, but, in a similar way to the dotcom bubble, people stopped discriminating in the scramble to climb aboard the bandwagon. Or perhaps they knew nothing about football in the first place.

I say that because I can't imagine anyone who knows anything at all about the game ever believing that live TV coverage of, with all due respect, Bradford City versus Barnsley would attract a large paying TV audience. The notion that ITV Digital would attract subscribers in sufficient numbers to make its Nationwide League deal financially viable was flawed from the start, as any genuine football fan could have told them.

Arguably, the advent of the transfer window currently under consideration by UEFA will have an even greater impact on the finances of clubs than the collapse of ITV Digital. The plan is to introduce two transfer windows, one in the summer and the other at Christmas. This would mean that clubs could buy or sell players only within those windows. Smaller clubs often experience cash-flow problems, one way out of which is to sell a player at short notice. If they have to wait up to six months to do so, it could well put some of them out of business.

Nationwide League clubs need to be allowed to develop young talent and given the opportunity for that emerging talent to filter through. Surely it would be far better for English football, and European football in general, if we had an international transfer window, but not a domestic one. This would help the finances of our game because our top clubs would be able to buy players from smaller clubs at any time, but foreign players during the two window periods only. Such a system would allow home-grown talent to move up the league ladder towards the Premiership, which can only benefit English football. We would still have the interest and skill that imports bring to the domestic game, and money would continue to circulate throughout the year. At the same time, young British talent would have the chance to shine. The plan in its current form can only damage both the game itself and the finances of smaller clubs.

If I had but one wish for football, it would be that the success of the Premiership and the national sides could be shared among every English football club. The almost daily news of another club on the brink of receivership saddens me greatly. Should the Burys, Swanseas and Mansfield Towns of English football disappear, it would be a tragic loss, not only for the people directly involved but also to the fabric of our society. Those who administer our game must do all they can to prevent that happening. The working man and woman must continue to have their ballet.

I have been especially pleased to see the England team emerge once again as a power in world football. We have some fine young players of true international quality and, in David Beckham, Michael Owen, Paul Scholes and Rio Ferdinand, players of world class. Under the careful and objective managership of Sven-Göran Eriksson I am very optimistic for the future of both the national side and English football in general.

I have been involved in football as a player, coach, manager, raffle-ticket seller and supporter for over fifty years. I've seen a lot of changes and will, no doubt, see many more. The game has altered irrevocably, but in essence it remains the same. Danny Blanchflower once said that football is about the pursuit of glory. That is true, but it is also about human endeavour, about passion, courage and emotion. Occasionally it is about pride and honour, and sometimes even humour. When played at its best and in a spirit of true sportsmanship, a football match becomes much more than a mere sporting contest. The truly beautiful game is a miracle of man's physical and mental capabilities. When that happens, the pitch becomes a nirvana.

I have been so very lucky. I have a loving and caring family who have been the hub around which my life has revolved. Robert is a sales executive for a timber merchant. Wendy is a sales representative for a shoe company and, in what spare time she has, is also a dressmaker to the entertainment industry. Julia is a solicitor in Cheshire. Ursula and I are keen gardeners and you'll find us outside most days attending to the beds and borders or mowing the grass. I always ensure the lawns are not too lush and that they'll take a short stud! We all enjoy watching movies. I often take my grandchildren to the cinema and consequently have become something of an expert on *Star Wars* and *Spiderman*.

Ursula and I love having the family over for a meal. I haven't inherited my mam's talent for cooking, nor have I learned from Ursula, who likes the kitchen to herself when she's cooking and packs me off to the lounge in order to avert a culinary disaster. I miss Mam. She died nearly twenty years since, but the legacy she left was one of love.

I have also been fortunate enough to have made a career in the greatest sport on earth. Football is a serious business, but the key to enjoying it to the full, and to surviving in the game, is not always to take it too seriously. That has been my philosophy in both football and life. Of course, seriousness has its place – any waiter will tell you that – but in life, as in football, to everything there is a season.

Football has given me an awful lot. I have played alongside and against some of the greatest names ever to have graced the game. No money could buy that wonderful experience and its store of golden memories that I will cherish for ever. It remains only to say thank you to every player, manager, official and supporter whose life I have touched and who, in turn, have touched mine. Collectively, you have given me so much more than a lad from Tinsley could ever have expected. Words could never express my true gratitude. Some people think there's no place for sentiment in football – there is now.

Career Record

Football League

CHESTERFIELD

1958–59

Date	Opponent		Score	Competition
29 Nov	Colchester United	(h)	2–2	
6 Dec	Carlisle United	(a)	0–0	FA Cup
10 Dec	Carlisle United	(h)	1–0	FA Cup (replay)
13 Dec	Norwich City	(h)	1–1	
20 Dec	Halifax Town	(a)	2–3	
26 Dec	Wrexham	(h)	1–1	
27 Dec	Wrexham	(a)	4–3	
1 Jan	Hull City	(h)	2–1	
3 Jan	Newport County	(h)	3–1	
10 Jan	Colchester United	(a)	0–2	FA Cup
17 Jan	Southend United	(a)	5–2	
24 Jan	Reading	(a)	2–1	
31 Jan	Notts County	(a)	1–3	
7 Feb	Mansfield Town	(h)	3–1	
14 Feb	Swindon Town	(a)	2–1	
21 Feb	Brentford	(h)	1–2	
28 Feb	QPR	(h)	2–3	
7 Mar	Rochdale	(a)	0–0	
14 Mar	Doncaster Rovers	(a)	1–2	
21 Mar	Plymouth Argyle	(a)	0–2	
27 Mar	Bury	(h)	3–0	
11 Apr	Bournemouth	(h)	1–0	
13 Apr	Stockport County	(h)	1–0	
18 Apr	Colchester United	(a)	0–1	
25 Apr	Reading	(h)	1–0	

| 29 Apr | Norwich City | (a) 1–2 |

Summary: League 23; FA Cup 3; Total 26.

LEICESTER CITY

1959–60

9 Sep	Blackpool	(h) 1–1	
12 Sep	Newcastle United	(a) 0–2	
17 Oct	Manchester City	(a) 2–3	
24 Oct	Arsenal	(h) 2–2	
31 Oct	Everton	(a) 1–6	
7 Nov	Sheffield Wednesday	(h) 2–0	
14 Nov	Nottingham Forest	(a) 0–1	
21 Nov	Fulham	(h) 0–1	
28 Nov	Bolton Wanderers	(a) 1–3	
5 Dec	Luton Town	(h) 3–3	
12 Dec	Wolves	(a) 3–0	
19 Dec	West Ham United	(h) 2–1	
26 Dec	Preston North End	(h) 2–2	
28 Dec	Preston North End	(a) 1–1	
2 Jan	Chelsea	(a) 2–2	
9 Jan	Wrexham	(a) 2–1	FA Cup
16 Jan	West Bromwich Albion	(h) 0–1	
23 Jan	Newcastle United	(a) 2–0	
30 Jan	Fulham	(h) 2–1	FA Cup
6 Feb	Birmingham City	(h) 1–3	
13 Feb	Tottenham Hotspur	(a) 2–1	
20 Feb	West Bromwich Albion	(h) 2–1	FA Cup
24 Feb	Manchester United	(h) 3–1	
27 Feb	Luton Town	(a) 0–2	
5 Mar	Manchester City	(h) 5–0	
12 Mar	Wolves	(h) 1–2	FA Cup
15 Mar	Arsenal	(a) 1–1	
19 Mar	Wolves	(h) 2–1	

2 Apr	Nottingham Forest	(h)	0–1	
6 Apr	Sheffield Wednesday	(a)	2–2	
9 Apr	Fulham	(a)	1–1	
15 Apr	Burnley	(a)	0–1	
16 Apr	Everton	(h)	3–3	
18 Apr	Burnley	(h)	2–1	
23 Apr	Blackburn Rovers	(a)	1–0	
30 Apr	Bolton Wanderers	(h)	1–2	

1960–61

20 Aug	Blackpool	(h)	1–1	
24 Aug	Chelsea	(a)	3–1	
27 Aug	Everton	(a)	1–3	
31 Aug	Chelsea	(h)	1–3	
3 Sep	Blackburn Rovers	(h)	2–4	
7 Sep	Wolves	(a)	2–3	
10 Sep	Manchester United	(a)	1–1	
14 Sep	Wolves	(h)	2–0	
17 Sep	Tottenham Hotspur	(h)	1–2	
24 Sep	Newcastle United	(a)	3–1	
1 Oct	Aston Villa	(a)	3–1	
8 Oct	Arsenal	(h)	2–1	
15 Oct	Manchester City	(a)	1–3	
22 Oct	West Bromwich Albion	(h)	2–2	
26 Oct	Rotherham United	(h)	1–2	League Cup
28 Oct	Cardiff City	(a)	1–2	
4 Nov	Preston North End	(h)	5–2	
12 Nov	Fulham	(a)	2–4	
19 Nov	Sheffield Wednesday	(h)	2–1	
26 Nov	Birmingham City	(a)	2–0	
3 Dec	Nottingham Forest	(h)	1–1	
10 Dec	Burnley	(a)	2–3	
17 Dec	Blackpool	(a)	1–5	
24 Dec	Bolton Wanderers	(a)	0–2	
26 Dec	Bolton Wanderers	(h)	2–0	

31 Dec	Everton	(h)	4–1	
7 Jan	Oxford United	(h)	3–1	FA Cup
14 Jan	Blackburn Rovers	(a)	1–1	
21 Jan	Manchester United	(h)	6–0	
31 Jan	Bristol City	(h)	5–1	FA Cup
4 Feb	Tottenham Hotspur	(a)	3–2	
11 Feb	Newcastle United	(h)	5–3	
18 Feb	Birmingham City	(a)	1–1	FA Cup
22 Feb	Birmingham City	(h)	2–1	FA Cup (replay)
25 Feb	Arsenal	(a)	3–1	
4 Mar	Barnsley	(h)	0–0	FA Cup
8 Mar	Barnsley	(a)	2–1	FA Cup (replay) (aet)
18 Mar	Sheffield United	(n)	0–0	FA Cup semi-final
23 Mar	Sheffield United	(n)	0–0	FA Cup (replay) (aet)
25 Mar	Preston North End	(a)	0–0	
27 Mar	Sheffield United	(n)	2–0	FA Cup (2nd replay)
31 Mar	West Ham United	(a)	0–1	
1 Apr	Burnley	(h)	2–2	
3 Apr	West Ham United	(h)	5–1	
8 Apr	Sheffield Wednesday	(a)	2–2	
10 Apr	Cardiff City	(h)	3–0	
15 Apr	Fulham	(h)	1–2	
19 Apr	Aston Villa	(h)	3–1	
22 Apr	Nottingham Forest	(a)	2–2	
26 Apr	Manchester City	(h)	1–2	
29 Apr	Birmingham City	(h)	3–2	
6 May	Tottenham Hotspur	(n)	0–2	FA Cup final

1961–62

19 Aug	Manchester City	(a)	1–3	
23 Aug	Arsenal	(h)	0–1	
26 Aug	West Bromwich Albion	(h)	1–0	
29 Aug	Arsenal	(a)	4–4	
2 Sep	Birmingham City	(a)	5–1	
5 Sep	Burnley	(a)	0–2	

9 Sep	Everton	(h)	2–0	
13 Sep	Glenavon	(a)	4–1	ECWC (1)
16 Sep	Fulham	(a)	1–2	
20 Sep	Burnley	(h)	2–6	
23 Sep	Sheffield Wednesday	(h)	1–0	
27 Sep	Glenavon	(h)	3–1	ECWC (2)
30 Sep	West Ham United	(a)	1–4	
7 Oct	Sheffield United	(h)	4–1	
9 Oct	York City	(a)	1–2	League Cup
14 Oct	Chelsea	(a)	3–1	
21 Oct	Blackpool	(h)	0–2	
25 Oct	Atletico Madrid	(h)	1–1	ECWC (1)
28 Oct	Blackburn Rovers	(a)	1–2	
4 Nov	Wolves	(h)	3–0	
11 Nov	Manchester United	(a)	2–2	
15 Nov	Atletico Madrid	(a)	0–2	ECWC (2)
18 Nov	Cardiff City	(h)	3–0	
2 Dec	Aston Villa	(h)	0–2	
9 Dec	Nottingham Forest	(a)	0–0	
16 Dec	Manchester City	(h)	2–0	
23 Dec	West Bromwich Albion	(a)	0–2	
26 Dec	Ipswich Town	(a)	0–1	
10 Jan	Stoke City	(h)	1–1	FA Cup
13 Jan	Birmingham City	(h)	1–2	
15 Jan	Stoke City	(a)	2–5	FA Cup (replay)
20 Jan	Everton	(a)	2–3	
3 Feb	Fulham	(h)	4–1	
10 Feb	Sheffield Wednesday	(a)	2–1	
17 Feb	West Ham United	(h)	2–2	
24 Feb	Sheffield United	(a)	1–3	
10 Mar	Blackpool	(a)	1–2	
17 Mar	Blackburn Rovers	(h)	2–0	
24 Mar	Wolves	(a)	1–1	
28 Mar	Ipswich Town	(h)	0–2	
4 Apr	Manchester United	(h)	4–3	
7 Apr	Cardiff City	(a)	4–0	

11 Apr	Chelsea	(h) 2–0
21 Apr	Aston Villa	(a) 3–8
23 Apr	Bolton Wanderers	(a) 0–1
24 Apr	Bolton Wanderers	(h) 1–1
28 Apr	Nottingham Forest	(h) 2–1
30 Apr	Tottenham Hotspur	(h) 2–3

1962–63

18 Aug	Fulham	(a) 1–2	
22 Aug	Sheffield Wednesday	(h) 3–3	
25 Aug	Nottingham Forest	(h) 2–1	
29 Aug	Sheffield Wednesday	(a) 3–0	
1 Sep	Bolton Wanderers	(h) 4–1	
4 Sep	Burnley	(a) 1–1	
8 Sep	Everton	(a) 2–3	
15 Sep	West Bromwich Albion	(h) 1–0	
19 Sep	Burnley	(h) 3–3	
22 Sep	Arsenal	(a) 1–1	
26 Sep	Charlton Athletic	(h) 4–4	League Cup
29 Sep	Birmingham City	(h) 3–0	
2 Oct	Charlton Athletic	(a) 1–2	League Cup (replay)
6 Oct	Ipswich Town	(a) 1–0	
13 Oct	Liverpool	(h) 3–0	
20 Oct	Blackburn Rovers	(a) 0–2	
27 Oct	Sheffield United	(h) 3–1	
3 Nov	Tottenham Hotspur	(a) 0–4	
10 Nov	West Ham United	(h) 2–0	
17 Nov	Manchester City	(a) 1–1	
24 Nov	Blackpool	(h) 0–0	
1 Dec	Wolves	(a) 3–1	
8 Dec	Aston Villa	(h) 3–3	
15 Dec	Fulham	(h) 2–3	
26 Dec	Leyton Orient	(h) 5–1	
8 Jan	Grimsby Town	(a) 3–1	FA Cup
30 Jan	Ipswich Town	(h) 3–1	FA Cup

9 Feb	Arsenal	(h)	2–0	
12 Feb	Everton	(h)	3–1	
19 Feb	Nottingham Forest	(a)	2–0	
23 Feb	Ipswich Town	(h)	3–0	
2 Mar	Liverpool	(a)	2–0	
9 Mar	Blackburn Rovers	(h)	2–0	
16 Mar	Leyton Orient	(a)	1–0	FA Cup
23 Mar	Tottenham Hotspur	(h)	2–2	
26 Mar	Sheffield United	(a)	0–0	
30 Mar	Norwich City	(a)	2–0	FA Cup
3 Apr	Leyton Orient	(a)	2–0	
8 Apr	Blackpool	(a)	1–1	
13 Apr	West Ham United	(a)	0–2	
15 Apr	Manchester United	(a)	2–2	
16 Apr	Manchester United	(h)	4–3	
20 Apr	Wolves	(h)	1–1	
27 Apr	Liverpool	(n)	1–0	FA Cup semi-final
4 May	West Bromwich Albion	(a)	1–2	
25 May	Manchester United	(n)	1–3	FA Cup final

1963–64

24 Aug	West Bromwich Albion	(a)	1–1	
28 Aug	Birmingham City	(h)	3–0	
31 Aug	Arsenal	(h)	7–2	
4 Sep	Birmingham City	(a)	0–2	
7 Sep	Stoke City	(a)	3–3	
11 Sep	Sheffield Wednesday	(h)	2–0	
14 Sep	Bolton Wanderers	(a)	0–0	
21 Sep	Fulham	(h)	0–1	
25 Sep	Aldershot	(h)	2–0	League Cup
28 Sep	Manchester United	(a)	1–3	
2 Oct	Sheffield Wednesday	(a)	2–1	
5 Oct	Burnley	(h)	0–0	
8 Oct	Nottingham Forest	(a)	0–2	
14 Oct	Wolves	(h)	0–1	

16 Oct	Tranmere Rovers	(a)	2–1	League Cup
19 Oct	Tottenham Hotspur	(a)	1–1	
26 Oct	Blackburn Rovers	(h)	4–3	
2 Nov	Liverpool	(a)	1–0	
9 Nov	Sheffield United	(h)	0–1	
16 Nov	West Ham United	(a)	2–2	
23 Nov	Chelsea	(h)	2–4	
27 Nov	Gillingham	(h)	3–1	League Cup
30 Nov	Blackpool	(a)	3–3	
7 Dec	Aston Villa	(h)	0–0	
14 Dec	West Bromwich Albion	(h)	0–2	
21 Dec	Arsenal	(a)	1–0	
26 Dec	Everton	(h)	2–0	
28 Dec	Everton	(a)	3–0	
4 Jan	Leyton Orient	(h)	2–3	FA Cup
11 Jan	Stoke City	(h)	2–1	
15 Jan	Norwich City	(h)	2–1	League Cup (replay) (aet)
18 Jan	Bolton Wanderers	(h)	1–0	
1 Feb	Fulham	(a)	1–2	
5 Feb	West Ham United	(h)	4–3	League Cup semi-final (1)
8 Feb	Manchester United	(h)	3–2	
22 Feb	Wolves	(a)	2–1	
29 Feb	Nottingham Forest	(h)	1–1	
23 Mar	West Ham United	(a)	2–0	League Cup semi-final (2)
28 Mar	Liverpool	(h)	0–2	
30 Mar	Ipswich Town	(a)	1–1	
31 Mar	Ipswich Town	(h)	2–1	
6 Apr	Chelsea	(a)	0–1	
15 Apr	Stoke City	(a)	1–1	League Cup final (1)
18 Apr	Aston Villa	(a)	3–1	
22 Apr	Stoke City	(h)	3–2	League Cup final (2)
25 Apr	Tottenham Hotspur	(h)	0–1	

1964–65

22 Aug	Sunderland	(a)	3–3	
26 Aug	Wolves	(h)	3–2	
29 Aug	Manchester United	(h)	2–2	
2 Sep	Wolves	(a)	1–1	
5 Sep	Chelsea	(h)	1–1	
9 Sep	Liverpool	(h)	2–0	
12 Sep	Leeds United	(a)	2–3	
19 Sep	Arsenal	(h)	2–3	
23 Sep	Peterborough United	(h)	0–0	League Cup
26 Sep	Blackburn Rovers	(a)	1–3	
30 Sep	West Bromwich Albion	(h)	4–2	
5 Oct	Blackpool	(h)	3–2	
8 Oct	Peterborough United	(a)	2–0	League Cup (replay)
10 Oct	Fulham	(a)	2–5	
17 Oct	Nottingham Forest	(h)	3–2	
31 Oct	Tottenham Hotspur	(h)	4–2	
4 Nov	Crystal Palace	(h)	0–0	League Cup
7 Nov	Burnley	(a)	1–2	
11 Nov	Crystal Palace	(a)	2–1	League Cup (replay)
14 Nov	Sheffield United	(h)	0–2	
21 Nov	Everton	(a)	2–2	
28 Nov	Birmingham City	(h)	4–4	
1 Dec	Coventry City	(a)	8–1	League Cup
5 Dec	West Ham United	(a)	0–0	
12 Dec	Sunderland	(h)	0–1	
26 Dec	Sheffield Wednesday	(h)	2–2	
28 Dec	Sheffield Wednesday	(a)	0–0	
2 Jan	Chelsea	(a)	1–4	
9 Jan	Blackburn Rovers	(h)	2–2	FA Cup
14 Jan	Blackburn Rovers	(a)	2–1	FA Cup (replay)
16 Jan	Leeds United	(h)	2–2	
20 Jan	Plymouth Argyle	(h)	3–2	League Cup semi-final (1)
23 Jan	Arsenal	(a)	3–4	
30 Jan	Plymouth Argyle	(h)	5–0	FA Cup

6 Feb	Blackburn Rovers	(h)	2–3	
10 Feb	Plymouth Argyle	(a)	1–0	League Cup semi-final (2)
13 Feb	Blackpool	(a)	1–1	
20 Feb	Middlesbrough	(a)	3–0	FA Cup
24 Feb	Fulham	(h)	5–1	
27 Feb	Nottingham Forest	(a)	1–2	
6 Mar	Liverpool	(h)	0–0	FA Cup
10 Mar	Liverpool	(a)	0–1	FA Cup (replay)
13 Mar	West Bromwich Albion	(a)	0–6	
15 Mar	Chelsea	(a)	2–3	League Cup final (1)
26 Mar	Sheffield United	(a)	2–0	
3 Apr	Everton	(h)	2–1	
5 Apr	Chelsea	(h)	0–0	League Cup final (2)
12 Apr	Manchester United	(a)	0–1	
17 Apr	West Ham United	(h)	1–0	
19 Apr	Aston Villa	(h)	1–1	
20 Apr	Aston Villa	(a)	0–1	
24 Apr	Tottenham Hotspur	(a)	6–2	

1965–66

22 Sep	Manchester City	(a)	1–3	League Cup
25 Sep	Sheffield United	(a)	2–2	
2 Oct	Northampton Town	(h)	1–1	
9 Oct	Stoke City	(a)	0–1	
16 Oct	Burnley	(h)	0–1	
23 Oct	Chelsea	(a)	2–0	
30 Oct	Arsenal	(h)	3–1	
6 Nov	Everton	(a)	2–1	
13 Nov	Manchester United	(h)	0–5	
20 Nov	Newcastle United	(a)	5–1	
27 Nov	West Bromwich Albion	(h)	2–1	
4 Dec	Nottingham Forest	(a)	0–2	
11 Dec	Sheffield Wednesday	(h)	4–1	
18 Dec	Burnley	(a)	2–4	
28 Dec	Fulham	(h)	5–0	

1 Jan	Stoke City	(h)	1–0	
8 Jan	Sheffield Wednesday	(a)	2–1	
22 Jan	Aston Villa	(a)	2–1	FA Cup
29 Jan	Liverpool	(a)	0–1	
5 Feb	Aston Villa	(h)	2–1	
12 Feb	Birmingham City	(a)	2–1	FA Cup
19 Feb	Sunderland	(a)	3–0	
5 Mar	Manchester City	(a)	2–2	FA Cup
9 Mar	Manchester City	(h)	0–1	FA Cup (replay)
12 Mar	Leeds United	(a)	2–3	
19 Mar	Sheffield United	(h)	1–0	
21 Mar	Chelsea	(h)	1–1	
26 Mar	Northampton Town	(a)	2–2	
8 Apr	Blackburn Rovers	(a)	2–0	
9 Apr	Manchester United	(a)	2–1	
12 Apr	Blackburn Rovers	(h)	2–0	
16 Apr	Newcastle United	(h)	1–2	
18 Apr	Fulham	(a)	4–0	
22 Apr	West Bromwich Albion	(a)	1–5	
30 Apr	Nottingham Forest	(h)	2–1	
7 May	Arsenal	(a)	0–1	
9 May	West Ham United	(h)	2–1	

1966–67

20 Aug	Liverpool	(a)	2–3	
22 Aug	Blackpool	(a)	1–1	
27 Aug	West Ham United	(h)	5–4	
30 Aug	Blackpool	(h)	3–0	
3 Sep	Sheffield Wednesday	(a)	1–1	
7 Sep	Chelsea	(a)	2–2	
10 Sep	Southampton	(h)	1–1	
14 Sep	Reading	(h)	5–0	League Cup
17 Sep	Sunderland	(a)	3–2	
24 Sep	Aston Villa	(h)	5–0	
1 Oct	Arsenal	(a)	4–2	

5 Oct	Lincoln City	(h)	5–0	
8 Oct	Nottingham Forest	(h)	3–0	
15 Oct	Burnley	(a)	2–5	
25 Oct	QPR	(a)	2–4	League Cup
29 Oct	Everton	(a)	0–2	
5 Nov	Burnley	(h)	5–1	
12 Nov	Leeds United	(a)	1–3	
19 Nov	West Bromwich Albion	(h)	2–1	
26 Nov	Sheffield United	(a)	1–0	
30 Nov	Manchester United	(h)	1–2	
3 Dec	Stoke City	(h)	4–2	
10 Dec	Tottenham Hotspur	(a)	0–2	
26 Dec	Fulham	(h)	0–2	
27 Dec	Fulham	(a)	2–4	
31 Dec	West Ham United	(a)	1–0	
7 Jan	Sheffield Wednesday	(h)	0–1	
14 Jan	Southampton	(a)	4–4	
18 Jan	Liverpool	(h)	2–1	
21 Jan	Sunderland	(h)	1–2	
28 Jan	Manchester City	(a)	1–2	FA Cup
4 Feb	Aston Villa	(a)	1–0	
11 Feb	Arsenal	(h)	2–1	
25 Feb	Nottingham Forest	(a)	0–1	
4 Mar	Everton	(h)	2–2	
18 Mar	Manchester United	(a)	2–5	
24 Mar	Manchester City	(a)	3–1	
25 Mar	Tottenham Hotspur	(h)	0–1	
28 Mar	Manchester City	(h)	3–1	
1 Apr	Newcastle United	(a)	0–1	
10 Apr	Leeds United	(h)	0–0	

Summary: League 293; FA Cup 34; League Cup 25; European Cup-Winners Cup 4; Total 356.

STOKE CITY

1966–67

22 Apr	Chelsea	(a)	0–1
29 Apr	Leicester City	(h)	3–1
6 May	Arsenal	(a)	1–3
13 May	Manchester United	(a)	0–0

1967–68

19 Aug	Arsenal	(a)	0–2	
23 Aug	Sheffield United	(h)	1–1	
26 Aug	Manchester City	(h)	3–0	
29 Aug	Sheffield United	(a)	0–1	
2 Sep	Newcastle United	(a)	1–1	
6 Sep	Leicester City	(h)	3–2	
9 Sep	West Bromwich Albion	(h)	0–0	
13 Sep	Watford	(h)	2–0	League Cup
16 Sep	Chelsea	(a)	2–2	
23 Sep	Southampton	(h)	3–2	
30 Sep	Liverpool	(a)	1–2	
7 Oct	West Ham United	(a)	4–3	
11 Oct	Ipswich Town	(h)	2–1	League Cup
14 Oct	Burnley	(h)	0–2	
23 Oct	Sheffield Wednesday	(a)	1–1	
28 Oct	Tottenham Hotspur	(h)	2–1	
1 Nov	Sheffield Wednesday	(a)	0–0	League Cup
4 Nov	Manchester United	(a)	0–1	
18 Nov	Wolves	(a)	4–3	
25 Nov	Fulham	(h)	0–1	
2 Dec	Leeds United	(a)	0–2	
9 Dec	Everton	(h)	1–0	
13 Dec	Leeds United	(a)	0–2	League Cup
16 Dec	Arsenal	(h)	0–1	
23 Dec	Manchester City	(a)	2–4	

26 Dec	Nottingham Forest	(a) 0–3
6 Jan	Newcastle United	(h) 2–1
20 Jan	Chelsea	(h) 0–1
27 Jan	Cardiff City	(h) 4–1	FA Cup
3 Feb	Southampton	(a) 2–1
17 Feb	West Ham United	(h) 0–3	FA Cup
26 Feb	West Ham United	(h) 2–0
13 Mar	West Bromwich Albion	(a) 0–3
16 Mar	Sheffield Wednesday	(h) 0–1
23 Mar	Tottenham Hotspur	(a) 0–3
30 Mar	Manchester United	(h) 2–4
6 Apr	Sunderland	(a) 1–3
13 Apr	Wolves	(h) 0–2
15 Apr	Coventry City	(a) 0–2
16 Apr	Coventry City	(h) 3–3
20 Apr	Burnley	(a) 0–4
23 Apr	Leeds United	(h) 3–2
1 May	Fulham	(a) 2–0
11 May	Leicester City	(a) 0–0
15 May	Liverpool	(h) 2–1

1968–69

10 Aug	Sunderland	(h) 2–1
14 Aug	West Ham United	(h) 0–2
17 Aug	Leeds United	(a) 0–2
28 Sep	Ipswich Town	(a) 1–3
5 Oct	Nottingham Forest	(a) 3–3
12 Oct	Burnley	(h) 1–3
19 Oct	Everton	(a) 1–2
26 Oct	Chelsea	(h) 2–0
2 Nov	Tottenham Hotspur	(a) 1–1
9 Nov	Coventry City	(h) 0–3
16 Nov	West Bromwich Albion	(a) 1–2
23 Nov	Manchester United	(h) 0–0
30 Nov	Sheffield Wednesday	(a) 1–2

7 Dec	Newcastle United	(h)	1–0	
14 Dec	Burnley	(a)	1–1	
21 Dec	Everton	(h)	0–0	
26 Dec	Nottingham Forest	(h)	3–1	
4 Jan	York City	(a)	2–0	FA Cup
11 Jan	Tottenham Hotspur	(h)	1–1	
25 Jan	Halifax Town	(h)	1–1	FA Cup
28 Jan	Halifax Town	(a)	3–0	FA Cup (replay)
1 Feb	West Bromwich Albion	(h)	1–1	
12 Feb	Chelsea	(a)	2–3	FA Cup
1 Mar	Sunderland	(a)	1–4	
15 Mar	Leicester City	(a)	0–0	
18 Mar	Coventry City	(a)	1–1	
22 Mar	Wolves	(h)	4–1	
24 Mar	Manchester United	(a)	1–1	
29 Mar	Manchester City	(a)	1–3	
5 Apr	Ipswich Town	(h)	2–1	
7 Apr	Liverpool	(a)	0–0	
8 Apr	West Ham United	(a)	0–0	
12 Apr	QPR	(a)	1–2	
19 Apr	Arsenal	(h)	1–3	
22 Apr	Sheffield Wednesday	(h)	1–1	

1969–70

9 Aug	Wolves	(a)	1–3	
12 Aug	Nottingham Forest	(a)	0–0	
16 Aug	West Ham United	(h)	2–1	
20 Aug	Nottingham Forest	(h)	1–1	
23 Aug	Derby County	(a)	0–0	
27 Aug	Coventry City	(h)	2–0	
30 Aug	Southampton	(h)	2–1	
3 Sep	Burnley	(h)	0–2	League Cup
6 Sep	Crystal Palace	(a)	1–3	
13 Sep	Sunderland	(h)	4–2	
17 Sep	West Bromwich Albion	(a)	3–1	

20 Sep	Liverpool	(a) 1–3	
27 Sep	Manchester City	(h) 2–0	
4 Oct	Leeds United	(a) 1–2	
6 Oct	West Ham United	(a) 3–3	
11 Oct	Arsenal	(h) 0–0	
15 Nov	Sheffield Wednesday	(a) 2–0	
22 Nov	Ipswich Town	(h) 3–3	
6 Dec	Newcastle United	(h) 0–1	
13 Dec	Sunderland	(a) 3–0	
20 Dec	Crystal Palace	(h) 1–0	
26 Dec	Derby County	(h) 1–0	
27 Dec	Southampton	(a) 0–0	
3 Jan	Oxford United	(a) 0–0	FA Cup
7 Jan	Oxford United	(h) 3–2	FA Cup (replay)
10 Jan	Liverpool	(h) 0–2	
17 Jan	Manchester City	(a) 1–0	
24 Jan	Watford	(a) 0–1	FA Cup
31 Jan	Leeds United	(h) 1–1	
7 Feb	Arsenal	(a) 0–0	
14 Feb	Wolves	(h) 1–1	
21 Feb	Tottenham Hotspur	(a) 0–1	
28 Feb	Manchester United	(h) 2–2	
7 Mar	Ipswich Town	(a) 1–1	
17 Mar	Chelsea	(a) 0–1	
20 Mar	Newcastle United	(a) 1–3	
27 Mar	Burnley	(a) 1–1	
28 Mar	Sheffield Wednesday	(h) 2–1	
30 Mar	Everton	(h) 0–1	
4 Apr	Coventry City	(a) 3–0	
13 Apr	Chelsea	(h) 2–1	
15 Apr	West Bromwich Albion	(h) 3–2	

1970–71

| 15 Aug | Ipswich Town | (h) 0–0 |
| 19 Aug | Newcastle United | (h) 3–0 |

22 Aug	Derby County	(a)	0–2	
26 Aug	West Bromwich Albion	(a)	2–5	
29 Aug	Crystal Palace	(h)	0–0	
2 Sep	Nottingham Forest	(h)	0–0	
5 Sep	Wolves	(a)	1–1	
9 Sep	Millwall	(h)	0–0	League Cup
12 Sep	Leeds United	(h)	3–0	
19 Sep	Manchester City	(a)	1–4	
3 Oct	Blackpool	(a)	1–1	
10 Oct	West Ham United	(h)	2–1	
17 Oct	Ipswich Town	(a)	0–2	
24 Oct	Tottenham Hotspur	(a)	0–3	
31 Oct	Huddersfield Town	(h)	3–1	
7 Nov	Manchester United	(a)	2–2	
14 Nov	Everton	(h)	1–1	
18 Nov	Leeds United	(a)	1–4	
21 Nov	Chelsea	(a)	1–2	
28 Nov	Southampton	(h)	0–0	
5 Dec	Coventry City	(a)	0–1	
12 Dec	Burnley	(h)	0–0	
19 Dec	Derby County	(h)	1–0	
26 Dec	Liverpool	(a)	0–0	
2 Jan	Millwall	(h)	2–1	FA Cup
9 Jan	Newcastle United	(a)	2–0	
16 Jan	West Bromwich Albion	(h)	2–0	
23 Jan	Huddersfield Town	(h)	3–3	FA Cup
26 Jan	Huddersfield Town	(a)	0–0	FA Cup (replay) (aet)
30 Jan	Southampton	(a)	1–2	
8 Feb	Huddersfield Town	(n)	1–0	FA Cup (2nd replay)
13 Feb	Ipswich Town	(h)	0–0	FA Cup
16 Feb	Ipswich Town	(a)	1–0	FA Cup (replay)
20 Feb	Chelsea	(h)	1–2	
23 Feb	Burnley	(a)	1–1	
27 Feb	Huddersfield Town	(a)	1–0	
6 Mar	Hull City	(a)	3–2	FA Cup
13 Mar	Everton	(a)	0–2	

20 Mar	Manchester United	(h)	1–2	
27 Mar	Arsenal	(n)	2–2	FA Cup semi-final
31 Mar	Arsenal	(n)	0–2	FA Cup (replay)
4 Apr	Crystal Palace	(a)	2–3	
7 Apr	Wolves	(h)	1–0	
10 Apr	Liverpool	(h)	0–1	
13 Apr	Blackpool	(h)	1–1	
17 Apr	West Ham United	(a)	0–1	
24 Apr	Manchester City	(h)	2–0	
27 Apr	Nottingham Forest	(a)	0–0	
1 May	Arsenal	(a)	0–1	
5 May	Tottenham Hotspur	(h)	0–1	
7 May	Everton	(n)	3–2	FA Cup 3rd place match

1971–72

14 Aug	Coventry City	(a)	1–1	
17 Aug	Southampton	(a)	1–3	
21 Aug	Crystal Palace	(h)	3–1	
25 Aug	Leicester City	(h)	3–1	
28 Aug	Arsenal	(a)	1–0	
31 Aug	Nottingham Forest	(a)	0–0	
4 Sep	Wolves	(h)	0–1	
11 Sep	Derby County	(a)	0–4	
18 Sep	Huddersfield Town	(h)	1–0	
26 Sep	West Ham United	(a)	1–2	
2 Oct	Liverpool	(h)	0–0	
6 Oct	Oxford United	(a)	1–1	League Cup
9 Oct	Sheffield United	(a)	3–2	
16 Oct	Coventry City	(h)	1–0	
18 Oct	Oxford United	(h)	2–0	League Cup (replay)
23 Oct	Ipswich Town	(a)	1–2	
26 Oct	Manchester United	(a)	1–1	League Cup
30 Oct	Tottenham Hotspur	(h)	2–0	
6 Nov	West Bromwich Albion	(a)	1–0	
8 Nov	Manchester United	(h)	0–0	League Cup (replay) (aet)

13 Nov	Chelsea	(h)	0–1	
15 Nov	Manchester United	(h)	2–1	League Cup (2nd replay)
20 Nov	Leeds United	(a)	0–1	
23 Nov	Bristol Rovers	(a)	4–2	League Cup
27 Nov	Newcastle United	(h)	3–3	
4 Dec	Everton	(a)	0–0	
8 Dec	West Ham United	(h)	1–2	League Cup semi-final (1)
11 Dec	Manchester United	(h)	1–1	
15 Dec	West Ham United	(a)	1–0	League Cup semi-final (2)
18 Dec	Wolves	(a)	0–2	
27 Dec	Manchester City	(h)	1–3	
1 Jan	Huddersfield Town	(a)	0–0	
5 Jan	West Ham United	(n)	0–0	League Cup (replay)
8 Jan	Arsenal	(h)	0–0	
15 Jan	Chesterfield	(h)	2–1	FA Cup
22 Jan	Southampton	(h)	3–1	
26 Jan	West Ham United	(n)	3–2	League Cup (2nd replay)
29 Jan	Leicester City	(a)	1–2	
5 Feb	Tranmere Rovers	(a)	2–2	FA Cup
9 Feb	Tranmere Rovers	(h)	2–0	FA Cup (replay)
12 Feb	Ipswich Town	(h)	3–3	
19 Feb	Tottenham Hotspur	(a)	0–2	
26 Feb	Hull City	(h)	4–1	FA Cup
3 Mar	Chelsea	(n)	2–1	League Cup final
18 Mar	Manchester United	(a)	1–1	FA Cup
22 Mar	Manchester United	(h)	2–1	FA Cup (replay) (aet)
25 Mar	Derby County	(h)	1–1	
28 Mar	Liverpool	(a)	1–2	
1 Apr	Manchester City	(a)	2–1	
4 Apr	West Ham United	(h)	0–0	
8 Apr	Leeds United	(h)	3–0	
15 Apr	Arsenal	(n)	1–1	FA Cup semi-final
19 Apr	Arsenal	(n)	1–2	FA Cup (replay)
22 Apr	Everton	(h)	1–1	
5 May	West Bromwich Albion	(h)	1–1	
8 May	Newcastle United	(a)	0–0	

1972–73

26 Aug	Everton	(h) 1–1	
30 Aug	Norwich City	(a) 0–2	
2 Sep	Coventry City	(a) 1–2	
6 Sep	Sunderland	(h) 3–0	League Cup
9 Sep	Leeds United	(h) 2–2	
13 Sep	Kaiserslautern	(h) 3–1	UEFA Cup
16 Sep	Ipswich Town	(a) 0–2	
3 Oct	Ipswich Town	(a) 2–1	League Cup
7 Oct	Tottenham Hotspur	(a) 3–4	
14 Oct	Newcastle United	(h) 2–0	
21 Oct	Liverpool	(a) 1–2	

Summary: League 194; FA Cup 27; League Cup 19; UEFA Cup 1; other sponsored cup competitions (not shown) 5; Total 246.

International Matches

1963

6 April	Scotland	Wembley	1–2
8 May	Brazil	Wembley	1–1
20 May	Czechoslovakia	Bratislava	4–2
20 June	East Germany	Leipzig	2–1
12 Oct	Wales	Cardiff	4–0
23 Oct	Rest of the World	Wembley	2–1
20 Nov	Northern Ireland	Wembley	8–3

1964

11 Apr	Scotland	Glasgow	0–1
6 May	Uruguay	Wembley	2–1
17 May	Portugal	Lisbon	4–3

27 May	USA	New York	10–0
4 June	Portugal	São Paulo	1–1
6 June	Argentina	Rio de Janeiro	0–1
3 Oct	Northern Ireland	Belfast	4–3

1965

10 Apr	Scotland	Wembley	2–2
5 May	Hungary	Wembley	1–0
9 May	Yugoslavia	Belgrade	1–1
12 May	West Germany	Nuremberg	1–0
16 May	Sweden	Gothenburg	2–1
10 Nov	Northern Ireland	Wembley	2–1
8 Dec	Spain	Madrid	2–0

1966

5 Jan	Poland	Liverpool	1–1
23 Feb	West Germany	Wembley	1–0
2 Apr	Scotland	Glasgow	4–3
4 May	Yugoslavia	Wembley	2–0
26 June	Finland	Helsinki	3–0
5 July	Poland	Chorzow	1–0
11 July	Uruguay (WC)	Wembley	0–0
16 July	Mexico (WC)	Wembley	2–0
20 July	France (WC)	Wembley	2–0
23 July	Argentina (WC)	Wembley	1–0
26 July	Portugal (WC)	Wembley	2–1
30 July	West Germany (WCF)	Wembley	4–2 (aet)
22 Oct	Northern Ireland (ECQ)	Belfast	2–0
2 Nov	Czechoslovakia	Wembley	0–0
16 Nov	Wales (ECQ)	Wembley	5–1

1967

15 Apr	Scotland (ECQ)	Wembley	2–3
21 Oct	Wales (ECQ)	Cardiff	3–0
22 Nov	Northern Ireland (ECQ)	Wembley	2–0
6 Dec	USSR	Wembley	2–2

1968

24 Feb	Scotland (ECQ)	Glasgow	1–1
3 Apr	Spain (ECQ)	Wembley	1–0
1 June	West Germany	Hanover	0–1
5 June	Yugoslavia (ECF)	Florence	0–1
8 June	USSR (ECF)	Rome	2–0
6 Nov	Romania	Bucharest	0–0

1969

15 Jan	Romania	Wembley	1–1
12 Mar	France	Wembley	5–0
3 May	Northern Ireland	Belfast	3–1
10 May	Scotland	Wembley	4–1
8 June	Uruguay	Montevideo	2–1
12 June	Brazil	Rio de Janeiro	1–2

1970

14 Jan	Holland	Wembley	0–0
25 Feb	Belgium	Brussels	3–1
18 Apr	Wales	Cardiff	1–1
21 Apr	Northern Ireland	Wembley	3–1
25 Apr	Scotland	Glasgow	0–0
20 May	Colombia	Bogotá	4–0
24 May	Ecuador	Quito	2–0
2 June	Romania (WC)	Guadalajara	1–0
7 June	Brazil (WC)	Guadalajara	0–1
11 June	Czechoslovakia (WC)	Guadalajara	1–0

1971

3 Feb	Malta (ECQ)	Valletta	1–0
21 Apr	Greece (ECQ)	Wembley	3–0
12 May	Malta (ECQ)	Wembley	5–0
15 May	Northern Ireland	Belfast	1–0
22 May	Scotland	Wembley	3–1
13 Oct	Switzerland (ECQ)	Basle	3–2
1 Dec	Greece (ECQ)	Athens	2–0

1972

29 Apr	West Germany (ECQ)	Wembley	1–3
13 May	West Germany (ECQ)	Berlin	0–0
20 May	Wales	Cardiff	3–0
27 May	Scotland	Glasgow	1–0

Total caps: 73.

Overall

	League	FA Cup	League Cup	Other	Total
Chesterfield	23	3			26
Leicester City	293	34	25	4	356
Stoke City	194	27	19	6	246
England					73
England Under-23s					2
TOTAL	510	64	44	10	703

Miscellaneous Statistics

Kept 162 clean sheets in 628 first-class matches in English domestic football.

Kept 35 clean sheets in 73 appearances for England and was on the losing side on only nine occasions.

Conceded 57 goals in 73 matches for England – an average of 0.78 per game.

Played in 23 consecutive matches for England between 1964 and 1967 without defeat.

Honours

OBE 1970
World Cup Winner 1966
League Cup Winner 1964, 1972
FA Cup runner-up 1961, 1963
League Cup runner-up 1965
English Football Writers' Association Player of the Year 1972
FIFA Goalkeeper of the Year 1966, 1967, 1968, 1969, 1970, 1971
NASL Goalkeeper of the Year 1977
Daily Express Sportsman of the Year 1971, 1972

Index